Wm. S. Wood

HELIOTYPE PRINTING CO. BOSTON.

Descendants
of the Brothers
Jeremiah & John
Wood

Compiled and
Originally Published
by

William S. Wood

SUPT. CITY SCHOOLS, SEYMOUR, IND.

HERITAGE BOOKS
2018

HERITAGE BOOKS
AN IMPRINT OF HERITAGE BOOKS, INC.

Books, CDs, and more—Worldwide

For our listing of thousands of titles see our website
at
www.HeritageBooks.com

A Facsimile Reprint
Published 2018 by
HERITAGE BOOKS, INC.
Publishing Division
5810 Ruatan Street
Berwyn Heights, Md. 20740

Originally published:
Press of Charles Hamilton
Worcester, Mass.
1885

International Standard Book Numbers
Paperbound: 978-0-7884-1646-0
Clothbound: 978-0-7884-8411-7

PREFACE.

The descendants of the brothers Jeremiah and John Wood are found in most of the States and Territories of the United States, as well as in some of the isles of the sea and distant lands.

The compiler has labored long and persistently to bring together the records of these various branches, and he hopes this volume may meet with a kind reception among those for whom it has been especially prepared.

It has been thought best to publish this pioneer Genealogy of the brothers Jeremiah and John Wood, not waiting for absolute perfection, hoping that it may give information and stimulate enquiry concerning our kindred, that we may be more strongly bound together as one great family, whether by the name of Wood or otherwise.

The compiler takes pleasure in saying that his respect and veneration for this family has been largely increased by his researches, and he believes it will bear favorable comparison with other great families whose genealogical records have been carefully preserved. May we all do what we can to perfect and preserve our own. In the language of Job, VIII. 8: "Enquire, I pray thee, of the former age, and prepare thyself to the search of their fathers."

I wish to thank all those who have contributed records and information, which includes hundreds of persons. I am particularly indebted to Charles H. Lane, of Templeton, Mass., who collected the Abel White records. I must acknowledge valuable suggestions from John Ward Dean, the librarian of the New England Historic Genealogical Society, Boston, Mass.

I call attention to the excellent mechanical execution of this volume by the printing establishment of Charles Hamilton, of Worcester, Mass., and I extend my sincere thanks for the uniform courtesy of the house, and for its superior work, under the well-known manager and proof-reader, Benjamin J. Dodge, who has done much to prevent mistakes of type and pen.

BOSTON, Mass., *August 14, 1885.*

EXPLANATIONS.

The figures *before* the name is the number given that name for reference.

The figures *after* the name refers back to the parents' number, excepting in the record of marriage it refers to that person's record in the following number.

The "Index of Heads of Families" refers to the name of the father, and the name of the mother before marriage, at the head of their family record in the book.

A part of the book is not numbered where references are not required, and some figures have been passed over in the numbering to facilitate the introduction of additional names in their proper place, up to the time of printing.

The abbreviations are as follows:—b. for born; bap. for baptized; m. for married; d. for died; res. for residence.

CONTENTS.

PART I.

JEREMIAH WOOD BRANCH.

PART II.

CAPT. JOHN WOOD BRANCH.

INDEX OF HEADS OF FAMILIES.

PORTRAITS.

PART FIRST.

2

JEREMIAH WOOD.

"JEREMIAH WOOD was married unto Dority Benett the 29th March 1709," as per Vol. 2, page 354, Lyme Town Records, and by his own Family Record now in possession of Isaac Wood of Boston, Mass.

The grandfather of Dorathy (Benett) Wood, Henry Champion, was born in England in 1611. He came to New England and was one of the first settlers of Saybrook and Lyme, Connecticut.

In the old Town Records of Saybrook we find the following:

Henry Champion was married in Aug. 1647. He had:

SARAW (Sarah), born in 1649.
MARY, born in 1651.
STEPHEN, born 1653; died in the beginning of May, 1660.
HENRY, Jun'r, born 1654 or 5.
THOMAS, born April, 1656.

Royal P. Hinman, in his "Early Puritan Settlers of Connecticut," says:—"Few families in the Connecticut Colony have been more prospered than that of Henry Champion, Sen., of Saybrook. When I speak of his family, I intend his numerous descendants." He speaks of descendants of Thomas, son of Henry, Sen., mentioning Col. Henry, Gen. Henry, Gen. Epaphroditus Champion, as fortunate in amassing wealth. Col. Henry, son of Thomas, bore an important part in the war of the Revolution; was appointed Commissary in 1775, in the commencement of the Revolution, assisted by his sons, who afterwards held an exalted position in Connecticut. E.

Champion was a Member of Congress from 1807 to 1817.

Henry Champion, Sen., removed to Lyme many years before his death. He was propounded for a freeman at Lyme in 1670. He had lands beyond "Little Stony Brook" in June, 1674, and other lands.

He married 21st March, 1698, second wife Deborah, and died at great age in Lyme, Conn., Feb. 17, 1708.

The papers concerning the final settlement of his estate are on file at the Probate Office, New London, Conn. The following named heirs signed a paper declaring themselves satisfied with the distribution of the estate: Deborah Champion, wife; Henry Champion; Henry Benet; Aaron Huntly; John Wade; Hannah Wade.

Lyme was settled about 1664; its first English name was East Saybrook. It was incorporated as a distinct town by the name of Lyme, in 1667.

Henry Benet, named above as one of the heirs of Henry Champion, Sen., married Sarah Champion, daughter of Henry Champion, Sen., 9th of December, 1673. Among the names of their children is Dorathy Benet, who married Jeremiah Wood.

As per Lyme Town Records, Henry and Sarah (Champion) Benet had:

CALEB, b. Oct. 11, 1675.
ROSE, b. Nov. 15, 1677.
JOHN, b. Dec. 26, 1680.
SARAH, b. Aug. 7, 1683.
LOVE, b. March 19th, 1685.
DORETE, b. May 19, 1688.
HENRY, b. July 29, 1691.

The History of New London, by F. M. Calkins, says: "Henry Bennet of Lyme died in 1726 leaving three sons and four married daughters." His Will and a record of "Deeds of Gift" to his children are to be found at New London, Conn., as also a "Deed of Gift" to Dorathy, his daughter, is found among the papers of her husband, Jeremiah Wood.

Children of Jeremiah (1) and Dorathy (2) (Benett) Wood:

3. SARAH, b. April 18, 1710; died Dec. 8, 1723.
4. ELIZABETH, b. Oct. 14, 1711.
5. JOSEPH, b. May 22, 1713.
6. LUCE, b. March 4, 1715.
7. BENET, b. March 15, 1717; d. Apr. 28, 1797.
8. JOHN, b. February 3, 1719; d. Apr. 8, 1758.
9. JEREMIAH, b. Dec. 1, 1721; d. Oct. 21, 1736.
10. SARAH, b. Feb. 7, 1724.
11. JONATHAN, b. Aug. 3, 1727; d. Oct. 18, 1797.
12. ELIPHALET, b. July 19, 1729; d. Apr. 16, 1817.

Jeremiah Wood lived in Stow, Mass., when his first four children were born, and the rest of his family were born in Littleton, Mass. The Stow Records were destroyed previous to 1713, consequently there is no Town record of the births of the first two girls. The first name on the Stow Town Record of Births is that of Joseph Wood, third child of Jeremiah and Dorathy Wood, b. May 22, 1713, as per Town and family records.

The Town record of the birth of Luce is identical with that found in Jeremiah's family record, including the spelling of the name. The Town and family records of those born in Littleton are the same. Jeremiah Wood died in Littleton, Mass., July 15, 1730, aged 52 years, 2 months and 8 days, as given upon his gravestone in Littleton.

His birth, therefore, must have been in May, 1678. He had a brother, John Wood, who married March 3, 1705, Elizabeth Buckminster, daughter of Col. Joseph Buckminster of Framingham, Mass., and the marriage is recorded there "both of this town." He first settled in Framingham, Mass., where the births of all of his children but the last are recorded. He afterwards settled in Hopkinton, Mass., where the present village of Woodville now stands, and where several of John Wood's descendants now reside.

In a memorandum of an agreement between Zachariah Whitman of Hull, and Jeremiah Wood, May 2, 1705, probably written by Whitman, it reads "Jeremiah Wood of 'Malborow.'" In his intention of marriage it reads "both of Lyme," Conn.; from 1710 to 1716, in records and accounts, he is of Stow, Mass. From 1716 until his death, of Littleton, Mass.

The following from Jeremiah Wood's papers:

"1705, May 2nd.

MEMORANDUM.

It is agreed upon betwixt Zechariah Whitman of Hull & Jeremiah Wood of Malborow ye s^d.^ Wood doth enter into possession & occupation of the same house and land and meadow formerly in the occupation of Thomas Daby of Stow for some years yet to come from the first of day of this instant May & sd. Wood is to pay or cause to be paid 7 £ per annum to said Whitman.

ZECHARIAH WHITMAN."

In 1707, by his account book, he worked three weeks and four days for James Levins. He received four weeks' board. "Sept. 20th day James Levins owes me eighty shillings."

In 1708, Feb. 13, a receipt in full for rent of estate in Stow is received from the agent of Zachariah Whitman.

An intention of marriage is found among Jeremiah's private papers:

"This: is: to give: notice: that there: is: a: purpose of marriage intended between Jeremiah Wood Sen. and Dorathy Benet both of Lyme.

March ye 20: day: 1709."

By the papers and accounts of Jeremiah Wood that we have seen, it is not improbable that he settled immediately after marriage upon the estate where he died. His residence was first in Stow, then in Littleton,—but this may have been caused by the establishing of the boundaries of the town, which was named Littleton, Dec. 3, 1715,—and in 1716, and ever after in his accounts we find Jeremiah Wood in Littleton. In Stow, in 1681, we find the names of twelve persons to whom allotments of land were made, one of whom was that of Joseph Daby, whose name appears later in this volume. The town extended from the ancient bounds of Sudbury to what is now Lunenburg. Stow was incorporated May 16, 1683. We find a receipt given to Jeremiah Wood *of Littleton*, for church purposes in 1716.

The birth of his daughter Luce, born March 16, 1715, is recorded in Stow; the birth of his next younger child, Benet, born March 15, 1717, is recorded in Littleton. One line of the lands of the Littleton estate crosses Beaver Brook.

"Whom it may concern.

This may certify that Jeremiah Wood hired of the Selectmen of Stow that part of common meadow belonging to sd. town lying on Beaver Brook for the year 1716.

Stow July the 9th 1716 THOMAS BROWN, Clark."

Jeremiah Wood was a Weaver, a Yeoman, Gentleman, as shown by his account book and papers. He was Constable and Collector, later Selectman, and for some years Treasurer of the town of Littleton. He was a member and supporter of the church in Littleton, and his estate, at the time of his death, was valued at almost a thousand pounds.

His brother John died about five years before him, and his estate, at what is now Woodville, Mass., was valued at nearly nine hundred pounds.

The account book and papers of Jeremiah Wood, and those of his son John, were discovered by the writer in searching for old papers of our ancestors. They are in the possession of Isaac Wood of Boston, Mass., who was not aware that he had them. He brought papers of his father and grandfather from the old homestead to Boston, but was not a little surprised to see records of six generations in his possession. He has my sincere thanks for the free use of all of them.

The account book was intended to be carried in the pocket, but is large for that purpose; it was bound in leather peculiar to those times, and had a copper clasp. It was commenced when he was young; some of the leaves are missing; the first pages are gone; the earliest account left in the book is in 1707. A part of another account book is found, but of later date. Other books are probably lost or destroyed. Of the first named book, on the second page of the cover, in his own handwriting, which was always very good, is the common entry in earlier times. When we recall the fact that he was born more than two hundred years ago, a more impressive meaning is attached to his statements on the cover. They are as follows:

> "Jeremiah Wood, His Book His hand.
> Jeremiah Wood, His Book and with his hand and pen he wret the same.
> Jeremiah Wood his hand and name and with my ink and pen writ the same."

To facilitate further research, I give some of the names of persons in this account book with whom I find he had dealings:

John Eveleth, minister of the town of Stow; John Barker of Concord, blacksmith; Samuel Wright of Concord; Joseph Daby of Stow; John Barker of Stow, 1710; James Keyes of Lancaster; Moses Whitney of Stow; Richard Euscnes, Sen., 1707; Capt. Prescott of Groton; Caleb Taylor; John Robins; Josiah Whitcombe of Lancaster; Hezekiah Whitcombe; Jonathan Whitcombe; Joseph Harris; Jonathan Prescott; Joseph Powers; Jonathan Hartwell; Jonathan Taylor; Moses Whitney,

Sen. of Stow; Elizabeth Whitcombe of Lancaster; Phineas Rice, 1711; David Wetherbee of Stow; Robert Robins; Benj. Shattuck; Joseph Whitcomb; John Perham; ——— Lawrence; Thomas Chamberlain; John Sayer of Lancaster; Widow Wetherbee of Stow; Ephraim Wetherbee; John Farr; John Cobliech, 1723; Thomas Whitney of Stow, 1722; Joseph Barker; Joseph Blancher; John Edwards; Joseph Whitney of Chelmsford; John Wood of Hopkinton, June and August, 1724.

We find among Jeremiah's papers a "Deed of Gift" to Dorathy Benet, from her father, Henry Benet of Lyme, Conn. It is recorded in the second book of Records, folio 347. This deed was signed Feb. 24, 1706–7.

Recorded 5th of March, 1707, by

JOSEPH PECK, Recorder.

Also, the following statement:

"LYME, Oct. 9, 1722.

Mr. Henry Benet Sen. hath given the one half of Volunteer lot in Voluntown unto me Jeremiah Wood who am his son-in-law, living in Littleton y[e] Massachusetts Bay in New England."

Henry Benet also remembers his daughter, Dorathy Wood, in his will.

"OCT. 27, 1725.

Received of Jeremiah Wood twenty shillings for y[e] five years tax of half a lot of land in Voluntown originally Henry Benett's which was sold for y[e] non payment of y[e] first two years Tax and was sold Thomas Dow of Voluntown and is acquitted from y[e] said seizment y[e] said Wood paying y[e] charge with y[e] interest sixteen shillings and four pence

01—16—4 JACOB BROWN, Treasurer."

A Deed of the above is found among the rest, it having been deeded to him after the back taxes had been paid. Deed dated March 28, 1726. The tract now comprising the town of Voluntown, Conn., was granted in 1696 to the Volunteers in the Narragansett war, and the town received its name from that circumstance. April 17, 1706, they went out to "draw lots." One hundred and fifty lots were laid out, some receiving but half a share. Henry Benet was one of the proprietors.

Jeremiah Wood purchased of the "Town of Littleton" his estate there Jan. 13, 1717, a part of which is still in the possession of his descendants. Several generations of the Wood family have been born there. The writer, his father, grandfather and great-grandfather were born there, and his great-great-grandfather, Jeremiah Wood, received the deed from the Town of Littleton, as explained in the deed itself. It is here given for the information it contains, and as a curiosity for coming generations. It is as follows:

DEED OF "TOWN OF LITTLETON" TO JEREMIAH WOOD.

"Be it known to all people before whom we send Greeting:

"That we Jonathan Prescott and Joseph Bulkley of Concord, Nathaniel Wilder of Lancaster, Eleazer Lawrence of Groton, Isaac Powers of Littleton all in the County of Middlesex in his majesty's Province of the Massachusetts in New England Gentlemen, Being a Committee be any Three of them authorized by the Grantors, owners, and proprietors of the Land in Littleton to Grant, sell, convey, and confirm by Deeds of Sale under our Hands and Seals as the Law directs in behalf of the owners and proprietors to such persons as Shall appear to purchase Land in Littleton, Have for the good Settlement of the Town and in consideration of Forty-one pounds in Current money To us in hand paid to our content for the use of the proprietors By Jeremiah Wood now Resident in Littleton in the County and Province above mentioned The receipt thereof we Do hereby acknowledge and y[e] show with we are fully Satisfied, Contented and paid and Do for ourselves and the Grantors & owners their heirs and assignes fully Clearly and absolutely acquit, Exonerate and discharge the aforesaid Jeremiah Wood his heirs and assigns of every part and parcel thereof forever, Have given, granted, bargained and sold allowed conveyed, made over and confirmed and do by these presents give grant bargain sell and convey, make over confirm Deliver and abdicate one Messuage or Tenement or Tract of Land containing upland, meadow Land and Swamp Land all in all in one entire piece and Is situate lying and being in the Town of Littleton and in County of Middlesex aforesaid and is laid out Butted and bounded as followeth Viz. The east corner is a stake and heap of stones at the west corner of Caleb Tailors Lott and from there partly south along sd. Tailors Line by divers marked Trees till it come to the highway to a white-oak tree marked standing before sd. Wood's Door then running southward along said Highway till it come to a heap of stones which is the southwardly corner of sd. Lott. Then turneth northwardly along by Divers old marked Trees till it come to a stake and heap of stones which is the west corner of the Lott, on the west side of Beaver Brook. Then turning eastward and running on a strait line to the first mentioned stake and heap of stones, Being by estimation one hundred acres be the same more or be the same less. To have and to hold the above granted and bargained premises as above Butted and bounded or Demised to be bounded with all appurtences, rights Titles Interest Privileges and commodity or discommoditiy to the same belonging or in any wise appertaining to him the sd. Jeremiah Wood his heirs and assigns forever to his and their proper only proper use benefit and behoof forever. And We the above named Committee ye Subscribers Do for ourselves and for the Grantors their heirs and Assigns Do covenant promise and Grant To & with the sd. Jeremiah Wood his heirs and assigns that before the Ensealing thereof we are the true sole and Lawfull owners of the above granted and bargained premises and are lawfully seized and possessed of same in our own proper right as a good perfect and absolute estate of inheritance in fee simple and have ourselves good right, full power and Lawful Authority to grant bargain Sell Convey and Confirm sd. bargained premises in manner as aforesaid and that the sd. Jeremiah Wood, his heirs and assigns Shall and may from time to time and at all times forever hereafter by virtue and force of these Grants Lawfully peaceably and Quietly Have, hold, use occupy possess and Enjoy the aforesaid demised and bargained premises free and clear and freely and clearly acquitted, Exonerated and Discharged from all and all manner of former &

other gifts grants, bargains, Sales Lease, mortgages, Wills, Entails Joyntures Doweries Judgments Executions, Incumbrances and Escheats.

Furthermore We the Subscribers in the behalf of y[e] Grantors their heirs Executors Adm[s] and assigns Do Covenant and engage the above Demised premises unto the Grantee his heirs Executors Adm[s] and assigns against the lawful claims and Demands of any person or persons whatsoever forever, hereafter to warrant secure and Defend.

In witness whereof we have hereunto Set our hands and Seals this thirteenth day of January One thousand seven hundred and sixteen aliaz seventeen.

JON.[a] PRESCOTT & a seal
ELEAZER LAWRENCE & a seal
ISAAC POWERS & a seal

Signed, sealed in presence of
Samuel Davis
Sam[ll] Dudley

Middlesex

Jonathan Prescott Eleazer Lawrence & Isaac Powers appeared before me and acknowledged the above written Instrument to be their act and Deed

Aug. 27, 1717

THOMAS HOW, *Justice of Peace.*

Cambr. Sept. 3, 1717
Rec[d] and accordingly Entered
By Sam[l] Phipps, Reg[r]."

John Daby of the Town of Stow, bought land of the same Committee a few days after.

Benjamin Shattuck, son of Dr. Philip Shattuck of Watertown, was the first ordained minister of Littleton, b. May 15, 1684, ordained 25th of December, 1717. He had probably preached there earlier, as I find a receipt, dated Sept. 1, 1716, for one pound some shillings, collected for Benjamin Shattuck of Jeremiah Wood.

I will now introduce a copy of a letter written one hundred and sixty-seven years ago. (1885). It was written by John Wood and wife to their brother. The direction was upon the outside as follows:

"This for
Mr. Jeremiah Wood
living in Littleton,
Deliver."

Inside.

"December the 18, 1718. Whithall.

After my love to you these lines are to inform you that I am in good health and mine also.

My wife and I have love for you and yours, but we show it not by our often meetings.

I pray mend these faults
And this for my part,
JOHN WOOD, your loven brother."

"And as for my part I would gladly have come to see you this fall but your Brother would not, nevertheless I would be very glad to see you both at our house.

Your loving sister
ELIZABETH WOOD."

The above letter from Jeremiah Wood's papers is important in establishing the relationship of Jeremiah Wood of Littleton and John Wood of Hopkinton, living at Whitehall.

In Jeremiah Wood's account book we find an account with his brother the year before John's death, as follows:

"June 3, 1724 John Wood of Hopkinton is debtor to me Jeremiah Wood of Littleton, To forty-three pounds of tobacco 1 £ 1s. 6d.

Aug. 1, 1724 To weaving twenty nine yards of all wool cloth at eight pence per yard 19s. 4d.

To weaving sixteen yards of Linen cloth four yards striped 16s. 4d."

In a paper of Capt. Amariah Wood, entitled "The Progenitors of Amariah Wood, as far back as he has knowledge thereof," written in 1856, he says: "I think my father, Dea. John Wood of Littleton has said that some of his relatives settled somewhere south, not far from Worcester, Mass., and some in Westminster, Mass." In my early days I heard the name of Hopkinton mentioned as perhaps the place of settlement; I therefore examined the records in Probate office at Cambridge, Mass. I found on file the settlement of Capt. John Wood's estate of Hopkinton. I was surprised in finding the same signature, Elizabeth Wood, as Administratrix, as in the letter named. She was married again about three years after John Wood's decease, and before the final settlement of the estate, and she signs again as Elizabeth Wood *alias* Rice.

She married Josiah Rice. I looked at the settlement of Rice's estate and his Will, and find the name "Elizabeth Rice and my son in law Joseph Wood Executors," and the same signature, Elizabeth Rice. I afterwards discovered that her maiden name was Elizabeth Buckminster, and a daughter of Col. Joseph Buckminster of Framingham, Mass. I looked at the settlement of his estate and found the name of Elizabeth Rice upon a paper acknowledging the receipt of one hundred and twelve pounds from the estate.

I then placed the four signatures before three men who were considered experts, the papers so folded that only the name appeared, and they unanimously agreed that these signatures were all written by the same person, viz: Upon the letter, and upon the settlement of the estates of John Wood, Josiah Rice, and Joseph Buckminster.

Whitehall, upon the letter, was the early name of the place where the village of Woodville now stands, and is at the outlet of Whitehall pond, a beautiful sheet of water of 620 acres and is the source of Sudbury river. The names of many of the descendants of John and Elizabeth (Buckminster) Wood and the ancestors of Elizabeth

Buckminster are found recorded in Part II. of this volume.

At the decease of Jeremiah Wood, his wife, Dorathy Wood, was appointed Administratrix.

Lieutenant Jonathan Hartwell, Mr. Jonathan Whitcomb, both of Littleton, and Mr. Ebenezer Prescott of Westford, were appointed to appraise the property.

The eldest son, Joseph, refused to accept the land set to him, alleging "that it is too highly appraised," and no other inclining to take it, the Judge directs the appraisers to set off to each an equal part, or else to settle it among the children in such proportion as shall be agreed on by the parties concerned. This was Feb. 24, 1734.

Joseph offers to let one of his brothers take his house at "as much as any man of judgment shall think it worth." He also desires the same appraisers to be further directed to "lay off my one part by itself." The eldest son, in those times, received two parts.

The Commissioners appointed to distribute the estate were Eleazer Lawrence, Lieut. Samuel Hunt, Abraham Patch and Jonathan Whetcombe, all of Littleton, and Ebenezer Prescott of Westford.

The Personal Property was appraised at 184 £, 16s.

The following is from the real estate minutes of the settlement of the *Real Estate* as per Probate records at Cambridge, Mass.:

"Set to John in Land	266 £	15 s.	— o
Set to Jeremiah in Land	218 £	9 s.	— o
Advanced to Elizabeth	63 £	4 s.	— 6d.
Joseph (Eldest son) in Land	121 £	6 s.	— o
	669 £	14 s.	6 d.
Deduct charges	37 £	5 s.	1 d.
	632 £	9 s.	5 d.
Which gives for a single share	63 £	4 s.	$11\frac{3}{10}$ d.

John to pay charges viz.	To the Widow	26 £.	13 s.	6 d.
	To Joseph	6 £	3 s.	7 d.
	To Commissioners	4 £	8 s.	

Then to pay			
Joseph	5 £.	3 s.	$10\frac{6}{10}$ d.
Bennet	63 £.	4 s.	$11\frac{3}{10}$ d.
Jonathan	63 £.	4 s.	$11\frac{3}{10}$ d.
Eliphalet	34 £.	11 s.	$2\frac{5}{10}$ d.
His own share	63 £	4 s.	$11\frac{3}{10}$ d.
	266 £	15 s.	

Jeremiah to pay			
Eliphalet	28 £	13 s.	$8\frac{8}{10}$ d.
Elizabeth	0 £.	0 s.	$5\frac{3}{10}$ d.
Sarah	63 £	4 s.	$11\frac{3}{10}$ d.
Lucy	63 £	4 s.	$11\frac{3}{10}$ d.
His own share	63 £	4 s.	$11\frac{3}{10}$ d.
	218 £	9 s.	0 d.

Memorandum: Joseph to be accountable to the heirs for the Narraganset Right which he sold and to be answerable to the Widow and heirs for the horse and clothing delivered to him valued at 13 £ 15s.

I will not record the distribution of Personal Property. The widow's thirds are not included in the above. The valuation of the estate at the time of final settlement was more than a thousand pounds.

The aforesaid portions to be paid by John and Jeremiah as they come of age & they are to pay interest in the meantime at the rate of 4 per cent to begin the 14th of July 1735."

The above account of settlement is the best evidence of relationship and may make us better acquainted with the family.

Dorathy, the wife of Jeremiah Wood, lived twenty-two years and two days after his decease. She was left with a large family; the youngest, Eliphalet, was four days less than a year old; the oldest child living, Elizabeth, in her nineteenth year, and the oldest son, Joseph, a little past seventeen. Dorathy was away from her early associations and home. Her oldest child, Sarah, had died less than seven years before, and her son, Jeremiah, to whom was assigned a portion of the real estate, died less than seven years after, not then fifteen years of age.

She did not despair; she did not go back to her early home by the river and the sea, but she cared for her children, and kept and improved the estate until its distribution.

We find the following allowances were made her:

"One acre of Land plowed up; Forty-six rods of Log and Brush fence,	5 £.
Seventy rods of Rail fence	4 £.
Twenty rods of Stone fence	3 £ 10 s."

In the inventory of her estate I notice sixteen barrels of cider. A gold necklace, appraised at fourteen pounds.

She was a good manager, and with much liberality towards her children and the poor; her estate, at her death, was appraised at £575, and fifty pounds more were given for it by Benet and John Wood than appraised, making £625 that was received from her thirds at her death, an increase upon what was left her by her husband twenty-two years before. She was no ordinary woman. Her influence was undoubtedly felt by her children. In uprightness of character, stability of purpose, sound judgment, and high regard for family and personal honor, the family of Jeremiah and Dorathy Wood was no ordinary family.

Jeremiah Wood died July 15, 1730; Dorathy Wood, his wife, died July 17, 1752. Their graves are side by side in Littleton, and near them are grouped the graves of some of their children, grandchildren, great-grandchildren and great-great-grandchildren.

Gravestones mark the resting-place of most of them. In the new Cemetery near by, are the graves of many more descendants, and upon gravestone and monument, separated by "mount and stream and sea," we read the names of their descendants and learn the fate of us all.

CHILDREN AND DESCENDANTS

OF

JEREMIAH AND DORATHY WOOD.

The record of their first born is upon the gravestone in Littleton, "Here lyes ye body of Sarah Wood daughter of Jeremiah & Dorathy Wood. Died Decem^{br} 8th 1723 aged 13 years 7 mo. & 8 ds." She was born in Stow, Mass., April 18, 1710.

Elizabeth Wood, second child of Jeremiah and Dorathy, m. Benjamin Robins; was of Groton, Mass., Dec. 1, 1738, and Dec. 20, 1748; was of Dunstable later. She was born in Stow, Mass., Oct. 14, 1711.

DESCENDANTS OF

JOSEPH AND GRACE WOOD.

Joseph Wood, third child of Jeremiah and Dorathy, b. in Stow, Mass., May 22, 1713; m. Grace Whettemore of Concord, Mass., dau. of Benj. and Esther (Brooks) Whettemore and sister of Rev. Aaron Whettemore, who was ordained 1737, and was for many years minister at Suncook (now Pembroke), N. H. Joseph first settled in Littleton, Mass., where their first child, Benjamin, was born Sept. 17, 1734.

In May, 1738, by the church records in Littleton, Joseph and wife were dismissed to the church in Suncook. Aaron was born in 1739. Grace was born in Concord, Mass., Dec. 1, 1741, as per Concord, Mass., records.

Joseph conveyed to Bennet Wood his right to the estate of his deceased brother, Jeremiah Wood, by deed dated May 9, 1738, as per records at Cambridge, Mass., and upon the same day Bennet Wood conveyed his right by deed in a lot of land in Narraganset Town.

Nov. 15, 1739, Joseph Wood acknowledged the receipt of amount Judge of Probate ordered John Wood to pay him, received from his honored mother, Dorathy Wood, Guardian of John.

Joseph died ———

His widow married Ephraim Stow of Concord, Jan. 14, 1745. A deed was given to Grace Wood of 60 acres of land, Nov. 19, 1745, for three hundred and fifty pounds, by Ephraim Stow, witnessed by Nathaniel Whettemore, Esther Whettemore, and E. Whettemore.

Benjamin Wood received a deed of about 23 acres of land in the northerly part of Concord, July 22, 1753, of his step-father, Ephraim Stow, and Grace Stow, his mother. Grace Stow, late of Carlisle, deceased. Appraisers were appointed and estate distributed July 14, 1757, perhaps two years after her decease. No children by second marriage. Ephraim Stow and ten others petitioned to be set back to Concord. It was done Jan. 11th, 1757, but was afterwards, May 8, 1780, set off, but perhaps not as before.

Aaron settled in Pepperell, probably upon land bought of Jonas Wheeler of Concord, one hundred acres, as per deed on record, 1762. This was Aaron Wood of Bedford, blacksmith. It was signed in presence of Benjamin Wheeler and John Wheat, Sept. 14, 1764.

Aaron married Rebekah Wheeler; they had children as follows:

Rebecca, b. June 13, 1764; m. (Parker).
Lucy, b. Mar. 22, 1766; m. (Shattuck).
Halah, b. Apr. 12, 1768.
Lydia, b. Feb. 23, 1770; m. (Blood).
Grace, b. Mar. 24, 1772; m. (Spaulding).
Hepzibah, b. Apr. 24, 1774.
Aaron, b. May 30, 1776.
Susanna, b. Apr. 29, 1778.
Benjamin, b. Aug. 22, 1780.
Joseph, b. Sept. 19, 1782.
Hannah, b. Sept. 23, 1784.
Sarah, b. Aug. 14, 1786.

Grace Wood, dau. of Joseph and Grace, m. William Wheeler, Jan. 18, 1763.

Children of Wm. and Grace Wheeler, as per Concord, Mass., Town Records:

Grace, b. Mar. 13, 1765.
William, b. Aug. 24, 1767.
Abigail, b. Feb. 22, 1770.
Timothy, b. Sept. 21, 1772.
Susanna, b. May 1, 1775.
Joseph, b. June 20, 1778.

Aaron Wood, son of Aaron, was born at Pepperell, Mass., May 30, 1776; m. Eady Curtis, b. Jan. 10, 1778. She died at Mason, N. H., Aug. 13, 1811. By this wife he had six children:

Becky, b. Oct. 11, 1800; d. Aug. 31, 1802.
Mary, b. Nov. 22, 1802; d. Apr. 29, 1851.
Aaron Curtis, b. Feb. 4, 1805; d. Mar. 25, 1819.
Suky, b. Jan. 2, 1807; d. Aug. 8, 1814.
Benjamin F., b. Mar. 16, 1809; d. Feb. 25, 1832; unmarried.
Eady, b. June 23, 1811; d. May 19, 1828; unmarried.

Wm Anson Wood

DIE VIRESCIT

Aaron Wood married 2nd wife, Rebeckah Wright of Westford, Mass., Feb. 2, 1812. He died at Rensselaerville, N. Y., June 4, 1848. They had eight children:

William Anson, b. Aug. 3, 1813; d. Nov. 18, 1884.
Walter Abbott, b. Oct. 23, 1815.
Eliphalet, b. Feb. 1, 1819.
Rebeckah Ann, b. May 16, 1821; d. Feb. 5, 1851; unmarried.
Sarah Jane, b. March 18, 1823.
Harriet Newell, b. July 30, 1825; d. Aug. 9, 1825.
Susan, b. Sept. 18, 1826; d. Aug. 7, 1828.
Luther Wright, b. Feb. 17, 1830; d. Feb. 3, 1835.

WILLIAM ANSON WOOD.

William Anson Wood, son of Aaron Wood and Rebeckah (Wright) Wood, was born at Mason, N. H., August 3rd, 1813.

His father, in his day, was a well-known and enterprising citizen, at the place of his birth, in Pepperell, Mass., and after his marriage and removal to Mason, N. H., where he resided for many years, engaged in his trade with marked success.

By reason of endorsements, he lost heavily, which induced him to leave Mason, locating for a short time at Washington, Berkshire, Co., Mass., thence he removed to New York State, and was among the first to manufacture the celebrated Jethro Wood Cast Iron Plow. Mr. Wood finally settled at Rensselaerville, Albany Co., where he found an intelligent, thrifty New England community, and fine schools for the education of his children. William Anson, the subject of this sketch, entered his father's shop at an early age, soon developing rare mechanical and inventive genius. When of age, he struck out for himself, locating at Hoosick Falls, N. Y., where for a long time he occupied a leading position as master mechanic in the well-known factory of Parsons & Wilder.

About the year 1850, he, with many others, caught the California fever, and decided to break the relations that had so long and pleasantly existed between Messrs. Parsons & Wilder and himself, and try his fortune in the "New Eldorado." Falling very ill on the steamer, he was compelled to land at New Orleans, where he stopped long enough to recover health, deciding meanwhile to abandon the trip and return North, which he did via the Mississippi river, thence to Cleveland, Ohio. He found here an old Rensselaerville friend, Col. Ethan Rogers, superintending the Cuyahoga Iron Works, and was by him induced to take a responsible place in the works.

Mr. Wood, in this position, made a reputation for genius of a high order, and attained great popularity as a citizen; was elected a member of the City Council, which trust he discharged with honor and fidelity, retiring with clean hands.

About the year 1856, the business of his brother, Walter Abbott Wood, had assumed such magnitude, that it became necessary to employ a competent superintendent. This qualification he knew his brother, Wm. Anson, possessed, and with the hope of improving his financial condition, he entered into an arrangement with Anson to take charge of the Reaper and Mower Factory at Hoosick Falls, with the additional duty of originating and adopting improvements in the Bureau of Invention. This responsible office he filled most creditably for fifteen years, at the expiration of which time he withdrew, having a reasonable competency. After a few years of retired life he was induced to engage in business with the late James S. Thayer, of New York, allowing the use of his name as the "William

Anson Wood Reaper and Mower Co.," Mr. Wood and his son Frank taking charge of the Patent and Mechanical Department, Thayer and Quackenbush the financial. This connection proved most disastrous, Mr. Wood advancing money and services without recovery; endorsing their paper without reserve, which soon worked his financial ruin, though he came out of the trial with a reputation for probity and integrity unsullied.

The Company was re-organized, and for two years continued their business at Albany, when it was sold out to capitalists of Youngstown, Ohio, in 1880, and established on a sound financial basis, Mr. Wood and his son, Frank Wood, filling the positions relatively, as at Albany, though at this date (1884) his failing health prevents him from giving much time or attention to the business; but the use of his name is of incalculable value to the concern, as Mr. Wood is well known among the celebrated inventors of the country, and is justly entitled to be ranked with those who have amassed fortunes.

Mr. Wood is in every sense of the word a self-made man; his early education being limited, and capital small in dollars and cents, but with an active brain and diligent hands, an unselfish heart and unswerving principles, he has battled the ills of life manfully for over seventy years, and none will deny him an honorable name. His motto was, "Whatever is done, let it be well done."

He never felt ashamed to be called a mechanic. Although frequently invited to take office from his fellow-citizens, with the exception of his service in the Council of Cleveland, he consented but once to be nominated for the assembly in Rensselaer Co. by the Democratic party in a strong Republican district, and narrowly escaped an election.

He was again, in 1878, unanimously nominated for Congress in the 17th district, but his brother, Walter A. Wood, being a candidate on the Republican ticket, he declined the honor.

Since the foregoing was written, William Anson Wood has passed this life's limits. He died November 18, 1884. His genial nature and obliging manners endeared him to many, many friends.

DESCENDANTS OF WILLIAM ANSON WOOD.

William Anson Wood, son of Aaron, was married at Rensselaerville, N. Y., Aug. 25, 1835, to Jane Dodge, dau. of Judge Luther Carter of Green Co., N. Y. They had three children. One died in infancy:

MARY JANETTE, b. Sept. 26, 1840.
FRANK, b. May 31, 1842.

Mary Janette m. Charles H. King, merchant of Wilmington, N. C., Sept. 29, 1869. They have one child:

ANSON WOOD KING, b. Apr. 25, 1873.

Frank Wood, son of Wm. Anson, m. Alice Crawford Thayer, dau. of Hon. Adin Thayer, Hoosick Falls, N. Y. They have:

ALICE THAYER, b. Feb. 4, 1871.
WILLIAM ADIN, b. June 26, 1872.
FRANK THAYER, b. Nov. 29, 1875.
ELIPHALET CRAWFORD, b. Feb. 25, 1880.

Frank Wood is noticed in the sketch of his father, Wm. Anson Wood.

WALTER ABBOTT WOOD.

WALTER ABBOTT WOOD, son of Aaron Wood and Rebeckah (Wright) Wood, was born at Mason, Hillsboro' Co., N. H., October 23rd, 1815.

At an early age his inclinations and tastes led him to engage in mechanical pursuits; remaining with his father until twenty years of age, he became master of his trade.

In the year 1835 he located at Hoosick Falls, N. Y., in the machine works of Parsons & Wilder, and soon found himself in a field of labor adapted to his genius and ambition, and by industry and close application took a high rank in the estimation of the firm and among his fellow-workmen; indeed, there was nothing in the line of his trade that he was unwilling to undertake and master.

One of the leading traits of his character was developed early, that was, never to give up what he undertook to do that would advance the science of mechanism. He always commanded the best wages in the factory, by reason of which (and the exercise of reasonable economy), he acquired a small capital, and soon established himself in business on his own account.

Farming implements became his "hobby," to the study of which he gave much time and attention, resulting in the introduction of the Manny Harvesting Machine, with Wood's Improvements; and in the year 1852 a hundred or two were made and sold by Mr. Wood. He continued to invent and improve upon Mowers and Reapers, so that in the year 1853 his sales amounted to five hundred. They were so well received by the farmers that he resolved to increase his works and manufacture on as large a scale as his means would warrant.

Notwithstanding these increased facilities, they were found insufficient to supply the demand. In the year 1859 his production and sales were 6,000; in 1869, 23,000; in 1879, 25,000; and in 1884, 48,300, and the total number made and sold since he commenced the business, sum up five hundred thirty-three thousand, which exceeds that of any other one establishment of the kind in the world.

His machines have found a market in every kingdom, and upon their working "the sun never sets."

From the small beginning named, it has now become the most extensive works known in the trade in this country or in Europe.

They occupy eighty-five acres of land for the workshops, store-houses and lumber yard; all parts of the works are connected by railway tracks of their own, five miles in length, and employing two powerful locomotives belonging to the company for transportation and shipping on their own grounds.

The average production of the factory exceeds two hundred and twenty-five machines daily, and the supply of material and shipping of machines is about twenty carloads every twenty-four hours.

The number of employés to man the works, fifteen hundred; add to this the number of those employed in their various branch establishments for the sale and distribution, the whole number employed will exceed two thousand. The yearly sales now exceed five million dollars.

Up to and including the year 1865, Mr. Wood conducted his business single handed; from 1866 to the present time, it has been organized under the laws of New York as a stock company, known as the "WALTER A. WOOD MOWING AND REAPING MACHINE CO.," with a capital of two million five hundred thousand dollars, Mr. Wood acting as President without intermission.

The writer is indebted to the "Encyclopædia of Contemporary Biography of New York," for the following extract:

"Mr. Wood early perceived the necessity for such implements abroad, particularly in the great grain districts of South-Eastern Europe, where the conditions so nearly correspond with those of the American grain-producing areas. In 1858 he established an office in London, and securing a competent representative, sent thither an invoice of fifty of his machines. They were the first implements of this class sent to Europe, and were speedily sold. The next year he sent out two hundred and fifty, which were disposed of with equal facility. Since that

Atlantic Publishing & Engraving Co. New York.

Walter A Wood

date the foreign sales have largely increased, the total number exported up to the close of 1872 being thirty thousand,—fully ninety per cent. of the whole number sold in that country by American makers."

Since which date a continued increased demand has been made upon his establishment until the aggregate exportation, to the present date, has reached one hundred and ten thousand!

In this connection it is just and very proper to say, that at all the great World's Fairs and Expositions in Europe, as well as in America, Wood's machines have been on exhibition and in competition with English and American machines, and also in field trials, where the most severe scientific tests have been applied, and with scarcely an exception Mr. Wood has received the highest awards.

At the Royal Agricultural Society of England, at the famous trial at Leeds in 1861.

At the London Exhibition they won the grand medal of merit, the highest award conferred.

At the Paris Universal Exposition, held in 1876, the display of the like implements far exceeded all former exhibits. The Walter A. Wood machines took the leading rank, and were awarded the grand Gold Medal of honor, also the Cross of Chevalier of the Legion of Honor.

And again at the great international field trial in France, Mr. Wood took the first prize against the world.

His next victory was achieved at the Vienna International Exhibition in 1873, which surpassed, if possible, all former competition in the number of machines on trial. After a sharp contest, Mr. Wood was unanimously awarded by the jury the highest prize, the Grand Diploma of Honor, and knighted with the Cross of the Imperial Order of Francis Joseph. At this trial Mr. Wood, for the first time, brought into the field his justly celebrated Harvester and Binder, which machine attracted universal attention, and was pronounced by all observers as the most complete consummation and perfection of labor-saving harvesting machines.

Again, at the World's Paris Exposition of 1878, Mr. Wood reaped the highest prize and honor, the prize being "an object of Art," and the honor of being promoted to "The Cross of Officer of the Legion of Honor."

It is unnecessary, in this brief sketch, to enumerate the many conquests that Mr. Wood has achieved over all American machines of the like kinds in this country, inasmuch as his name has become a household word throughout the length and breadth of the land. His exhibits at the Centennial Show at Philadelphia, in the year 1876, and at State and County Agricultural Fairs innumerable, have brought to him over fifteen hundred invaluable prizes.

His palatial mansion at Hoosick Falls is a perfect museum of Rewards of Merit, which fails to move him to pride or vain-glory.

The Church never lacks a warm and liberal friend, or the State a good citizen; his hand is always open to the wants of the poor; and mechanics and clerks in his employment who make an honest effort to advance in the world, always find favor and encouragement at his hands. Being a self-made man, nothing delights him more than to see others succeed.

During the thirty-six years of his active business life, Mr. Wood has never failed to meet his engagements; although one disaster after another came upon him, sometimes in quick succession, which might discourage and overwhelm others, he rallied all his energies and soon overcame them. For tenacity of purpose he was most remarkable.

In the year 1860, his entire works were destroyed by fire, with partial insurance, and at a time approaching a harvest, when, under obligations to supply machines to his customers, with a will and purpose peculiar to himself, he rallied his men and took the lead personally to clear away the rubbish, and in the short space of eighty days the shops were reconstructed and in working order. Again, in 1870, the same calamity overtook the works, and in like manner they were restored in sixty days.

The true secret of Mr. Wood's success may be attributed to the fact that he never would allow a machine to be sold to the farmers until he had fully tested its merits and was personally certain that it would do the work claimed for it.

Mr. Wood is not, in the narrow sense of the word, a politician, his business interests engaging most of his time. During the Rebellion, he made his influence felt in the right direction, and rendered valuable service in helping the families of those who enlisted in their country's cause, and since that time has been a declared Republican.

During his absence from the country, attending the World's Fair at Paris, in 1878, he was nominated for Congress by his party in the 17th Congressional district, composed of Washington and Rensselaer Counties. Upon his return in October, previous to the election in November following, there was no time left for him to consider the matter; his reception at his home at Hoosick Falls was so cordial and overwhelming, that he yielded to the wishes of his friends and accepted the honor. Notwithstanding the district had, the year previous, elected a democratic Senator, Charles Hughes, by about five hundred majority, he came out of the canvass with seven thousand majority. He was re-nominated in 1880 and was re-elected by a majority of seventeen thousand.

During his four years in Congress he faithfully represented his constituents and his party, and expressed no regrets when his term expired, as his tastes and habits of life made it more congenial for him to be about his own business and in the enjoyment of his home and family, than in the whirlpool of politics.

Incidents occur in the life of most men that demonstrate their peculiar characteristics, by means of which they make lifelong impressions and friendships.

When Mr. Wood was a young man, and in the employ of a prominent manufacturer, and turned out a larger number of pieces than any other employé, it was remarked to him, in a playful manner, that he exceeded all others in the number of pieces daily. He quickly replied, "Does not the scriptures say, 'blessed are the peace-makers,'" &c. This man, who lived to a good old age, never failed to interest himself in Mr. Wood's success in all his business enterprises, and often reminded him of the "piece-makers." May not our young men seek for an incentive to industry that excels!

It is difficult to estimate the immense value the Wood inventions have been to the world. It is perfectly safe to say that hundreds of millions of dollars is not excessive in making up the account, and some parties claim that the sum total would more than pay our present national debt! May we not claim for Mr. Wood that he has been a benefactor to his own country and to the agricultural world, and now lives to see the words of Revelation fulfilled: "He that is diligent in his calling shall stand before kings."

DESCENDANTS OF WALTER ABBOTT WOOD.

Walter Abbott Wood, son of Aaron, married Betsey A. Parsons, dau. of the Hon. Seth Parsons of Hoosick Falls, N. Y., 1842. They had two children:

JAMES T., b. Aug. 24, 1843, at Hoosick Falls, N. Y.; d. Aug. 31, 1848.

LYN P., b. Apr. 30, 1850, at Brattleboro', Vt.

Mrs. Betsey A. Wood, b. at Hoosick Falls, June 19, 1821; d. May 24, 1867.

Walter A. Wood was married to his second wife, Lizzie Warren Nichols, dau. of the Rev. George Nichols of Hoosick Falls, Sept. 2, 1868. They have two children:

WALTER A., b. June 2, 1871.
JULIA N., b. June 9, 1874.

Lyn P. Wood, son of Walter A., was married to Mary E. Jack, Aug. 21, 1873. Their child:

BESSIE LYN, b. Dec. 20, 1876.

Lyn P. Wood d. Apr. 22, 1877. The widow and child reside with a sister, Mrs. E. H. Valentine, Chicago, Ill.

ELIPHALET WOOD.

ELIPHALET WOOD, son of Aaron Wood and Rebeckah (Wright) Wood, was born February 1st, 1819, at Washington, Berkshire Co., Mass. Unlike his brothers, William Anson and Walter Abbott, he did not take to the workshop, but at an early age decided to be a merchant, and, suiting the action to the word, found a situation behind the counter of a dry goods house in the city of Albany, N. Y., in the year 1835.

His diligent attention to business in the old established and well known wholesale dry goods house of Gaylor & Smith Sheldon, secured to himself a position as junior partner in the year 1840, under the title of Gaylor, Sheldon & Co., subsequently it was changed to that of Sheldons & Wood, where he continued in active business relations until March, 1854, when he parted with his interest to Sheldons & Co., and in May removed with his family to the growing city of Chicago, entering the lumber business under the name and title of the "Newaygo Co."

The mills and landed estate of the Company were located in Michigan, at Newaygo, on the Muskegon river; the company erected the first gang-saw-mill west of Saginaw, running one hundred and fifty saws, with a capacity to manufacture one hundred thousand feet of pine lumber daily.

Eliphalet Wood was the sole resident partner at Chicago, where their sales of their own make of lumber, for eighteen years, averaged over ten million feet yearly.

The introduction of gang-sawed lumber into that market gained rapid favor, so that very soon thereafter all the enterprising manufacturers adopted the use of gang-saws. The advantage gained in their use over all other saws then in vogue, was in the economy of timber and the producing of lumber free from "stub-shots," smooth, and of uniform widths and thickness.

Eliphalet Wood took a prominent part in the organization of the first Lumberman's Board of Trade in that city, and in the introduction of uniform rules of inspection, and acted as Secretary to the Board. He was also well known in the political circles of the city, always holding to conservative opinions, acting with the Bell and Everett party, and was nominated for the office of Mayor of Chicago by that party in the spring of 1860, but declined the honor on account of large business responsibilities.

When the civil war came upon the country in April, 1861, Eliphalet Wood was among the first of the loyal and patriotic citizens to "rally around the old flag" for the protection of the union of States, "one and inseparable," and was appointed a member of the "Union Defence Committee" at the first mass meeting called for the purpose of raising funds for the arming and equipping soldiers for the war, and by that committee selected to serve on the Finance and Military Organization Department. This organization was rendered indispensable in the absence of regular army officers, and did most invaluable service in raising money and men at a critical time in the history of the country, acting as they did, under orders from the Governor of the State of Illinois, and from General Frémont, who was in command of that division of the U. S. Army, and located at St. Louis.

The "Union Defence Committee" were remarkably efficient in the work of inducing volunteers into the army and succeeded in dispatching a regiment to Cairo, under the command of Col. R. K. Swift, in time to keep that strategetic point out of the hands of the confederates. They also sent into the State of Missouri several regiments and batteries at a critical time, where they rendered invaluable service in retaining that State in the Union.

The "Union Defence Committee" was composed of twelve distinguished citizens of each of the two leading parties, and one Bell and Everett partisan; they devoted their time for nearly two years without pay or emolument. At the final closing of their business connection with the Government, Eliphalet Wood, in conjunction with Col. James H. Bowen and Charles G. Wicker, was commissioned by the committee to visit Washington and conclude a final settlement with the Government, covering all their transactions. Such settlement was honorably concluded after seven weeks of indefatigable labor, Eliphalet Wood, only, remaining to the last, receipting for the money paid by the Government, amounting to several hundred thousand dollars, and then safely returned the same to the officers of the "Union Defence Committee" (who disbursed it quickly to the almost numberless creditors of the Government), for which service he received the unanimous vote of thanks of the Committee.

Mr. Wood was active and liberal in all church relations, holding the office of trustee and treasurer of the Presbyterian Northwest Theological Seminary of Chicago at a time in its history when greatly embarrassed; he also served on the Building Committee, retaining his position until he left that city, in 1869, to reside at Irvington-on-the-Hudson, where he still lives comparatively retired from the active business of a busy life, which has by no means been free from anxiety, perplexity and toil. During his residence at Irvington, he has taken a deep interest in the schools in the township, and served nine years with zeal on the Board of Education, during most of the time as President of the Board.

At the present time he holds the office of Manager of the Walter A. Wood Mowing and Reaping Machine Co., in New York City, in which company he is a stockholder, and for many years has felt a lively interest.

Success he considers man's general highest ambition; "but that a good name *with success* is far better, and none can attain unto it without a struggle."

DESCENDANTS OF ELIPHALET WOOD.

Eliphalet Wood, above named, married in Albany, N. Y., Aug. 31, 1841, Mary J. Grant, dau. of Sweton Grant of Hobart, Delaware Co., N. Y. They had eight children; seven died in infancy and childhood, as follows:

ELIPHALET GRANT,
ELIPHALET GRANT,
MARY ALICE,
WALTER BOYNTON,
WILLIAM SPRAGUE,
CHARLES FREDERICK,
WALTER ANSON.

Caroline Whitely Wood, the only surviving child, was married to Joseph Ormsby Rutter of Chicago, Ill., by Wm. B. Sprague, D.D., at Irvington-on-the-Hudson, Mar. 10, 1874. Their children:

MARY, b. June 22, 1875; d. Sept. 11, 1875.
ESTHER, b. Jan. 1, 1877.
CAROLINE, b. Feb. 7, 1880.
REBECKAH, b. July 20, 1881.
JOSEPH WOOD, b. Apr. 6, 1883.

Mr. Rutter is the oldest son of Dr. Rutter, originally of Philadelphia, Pa., but for many years a resident of Chicago, Ill., holding a high place in his profession, and an influential and well-known citizen.

Joseph O. Rutter, for many years, as at present, a leading banker in the city of Chicago, and President of the Traders' Bank, is well known in commercial circles of the Northwest as a man of influence and probity.

Sarah Jane Wood, dau. of Aaron², married E. D. Selden, a retired gentleman. They reside at Saratoga Springs, N. Y. They have no children. Their home is supplied with all the surroundings and comforts of modern times, where they dispense true New England hospitality.

DESCENDANTS OF LUCY WOOD (6).

Lucy Wood, the fourth child of Jeremiah and Dorathy, b. in Stow, Mass., Mar. 4, 1715; m. George Chase of Littleton. They had:

Francis, b. Oct. 14, 1734.
Lucy, b. July 25, 1739.
Abigail, b. Sept. 9, 1741.
Joshua, b. Aug. 31, 1743.
Elizabeth, b. Mar. 30, 1745.
Charles, b. Aug. 8, 1747.
Sarah, b. July 14, 1749.
Hannah, b. Aug. 5, 1751.
Abel, b. June 3, 1754.
Abraham, b. June 24, 175—, the last figure illegible.

—[Littleton Town Records.]

Afterwards the family probably settled in Shirley, Mass.

BENNET WOOD (7) AND DESCENDANTS.

Bennet Wood, the fifth child of Jeremiah and Dorathy, was born in Littleton, Mass., Mar. 15, 1717; he was married to Lydia Law of Acton, Mass., in Jan., 1739, by Rev. John Swift, the first minister of Acton. Bennet was a housewright. After the death of his younger brother, Jeremiah, he bought most of the shares falling to his brothers and sisters. Their deeds to Bennet are recorded at Cambridge, Mass.

Children of Bennet and Lydia (Law) Wood:

DORATHY, b. Jan. 10, 1740; d. Mar. 8, 1740.
DORATHY, b. Mar. 7, 1741; m. Deliverance Davis of Littleton.
JEREMIAH, b. June 10, 1744; d. Feb. 25, 1767.
THOMAS, b. Oct. 23, 1746; d. Mar. 2, 1794.
SUSANNA, b. Apr. 14, 1750; m. Samuel Foster of Ashburnham, Mass.

Lydia, wife of Bennet, and mother of his children, died Feb. 27, 1765, aged 54 yrs., 1 mo., 13 da., and is buried among the Wood families in Littleton.

Bennet m. second wife, Mrs. Isabel Taylor, the daughter of the first Dea. John Wood and Sarah, his wife, of Littleton. Her first husband was Oliver Taylor, who died June 2, 1759, in his 45th year.

I find nothing to show that the first Dea. John Wood, who married Sarah, was any connection of our branch. He was neither father, brother nor son of Jeremiah. He was one of the Selectmen with Jeremiah, as shown by their orders upon the Treasurer.

Bennet was a prominent and enterprising citizen, as his numerous deeds and business transactions show. He was interested in the church and formation of the new town of Boxboro', and did much to make success certain.

From the gravestones of Bennet Wood and his second wife, in the cemetery at Boxboro', I extract the following:

"In memory of
Mr. BENNET WOOD,
who departed this life
Apr. 28, 1797.
in the 81st year of his age."

"In memory of
Mrs. ISABEL WOOD
Relict of Mr. Bennet Wood
who departed this life
Dec. 14, 1797
in the 84th year of her age."

Near them is buried Lois Wood, dau. of Jeremiah and Elizabeth Wood, and granddaughter of Bennet Wood, who died Feb. 1, 1782, at the age of 15 years, 2 months and 22 days.

Ebenezer Bennet Davis, son of Deliverance and Dorathy (Wood) Davis, and grandson of Bennet Wood, b. Feb. 4, 1761. Oliver Taylor Davis, son of Deliverance and Dorathy (Wood) Davis, b. Nov. 22, 1762; m. Mary Sawyer of Harvard, Mass. He settled upon the homestead of Bennet Wood, which was a part of the purchase of Bennet's father, Jeremiah Wood. Oliver Taylor Davis d. 1841; had Eli, Sally, Sophronia, Clarissa, Dorathy, Lydia, Oliver and Mary, all now deceased. Of these children:

1. ELI, m. Aseneth Jewett; had Wm. Jerome, Oliver T. d., Eli Francis, Angeline d., Julia A. who m. a Davis, Ellen d. and others that died young.
2. SALLY, and 3, SOPHRONIA, d. unmarried.
4. CLARISSA, m. Wm. Clark; had Wm. Mayhews, d., John Saltenstall, res. Peoria, Ill., Sarah (Clark) Dodge d.
5. DORATHY, m. Wm. A. Kelley; had Mary Jane, who m. John Reed, who had Mary J. Reed, who married Dea. Boynton of Lowell, Mass.

6. LYDIA, m. John Brooks of Chester, Vt.; had John D., became a physician, d., Mary H. d., Martha d.
7. OLIVER, m. ———; had Marshall, res. Lexington, Mass.; Jane Elizabeth, m. —— Robertson, res. Hudson, Mass.
8. MARY, b. in Boxboro', Mass., Sept. 4, 1797; d. Sept., 1872; m. George Sawyer, b. in Harvard, Mass., May 15, 1793; d. in Dorchester, Mass., July 17, 1855; had George A. Sawyer (Proprietor of Sawyer's Commercial College, 161 Tremont St., Boston, Mass.); Edwin d. an infant; Henry Edwin d. 1847; Ellen d. an infant; Chancy B.; Mary Jane d. 1858, aged 24 yrs.; Martha W.

Thomas Wood, son of Bennet, had by wife Mary:

THOMAS, Jr., b. Dec. 21, 1776, in Littleton, Mass.
MARY, b. Dec. 24, 1778, in Littleton.
LYDIA LAW, b. Sept. 19, 1780, in Littleton; d. 1801, unmarried.
JEREMIAH, b. Oct. 6, 1782, in Littleton.
LOIS, b. Jan. 2, 1784, in Littleton.
SUSANNA M., b. Nov. 29, 1785.
ZACHARIAH, b. Oct. 13, 1787.
BENNET, b. Oct. 30, 1789; d. Apr. 26, 1794.
DANIEL, b. Oct. 8, 1791; d. July 30, 1795.
ELIZABETH, b. Jan. 7, 1793; d. July 31, 1795.
SALLIE, b. May 20, 1794.

Thomas Wood, father of the above, died March 2, 1794.

Thomas Wood, Jr., was drafted into the army and died of yellow fever while on his way from Maine to Boston, or about the time the vessel landed. He left two sons, Samuel and Jackson. Samuel married and had a family of children. He lived in Brownsville, Maine, owning a large farm there. Jackson was unmarried in 1847 when he was visiting in Massachusetts.

Jeremiah Wood, son of Thomas, Senior, was drowned, with many others, in a severe storm, while on his way from South Carolina. He was a carpenter, was married, but my informant thinks he had no children.

Zechariah Wood, son of Thomas, Senior, was in the war of 1812; was taken prisoner by the Indians; his fate was never known; was not married.

Mary Wood married a Mansfield and lived in New Hampshire, and had a large family of children. One daughter married a man by the name of Start. They removed to Brownsville, Me., and had a large family; several died young, and Mrs. Start was dead in 1847.

I have no information at hand of the two remaining daughters whose names are found in the family record of Thomas Wood, son of Bennet.

Susanna Wood, dau. of Bennet, m. Samuel Foster, July 6, 1769; he was b. Jan. 9, 1743, and d. Apr. 15, 1793. Their children were as follows:

Abraham, b. Apr. 8, 1770; d. Dec. 12, 1837.
Nathaniel, b. Dec. 26, 1771; d. Sept. 30, 1836.
Jeremiah B., b. Oct. 14, 1773; d. May 3, 1846; unmarried.
Samuel, b. Feb. 9, 1776; d. Apr. 24, 1868.
Hosea, b. Aug. 1, 1778; d. Feb. 23, 1855.
Joel, b. Aug. 21, 1780; d. Sept. 6, 1859.
Amos, b. Nov. 16, 1782; d. Sept., 1812; unmarried.
Obadiah, b. Oct. 25, 1786; d. July 23, 1809; unmarried.
Susanna, b. Sept. 25, 1789; d. Mar. 15, 1867.
Dorathy, b. Nov. 25, 1793; d. Apr. 14, 1867.

Abraham Foster, son of Samuel and Susanna (Wood) Foster, m. a wife by the name of Willard. Their children were John, Sally, Mary and Willard. Willard Foster lives in Gardner, Mass., where one or more of his children still reside.

Nathaniel Foster, second son of Samuel and Susanna Wood, m. Hepsibath Cotting. Their children:

1. Rhoda; m. Asa Smith of Gardner; had one son.
2. Samuel; d. 1870; he m. Emeline Kibling; had five children, only one of whom is living.

3. EMMA; m. Thomas Bennett of Gardner; had eight children.
4. EUNICE; m. Henry Carter of Leominster, Mass.; had four children.
5. NANCY; m. Metephor Kendall of Leominster; d. 1843; had five children.
6. MARY, b. 1807; d. 1882; m. Stillman D. Benjamin of Shirley, Mass. Their children are:

Sidney W., b. 1833; m. Mary Harris of Ashburnham, 1873, and now resides in Shirley.
Viola D., b. 1836; resides in Everett, Mass.
Mary Jane, b. 1841; m. L. L. Brown, 1865; resides in Harvard, Mass.
Frances Ann, b. 1845; resides in Shirley.

7. ADALINE; m. Albert Lamb of Leominster.
8. ELVIRA F.; m. Stephen Dodge of Leominster.
9. LEONARD; m. Melvina Lawrence of Ashburnham.

Leonard Foster is still living at Ashburnham, where for many years he has been a prominent business man.

Samuel Foster, son of Samuel and Susanna (Wood) Foster, m. Lydia Stearns, b. Mar. 24, 1780, who was dau. of Wm. Stearns, son of Hon. Isaac Stearns, son of John, son of Capt. John, son of John born in England between 1628 and 1633, and one of the first settlers of Billerica, Mass., whose father, Isaac Stearns, was the emigrant ancestor, born in the Parish of Wayland, County of Suffolk, England. He came to America in the same ship (the *Arbella*) with Gov. Winthrop, in 1630, and settled in Watertown, Mass.

Children of Samuel and Lydia Stearns Foster, all born in Stoddard, N. H.:

STEARNS, b. Dec. 26, 1799; m. Cynthia Willson, b. Sept. 8, 1804, m. Feb. 3, 1825; she d. July 9, 1844; second wife, Mary Fuller, b. June 13, 1813; m. Dec. 3, 1845.

LYDIA, b. Aug. 22, 1801; m. Nov. 24, 1824, Dea. Luke Joslin, b. Dec. 22, 1797.

MARIA, b. Apr. 29, 1804; m. Nov. 4, 1823, in Stoddard, N. H., Stephen Wood, b. Jan. 11, 1800; he d. Apr. 30, 1874.

HOSEA, b. Apr. 13, 1806; m. Mary G. Rice, Nov. 7, 1833, b. Mar. 14, 1816; he d. Feb. 7, 1872.

SELINA, b. July 5, 1809; m. Feb. 16, 1830, Mark Bowers; settled in Hancock, N. H.; he d.

EMILY, b. Dec. 19, 1811; m. Oct. 10, 1833, Dea. Edward Hayward, b. Apr. 26, 1810; residence, until 1869, Hancock, N. H.; he d. Nov. 6, 1883, at Hyde Park, Mass.

SAMUEL, b. Nov. 29, 1815; m. Nov. 5, 1845, Mary S. Palmer, b. Aug. 23, 1823; he d. Aug. 5, 1850; his wife d. Sept. 25, 1846. Had: Mary Alice, b. Sept. 20, 1846; d. in infancy. Merchant in Boston; d. there; buried with his family in Mt. Auburn.

ELECTA, b. Nov. 10, 1817; d. Dec. 25, 1818.

ELECTA, b. June 10, 1825; m. June 15, 1850, James Downing, b. Apr. 8, 1815.

Children of Stearns Foster by first wife, Cynthia (Wilson) Foster:

HENRY, b. Mar. 2, 1826; d. Mar. 3, 1826.

EDWIN, b. Nov. 18, 1828; d. Feb. 8, 1832.

GEORGE, b. June 10, 1830; m. Feb. 25, 1857, Dollie E. Whicher, b. Mar. 15, 1837.

AMELIA, b. June 3, 1838; d. Nov. 9, 1838.

EMMA L., b. Sept. 16, 1843; d. Sept. 17, 1844.

By second wife, Mary (Fuller) Foster:

MARY A., b. June 25, 1849.

WILLIAM S., b. Sept. 1, 1851.

Children of Lydia Foster and Luke Joslin:

GILMAN, b. Dec. 25, 1825; m. Feb. 20, 1851, Susan A. Williams; he d. Nov. 16, 1867. They had: Oscar A., b. Aug. 20, 1855, and Mary A., b. Aug. 5, 1862.

ALBERT, b. Oct. 27, 1828; d. July 13, 1850.

Elsie, b. July 21, 1832; m. Jan. 22, 1855, Ira F. Prouty, M.D., b. Nov. 9, 1812; she d. Jan. 17, 1882. They had: Ira J., b. Aug. 15, 1857, who m. Etta M. Humphrey, July 19, 1882.

Ira F. Prouty, M.D., graduated from Dartmouth Medical School, 1837.

Ira J. Prouty, M.D., graduated at Medical Department University, City of New York, 1882; now practising in Keene, N. H.

CHILDREN AND DESCENDANTS OF MARIA FOSTER AND STEPHEN WOOD.

Records found in the Salmon Wood branch (2509).

Children of Hosea and Mary G. (Rice) Foster:

Alvin R., b. Oct. 14, 1834; m. Feb. 2, 1866, Mary J. Sargent. Had: Herbert A., b. Mar. 27, 1867; Nellie M., b. Sept. 17, 1872. The mother, Mary J., d. June 15, 1877. Alvin R. m. June 13, 1880, second wife, Mrs. Eliza A. Scott.

Sarah M., b. Apr. 9, 1837; d. Nov. 23, 1858.

Edwin S., b. Dec. 21, 1840, m. Nov. 26, 1868, Ella S. Houghton. Had: Frank H., b. Sept. 10, 1869; Harry S., b. May 17, 1871; George E., b. Aug. 13, 1872; Louisa Belle, b. Aug. 13, 1876; Carl H., b. Jan. 3, 1883; Grace A., b. Feb. 23, 1884.

Charles M., b. Nov. 16, 1843.

Horace E., b. Aug. 22, 1846; d. Jan. 9, 1853.

Ella F., b. Feb. 20, 1856.

Children of Selina Foster and Mark Bowers:

George, b. Oct. 10, 1831, m. Dec. 28, 1858, Urania E. Brackett; settled in Nashua, N. H.; graduated at the Philadelphia College, receiving the degree of Doctor of Dental Surgery, 1865. Had: Adelbert V., b. Mar. 29, 1860, d. Jan. 18, 1865; Lucy A., b. Feb. 12, 1862, d. Jan. 29, 1867; Horace A., b. Dec. 15, 1863, grad. Nashua High School, 1881, and in the University of Penn., 1884, receiving the degree of Doctor of Dental Surgery; George A., b. Mar. 31, 1866, grad. Nashua High School, 1884.

ALMIRA, b. Oct. 14, 1832; m. Reuben M. Sawyer, June 17, 1856; settled in Nashua, N. H. Had: Frank M., b. Apr. 21, 1861, d. July 18, 1879.

CAROLINE, b. Apr. 30, 1835; m. June 17, 1856, Adams A. Roberts; settled in Kansas; d. May 24, 1862. Children: Three, d. in infancy.

ALBERT, b. Apr. 11, 1837; m. Melvina E. Hart, June 22, 1869. Grad. at Dartmouth College in 1863, and at Andover Theological Seminary in 1868. Settled in Macon, Mo., the same year, as Pastor of a Congregational Church, where he remained about five years, then removed to Huntington, West Virginia, where he was pastor of a flourishing parish about eleven years. Then he removed (1884) to Ruggles, Ohio. Children: Roy E. and Berta H.

CYNTHIA, b. May 17, 1839; m. Asa D. Wood, June 21, 1859; settled in Hancock, N. H.

HORACE S., b. July 17, 1841; enlisted in a Mass. regiment, 1861; d. Feb. 28, 1862.

SAMUEL O., b. Dec. 13, 1843; m. Susan Sharp, May 27, 1871; settled in Hillsboro', N. H.; profession, dental practice. Had: Elgin M., b. Oct. 11, 1873.

Children of Emily Foster and Dea. Edward Hayward:

SARAH M., b. July 27, 1835; m. June 5, 1855, J. Ellery Piper of Boston, Mass., b. Nov. 29, 1830. Had: Edward Ellery, b. Dec. 13, 1856; Alice Greenwood, b. Apr. 22, 1860, who m. Oct. 22, 1879, Fred. Young French, and had Arthur Hartwell French, b. Aug. 1, 1880, and Fred. Y., Jr., b. July 14, 1882; Marion Sarah, b. May 22, 1864; Arthur Willard, b. Aug. 21, 1866; Mabel Emily, b. Sept. 24, 1869.

SYLVIA A., b. July 4, 1837; d. Apr. 3, 1838.

CYNTHIA F., b. Sept. 10, 1839; m. Jan. 12, 1865, Luke Putnam Willard of Boston, Mass. Children: Annie Wellington, b. Oct. 29, 1869; May Lillian; Frederick William; Ralph Putnam, b. Feb. 24, 1878; d. in infancy.

EDWARD S., b. June 30, 1841; m. Oct. 18, 1866, Emma Washburn, b. Mar. 2, 1846, in Belfast, Me. Had: Harrison W., b. Jan. 1, 1873.

MILAN A. and MARY A., twins, b. June 7, 1843; Milan A. d. June 25, 1843; Mary A. d. July 14, 1843.

LYDIA ALICE, b. Oct. 24, 1847; d. Sept. 13, 1853.

FRED. A., b. Jan. 31, 1856; d. June 14, 1860.

Children of Electa Foster and James Downing:

ALBERT S., b. June 22, 1851.

GEORGE E., b. Sept. 11, 1854.

HERBERT J., b. July 12, 1858.

ELLEN C., b. Oct. 24, 1865.

Hosea Foster, son of Samuel and Susanna Wood, m. Polly Joslin and emigrated to Verona, Oneida Co., N. Y. Their children were Polly, Susan, Caroline and Hosea.

POLLY FOSTER, m. Justus Brewster of Verona, N. Y., had Amos F., Mary, Susan F., Polly J. Amos F. Brewster has Susan, Jenny, Julia and Foster. Jenny m. ——— Knight; Julia m. David Broughton, of Little Falls, N. Y., have a daughter Reba.

Mary Brewster, dau. of Justus and Polly, m. Almon Stewart, — had 10 children.

Susan F. Brewster, m. Benjamin F. Wilson of Verona, N. Y. Their children are George, Emma, James, Frank, Alice, Julia, Herbert and Seymour.

Emma Wilson, m. Willard Soper; have two children.

Alice Wilson, m. John Brewster; have two children.

Frank Wilson, m. Emma Soper.

Polly J. Brewster, m. David Williams; had Eva, Emma, Clarence and Imogene.

SUSAN FOSTER, m. Ed. S. Latham of Seneca Falls, N. Y.; had Hosea Foster Latham, Imogene Latham.

Hosea F. Latham graduated at Hobart College, Geneva, N. Y.

Imogene Latham, m. J. Marshall Guion of Seneca Falls, N. Y.; had Ed. L. Guion and John M. Guion.

CAROLINE FOSTER, m. Oscar Granger, Feb. 21, 1833; had Antoinette S., Lyman F., and O. Foster Granger. Antoinette S., m. June 20, 1854, John T. Carr of Saratoga Springs, N. Y. Their children are Clarence G., Carrie and Lora W.

Clarence G. Carr graduated at University of Rochester, N. Y. and Carrie at N. E. Conservatory of Music; both reside in Minneapolis, Minn.

O. Foster Granger, m. Alice C. Scott. Their children are Imogene, Oscar and Carrie.

Lyman F. Granger, m. Elizabeth Hoyt; had Adelbert and Adella.

HOSEA FOSTER, m. Cornelia Scaden. Their children were Cornelia, Wesley, Emma C., Jennie E., Velton, Edward and Imogene.

Wesley Foster, m. Dec. 16, 1874, Frank Wilcox of Clockville, Mad. Co., N. Y.; have a dau., Grace Foster.

Joel Foster, son of Samuel and Susanna Wood Foster, b. at Ashburnham, Mass., Aug. 21, 1780, m. Dolly Wetherbee of Ashby, Mass., who was b. Feb. 21, 1774, and d. May 23, 1838. Their children were:

HARRIET, b. Sept. 10, 1806; m. James Hayward of Ashby, Mass., Apr. 1, 1830. She d. Apr. 10, 1839.

JOEL FOSTER, b. July 15, 1808; d. Mar. 31, 1814.

JEROME W. FOSTER, an honored and prominent citizen of Ashburnham, b. Dec. 15, 1810; m. Mary Colson Apr. 23, 1834. He d. Mar. 23, 1871. They had:

GEORGE C. FOSTER, a prominent citizen of Ashburnham, Mass., b. Jan. 21, 1835; m. Aug. 10, 1856, Sarah E. Bemis. Had:

CHARLES W., b. May 16, 1858.

GEORGE O., b. June 17, 1862; d. Feb. 12, 1883.

MARY C. FOSTER, b. Mar. 12, 1838; m. Feb. 9, 1858, Josiah P. Sawtelle, New York City; had:

NETTIE A., b. Sept. 25, 1868; d. May 25, 1871.
ANNIE C., b. Sept. 4, 1872; d. Apr. 6, 1876.

JEROME W. FOSTER, b. Nov. 5, 1839; d. Apr. 5, 1841.
HARRIET M. FOSTER, b. July 28, 1843; m. July 1, 1875, Goldsbury H. Pond.
SUSAN R. FOSTER, b. Nov. 12, 1844; d. Aug. 14, 1866.
C. LUCRETIA FOSTER, b. June 1, 1846.
ELLA JANE, b. Nov. 11, 1847; d. May 29, 1861.
D. JOSEPHINE, b. Dec. 26, 1849; d. Nov. 18, 1869.
EMMA DELPHIA, b. Feb. 6, 1852; d. Sept. 14, 1852.
EMMA, b. June 15, 1853; d. Sept. 7, 1861.
JEROME, b. June 5, 1856; d. Oct. 29, 1856.

DORATHY FOSTER, dau. of Joel and Dolly, b. Sept. 6, 1813; m. June 1833, Lewis Houghton of Ashby, Mass. She d. Dec. 31, 1863.

Susannah Foster, dau. of Samuel and Susanna (Wood) Foster of Ashburnham, Mass., m. in 1811, Francis Lane. Their children were as follows:

ALLEN F., b. 1812.
HEPSIBATH C., b. 1813.
AMOS F., b. 1815; d. 1878.
SAMUEL, b. 1817; d. 1856.
MILTON, b. 1819; d. 1876.
LEONARD, b. 1821.
HOSEA, b. 1823; d. 1828.
SUSAN W., b. 1825.
REBECCA C., b. 1827.
ELEANOR J., b. 1829.
HOSEA F., b. 1831.
CHARLES W., b. 1833.

Descendants of these children are as follows:

Allen F. Lane, m. Laura Tyler and had:

HENRY T., b. 1841; d. in the Civil War, 1864.
LAURA A., b. 1844; m. Wm. Richardson of Fitchburg.
EMMA L., b. 1847; d. 1847.

Ellen, b. 1849; m. Charles T. Harding, Fitchburg.
Albert, b. 1853.
James A., b. 1854.
Francis W., b. 1858.
Justin E., b. 1861; d. 1861.

Hepsibath C. Lane m. 1843, I. A. Packard, and had:

Charles F., b. 1844.
Frances S., b. 1846; m. A. Burnham, Westminster.
Susan R., b. 1848; m. Augustus Scales, Minneapolis, Minn.
Henry A., b. 1852.
Mina A., b. 1856; d. 1866.

Amos F. Lane m. Martha Ward; had:

William W., b. 1841.
Albert F., b. 1844; d. 1847.
Sarah N., b. 1846; d. 1847.
George F., b. 1848.
Elmira J., b. 1850.
Oman F., b. 1853.
Mary E., b. 1856.
Walter A., b. 1858.
Samuel A., b. 1860; d. 1860.
John F., b. 1861; d. 1864.

Samuel Lane m. Nancy H. Eaton of Shirley. Had:

Joel E., b. 1843; d. 1859.
Mary S., b. 1845; d. 1845.
Edward S., b. 1846.
Frederick D., b. 1849; teacher in Cushing Academy, Ashburnham.
Susetta, b. 1850; d. 1858.

Milton Lane m. Mary Parkhurst of Fitchburg; had:

Ella M., b. 1855.
Hattie P., b. 1857.
Delia M., b. 1863.
Genery M., b. 1860.
Gertrude E., b. 1867.
Herbert, b. 1869.

Gertrude and Herbert being children of a second marriage.

Leonard Lane m. Lucy Pollard. Their only child was:

Ada E., b. 1859; d. 1863.

Rebecca C. Lane m. Merrick Eaton of Ashburnham.

Eleanor J. Lane m. Daniel W. Lane of Ashburnham.

Hosea Foster Lane, now, and for twenty-nine years, Principal of Templeton, Mass., High School, m. Elizabeth E. Fairbanks of Ashburnham. Their children are:

Charles H., b. 1859.
Arthur Francis, b. 1861; d. 1862.

Charles W. Lane m. Philena (Howard) Packard of Hinsdale, N. H. Had:

Harry, b. 1871.

Dorathy Foster, youngest child of Samuel and Susanna (Wood) Foster, became the wife of Ezekiel Metcalf of Ashburnham. Their children were:

Otis, b. 1816; d. 1872.
Joel F., b. 1819.
Mary Ann, b. 1821; d. 1875.
Sultina S., b. 1824; d. 1840.
Lavina, b. 1835, d. 1848.

Otis Metcalf, son of Ezekiel and Dorathy, had three children:

George Otis, b. 1840; d. 1870.
Sultina S., b. 1842.
Augusta, b. 1844.

Joel F. Metcalf, son of Ezekiel and Dorathy, lives in Leominster, Mass. Had:

Emily, b. 1841.
Sarah, b. 1843.
Martha Ann, b. 1845; d. 1864.
Maria, b. 1846.
Walton J., b. 1854.

Mary Ann Metcalf, dau. of Ezekiel and Dorathy, m. Orrin Morton of Ashburnham; had Clara, Edward and Lavina.

JOHN WOOD.

JOHN WOOD, sixth child of Jeremiah and Dorathy Wood, was born Feb. 3, 1719, in Littleton, upon the estate now owned in part by his descendants. He was in his twelfth year when his father, Jeremiah, died.

A large portion of the real estate was set to him. His mother, Dorathy, was made his guardian,—her thirds set next to his portion, and at her decease, in 1752, her real estate was divided between Bennet and John. John was to pay the shares of his sisters Mrs. Elizabeth Robins, wife of Benjamin Robins; Mrs. Lucy Chase, wife of George Chase, and Mrs. Sarah Chase, wife of Joseph Chase, and a part of the share of Eliphalet. Bennet was to pay the remainder of Eliphalet's share, Joseph's heirs, and Jonathan. Joseph's children were Benjamin, Aaron and Grace.

The above were the heirs of the widow of Jeremiah Wood in 1752. [Entered Lib. 43, p. 460.]

John Wood, son of Jeremiah, married in Harvard, Mass., Oct. 19, 1743, Lydia Davis, daughter of Ebenezer and Sarah Davis of Harvard. She was born Sept. 7, 1724.

They had seven children, as follows:

491. SARAH, b. Aug. 2, 1744; d. Nov. 2, 1746.
492. LYDIA, b. Apr. 22, 1746; m. Oliver Davis.
493. JOHN, b. Sept. 3, 1747; d. May 4, 1826.
494. TIMOTHY, b. July 29, 1749; d. July 18, 1801.
495. SARAH, b. July 27, 1751.
496. EBENEZER, b. Jan. 20, 1754; d. Dec. 28, 1840.
497. SALMON, b. Aug. 15, 1758; d. Feb. 25, 1823.

We find John Wood, the father of the above named children, Constable and Collector at the age of twenty-four, a prominent and successful man, had pleasant surroundings for those times, and had a promising young family, but death called him away in his fortieth year. He died Apr. 8, 1758. His wife remained a widow for several years, then "May ye 21, 1765, Capt. David Goodridge of Fitchburg, and Mrs. Lydia Wood was joined in marriage by the Rev. Mr. Daniel Rogers of Littleton, as by a certificate under his hand." She outlived her second husband. David Goodridge made his will Apr. 28, 1782. He named sons and daughters in his will as follows: David Goodridge, Ebenezer Goodridge, Abijah Goodridge, Hannah Mellen, Eunice Farwell and John Goodridge.

His widow gave Power of Attorney to her son, John Wood, Apr. 6, 1787, expressly on account of her Dowry.

In the settlement of the estate of her first husband, John Wood, the heirs were John Wood, Timothy Wood, Ebenezer Wood, Salmon Wood, and Lydia Davis.

The brother of their mother, Zadok Davis, was guardian for John and Timothy. John had the homestead, including the widows' third, when he became of age, which was after her marriage to David Goodridge.

In the distribution of the mother's personal property, in 1792, she remembered her four sons by John Wood, and her granddaughter Sarah Gary, and gave six shillings each to the six brothers of Sarah Gary.

John and Lydia are both buried among the Wood families in Littleton. The following is from their gravestones:

"Here lies buried the body of
John Wood,
who departed this life
April ye 8, A. D., 1758,
& in ye 40th year of his age."

"In memory of
MRS. LYDIA WOOD,
wife of
MR. JOHN WOOD,
and late wife to
DEA. DAVID GOODRIDGE,
of Fitchburg,
who died
Jan'y 13, 1792,
aged
67 years, 4 months and six days."

DEA. JOHN WOOD.

493. JOHN WOOD, son of John and Lydia (Davis) Wood, was born in Littleton, Mass., Sept. 3, 1747, O. S. He married Lucy Martin in 1769, and had eleven children. He settled upon the home place and prospered. He built for himself a very fine residence about 1790, which is still in excellent condition.

John Wood was a highly respected citizen, holding various offices of trust. We notice by receipts that he was Clerk of the Littleton Company in the Revolution. Among his papers we find the evidence of his being guardian for more than a dozen children besides his own.

In the Church records of Littleton I find the following:

"24 May, 1793. At a meeting of the Church for the purpose of choosing one or more persons to serve in the office of Deacon, the question was put whether the church would proceed to the choice of a person, or persons to serve in that office, and it passed in the affirmative. After looking up to heaven for direction in the important business before us, the church proceeded, with great unanimity, and made choice first, of Mr. John Wood, and secondly, of Mr. Daniel Kimball to that office."

"Sept. 22, 1822. Stayed the Church after divine service to hear and act on the request of Dea. John Wood and Samuel

Hoar to be released from further providing the Sacramental Elements, and from serving at the Table in the seasons of communion, and other persons might be chosen in their stead.

"The Church voted to release them from the above duties in the future.

"The Church then voted their thanks to 'Deacon John Wood and Deacon Samuel Hoar for their long and faithful service they had rendered to the church in this place.'

"The Church then, Oct. 14, 1822, Chose Benjamin Dix and Martin Wood, a son of Dea. John Wood, to fill the vacancies."

Deacon John Wood died in Littleton, May 4, 1826, in the 79th year of his age. Upon his gravestone in Littleton, is the following:

"Farewell dear friend and children too,
God has called me home.
In a short time he'll call for you,
Prepare yourselves to come."

502. Lucy Martin, wife of Dea. John Wood, was daughter of George Martin and Eunice Burnham, his wife. Lucy (Martin) Wood was born in Old Ipswich, Mass., July 11, 1751, O. S. She died in Littleton, Mass., Feb. 20, 1836. Upon her gravestone is the following:

"Farewell my friends, my children dear,
My Savior calls me home.
My Savior calls my children too,
Prepare yourselves to come."

At her decease she had eight children living and three dead; sixty-nine grandchildren living and twenty-two dead; forty-seven great-grandchildren living and eleven dead. Total descendants living, one hundred twenty-four; dead, thirty-six. Total living and dead, one hundred and sixty.

Her father died previous to 1781, and was probably living in 1777, from some business transactions in Dea. John Wood's accounts.

Eunice (Burnham) Martin, her mother, died in Littleton, Dec. 2, 1818, and was buried in Lunenburg, Mass.

I quote from the Burnham Genealogy, which includes the birth of Eunice Burnham and her marriage to George Martin:—

"From the best information obtainable at the present day it would appear that the three boy brothers, John, Thomas and Robert, sons of Robert and his wife, Mary (Andrews) Burnham of Norwich, Norfolk Co., England, came to America early in 1635; that they came in the ship *Angel Gabriel*, in charge of their maternal uncle, Capt. Andrews, master of the said ship; that they were wrecked on the coast of Maine; that with the freight thrown overboard to relieve the vessel at the time of the disaster, was a chest (containing valuables) belonging to the three boys; that the boys came to Chebacco, in the Colony of Massachusetts Bay, with their uncle, Capt. Andrews, who, having lost his ship settled there, the boys remaining with him; John and Thomas served (boys as they were) in the Pequot expedition. When grown to manhood, John and Thomas remained at Chebacco and became Freemen there. *Robert* removed to Boston, and while there became one of the company who purchased the town of Dover, N. H., to which place he removed, erected his 'garrison house' at Oyster river, became an inhabitant, and his descendants are still there.

John was appointed deacon of the church at Chebacco. He became the owner of a large tract of land lying on the east side of what is now known as 'Haskell's Creek.' Many of his descendants removed from Chebacco and settled in other places. Ebenezer, his grandson, removed to Windham Co., Conn., and himself became the ancestor of a numerous progeny. Others removed to New Hampshire and Maine.

Thomas was commissioned as Lieutenant, was deputy to the General Court, was Selectman and on Town Committees.

He owned much land, both in Chebacco and Ipswich, and a saw-mill upon Chebacco river.

In the town of Essex, Mass., a large proportion of its inhabitants are Burnhams, and are descended from Lieut. Thomas,

Sen., through his son John. The Norwich, Conn., Burnhams are descendants from Lieut. Thomas, Sen.

There are also many of the name of Andrews, probably descended from Capt. Andrews, brother of the mother of the three Burnham boys."

The descendants of these three brothers have made various attempts to obtain the immense estate believed to be still held in England for heirs of the Burnham descent now in America, but as yet without success. Meetings have been held, counsel employed, and correspondence entered into; some of which is published in the Burnham Genealogy.

Lieut. Thomas Burnham, the emigrant who settled at Ipswich, Mass., was in Chebacco (Ipswich), Mass., 1636, b. in England, 1623; d. June, 1694, Æ 71 years; m. 1645, Mary, dau. of John Tuttle, b. 1624.

The houses and farms of Lieut. Thomas Burnham, Sen., were divided between his sons Thomas and James.

John (son of Thomas, Sen.), of Chebacco, b. 1648; d. Jan. 12, 1704; m. June 6, 1668, Elizabeth Wells, b. ——; d. 1717.

John Burnham, from whom most of the Burnhams in Essex, and many others descended, settled in Chebacco, first near the head of Whittridge Creek, and afterwards removed to the Falls. He became proprietor of a grist-mill there, and other real estate in the vicinity, which has ever remained with him and his descendants. He had John, m. Sarah Choate; Thomas, m. Susannah ——; Joseph, unmarried. Abigail, m. Eben Whitman; Jacob, m. Mehitable Perkins; *Jonathan, m. Mary Perkins;* and 2nd., m. Martha Foster. David, m. Elizabeth Perkins; 2nd., m. Elizabeth Barrett; Mary, m. Samuel Weymouth.

Of the above mentioned: Capt. Jonathan Burnham, son of John, and grandson of Thomas, Sen., was born Oct. 10, 1685; d. April 3, 1773; m. Mar. 17, 1710, Mary

Perkins. She died and Capt. Jonathan m. May 13, 1730, second wife, Martha Foster, b. 1700; d. Feb. 20, 1790, Æ 90 years.

CHILDREN OF FIRST WIFE.

JONATHAN, b. 1716; m. Oct. 4, 1737, Elizabeth Proctor; d. Mar. 26, 1802.

MARY, b. Dec., 1718; m. Oct. 22, 1741, Job. Smith; d. Mar. 27, 1816.

FRANCIS, b. 1721; m. Apr. 25, 1754, Mary Cavies; d. 1808.

Eunice, b. Apr. 24, 1726; m. Oct. 22, 1745, *George Martin.*

LUCY, b. Sept. 17, 1727; m.

CHILDREN OF SECOND WIFE.

MARTHA, b. July 4, 1731; d. in infancy.

MARTHA, b. Mar. 11, 1733; m.

LUCY, b. Dec. 29, 1734; m. Feb., 1757, Enoch Haskell.

JOSEPH, b. May 21, 1736; d. in infancy.

ELIZABETH, b. Mar. 15, 1741; d. in infancy.

ELIZABETH, b. Aug. 21, 1743; m.

ABIGAIL, b. June 2, 1745; m. Mar. 12, 1767, Dea. Grover Dodge; d. Mar. 31, 1836.

Capt. Amariah Wood, son of Dea. John and Lucy (Martin) Wood, says in a paper to the writer, January 3, 1856:

"My mother's name was Lucy Martin. Her father, George Martin, lived in old Ipswich; moved from there to Lunenburg, Mass.

Her mother's name was Burnham. Her ancester, Martin, was a weaver in England; his wife was one of the higher classes; her parents were opposed to her marrying a weaver, and they came to America. My mother's great-grandfather's name was Dergy; he was the King of England's Cup-bearer.

My mother's brother Jonathan was settled on his father's place; had a numerous family, whose descendants are, some in

Gardner, Mass.; some in Worcester, Mass.; one in Westfield, Mass., many of whom are great musicians and teachers of penmanship.

Her brother, John Martin, was a Doctor. He was sick at sea the last he was heard from. Joseph was a Doctor, — went to Connecticut. My mother's sister Eunice married Abijah Goodridge; settled in Fitchburg, Mass., had a numerous family. My mother's sister Polly married Mr. Jones, settled in Rindge, N. H., and I believe had the greatest number of children of any of the family."

I record some names found in account books of Dea. John Wood, which may help in future genealogical work: Capt. David Goodridge, Timothy Wood, Ebenezer Wood, Salmon Wood, 1789, widow Eunice Martin, 1786, Joseph Martin, 1784, Jonathan Martin, 1781, George Martin, 1777, Thomas Wood, Deliverance Davis, Capt. John Goodridge, Bennet Wood, Ebenezer Davis, Benjamin Robbins, Abijah Goodridge, widow Lydia Goodridge, Elisha Robbins, Oliver Davis, 1775; Martin Wood, Amariah Wood, Zadok Davis, Nathaniel Edwards of Acton, Mass., who made his eight-day brass clock in 1793, now in possession of his grandson, Isaac Wood of Boston, Mass.; Hannah Mellen and Eunice Farwell, daughters of Dea. David Goodridge, Eliphalet Wood and many others.

DESCENDANTS

OF

DEA. JOHN WOOD

AND

LUCY (MARTIN)

HIS WIFE.

FOURTH GENERATION.

CHILDREN OF JOHN (493)

AND

LUCY MARTIN (502) WOOD.

503. Lucy, b. in Littleton, Mass., Nov. 17, 1770; m. Peter Fletcher (504); d. Feb. 8, 1856.

504. Peter Fletcher, b. Jan. 12, 1767; d. Nov. 21, 1811. He was the son of Peter and Martha (Dix) Fletcher of Littleton, — the father was son of Capt. Samuel, son of William, son of Samuel, who came to this country from England, with his father Robert who settled in Concord, 1630.

505. Sarah, b. in Littleton, Mass., May 26, 1772; m. Abel White (506); d. Aug. 26, 1846.

506. Abel White, b. Sept. 18, 1774; d. May 4, 1844.

507. Martin, b. in Littleton, Mass., Feb. 15, 1774; m. Nancy Hunt (508), and 2nd., Abigail Willard (509); d. Dec. 27, 1853.

508. Nancy Hunt, b. Apr. 8, 1780; d. Nov. 3, 1819.

509. Abigail Willard, b. Sept. 24, 1783; d. Apr. 16, 1874.

510. Carshena, b. in Littleton, Mass., Nov. 19, 1776; m. Betsey Lawrence (511) and 2nd., Tryphena Lawrence (512); d. July 13, 1854.

511. Betsey Lawrence, b. Feb. 4, 1784; d. Oct. 23, 1810.

512. Tryphena Lawrence, b. Jan. 11, 1792; d. Aug. 30, 1870.

513. John, b. in Littleton, Mass., Sept. 12, 1779; m. Mary Hayward (514); d. July 1, 1807. Had two children: John and Mary Ann.

514. Mary Hayward, b. in Boxborough, Mass.; d. Sept. 2, 1854, aged 70; m. 2nd husband, Jonathan Nourse of Bolton, Mass., and had a large family: Franklin, Steadman, Parkman, Hayward, Louisa m. Whitcomb, Susan m. Sawyer, and perhaps others.

515. EUNICE, b. in Littleton, Mass., May 16, 1781; m. James Hayward (516); d. Oct. 30, 1846.

516. JAMES HAYWARD, b. in Boxborough, Mass., Jan. 2, 1779; d. Nov. 11, 1846.

517. AMARIAH, b. in Littleton, Mass., June 14, 1782; d. March 8, 1783.

518. AMARIAH, b. in Littleton, Mass., Apr. 19, 1784; d. Dec. 5, 1784.

519. AMARIAH, b. in Littleton, Mass., Sept. 9, 1785; m. Hannah Smith (520), and 2nd, Lois Eames (521).

520. HANNAH SMITH, b. in Weston, Mass., Apr. 18, 1787; d. July 24, 1849. Her mother's maiden name was Hobbs, dau. of Nathan and Elizabeth (Fisk) Hobbs, who was daughter of Dea. Samuel and Anna (Bemis) Fisk of Waltham, Mass.

521. LOIS EAMES, b. Aug. 15, 1794.

522. MARY, b. in Littleton, Mass., June 28, 1788; m. Frank Priest (523); d. Aug. 15, 1874.

523. FRANK PRIEST, b. in Littleton, Mass., Feb. 26, 1784; d. in Parishville, N. Y., Aug. 7, 1850.

524. FREDERICK, b. in Littleton, Mass., Nov. 4, 1791; graduated at Dartmouth College, 1813; was A. M. and M. D.; d. Apr., 1864; unmarried.

Martin Wood (507) was well posted in common historical subjects, and had a very complete knowledge of the Bible. He was a Deacon in the Church, and a Teacher of the Bible Class for men and women in the Sunday School for many years. He was a man of sterling integrity, thoroughly honest and earnest in whatever engaged. He had quite a mechanical talent; was ingenious in making various implements and instruments, was a good carpenter, blacksmith, and cooper. He built several of the school-houses of the town. Several pieces of public roads were contracted for and built by him.

He was a skilful surveyor, and was often called upon to settle disputed boundary lines, where other good surveyors would not agree.

He held, at different times, all the important places of trust in his town, as Committee-man, Assessor, Selectman.

FIFTH GENERATION.

DESCENDANTS OF MARTIN (507) AND NANCY HUNT (508) WOOD.

CHILDREN.

525. Nancy M., b. in Littleton, Mass., Dec. 7, 1801; d. June 14, 1872; unmarried.
526. Josephus, b. in Littleton, Aug. 21, 1803; d. Dec. 14, 1882; unmarried.
527. George, b. in Littleton, Jan. 11, 1805; d. Jan., 1885; unmarried.
528. Amasa, b. in Littleton, Sept. 10, 1806; d. July 26, 1807.
529. Amasa, b. in Littleton, May 2, 1808; m. Nancy G. Mills (530); d. Sept. 18, 1852.
530. Nancy G. Mills of Lowell, Mass.
531. Lucy, b. in Littleton, Nov. 18, 1809; m. Benson Bigelow (532); d. Dec. 7, 1859.
532. Benson Bigelow, b. in Westminster, Feb. 16, 1806; d. Jan. 26, 1880, aged 73 yrs. 11 mo.
533. Mary, b. in Littleton, Oct. 16, 1811; unmarried.
534. John, b. in Littleton, Feb. 4, 1813; d. May, 1874; unmarried.
535. Harriot, b. in Littleton, Aug. 19, 1816; d. July 24, 1817.
536. Harriot, b. in Littleton, July 24, 1819; d. Oct. 5, 1823.

CHILDREN OF MARTIN (507) AND ABIGAIL WILLARD (509) WOOD.

537. Infant son, b. March 3, 1825; d.
538. Cornelius Elliot Wood, A. M., b. in Littleton, Dec. 1, 1827. Graduate of Harvard University, 1850, and afterwards of Harvard Law School; m. Catherine Maria McGovern (539).
539. Catherine Maria McGovern, b. Oct. 7, 1844.

SIXTH GENERATION.

CHILDREN OF AMASA (529)

AND

NANCY G. MILLS (530) WOOD.

540. Carrie A.
541. Lucy Jane; m. ——— Givens.

CHILDREN OF LUCY WOOD (531)

AND

BENSON BIGELOW (532).

542. Nancy Elmira, b. Dec. 7, 1851; d. Feb., 1864.
543. Edward Benson, b. Sept. 1, 1855.

CHILD OF CORNELIUS E. (538)

AND

CATHERINE M. McGOVERN (539) WOOD.

544. Amelia Eldora, b. in Littleton, Jan. 6, 1863; d. June 14, 1880.

FIFTH GENERATION.

DESCENDANTS OF PETER (504)

AND

LUCY WOOD (503) FLETCHER.

CHILDREN.

545. LUCY, b. Aug. 1, 1795, in Phillipston, Mass.; m. Edmund Fletcher (546); d. Oct. 14, 1871.
546. EDMUND FLETCHER of Littleton, Mass., b. Feb. 19, 1791.
547. SARAH, b. Sept. 29, 1796; m. Silas Nourse (548); d. Nov. 9, 1860.
548. SILAS NOURSE of Bolton, Mass.
549. MARTHA, b. Dec. 4, 1797; d. March 11, 1876; unmarried.
550. PETER, b. Feb. 22, 1799; m. widow Betsey Warren Patch (551); widow Harriet Tower Whitney (552).
551. BETSEY WARREN PATCH, b. March 2, 1797; d. Sept. 21, 1856.
552. HARRIET TOWER WHITNEY, b. May 28, 1789; d. March 16, 1873.
553. JOHN (twin to Peter), b. Feb. 22, 1799; d. Sept. 11, 1799.
554. JOHN, b. July 11, 1800; m. Hulda T. Fletcher (555); Matilda Bowker (556); d. Sept. 5, 1881.
555. HULDA T. FLETCHER, b. March 23, 1806; d. June 3, 1838.
556. MATILDA BOWKER, b. July 20, 1809; d. May 16, 1872.
557. FREDERICK, b. March 30, 1802; d. Sept. 1, 1831; unmarried.

558. Dix, b. Sept. 14, 1803; m. Louisa Patch (559).

559. Louisa Patch, b. in New Salem, Mass., Feb. 10, 1808; d. Jan., 1884.

560. Martin Wood, b. Feb. 10, 1806; d. Mar. 30, 1837; unmarried.

561. Carshena, b. May 22, 1807; d. Aug. 30, 1825; unmarried.

562. Cynthia, b. Sept. 22, 1809; m. Abram Wilder (563); d. Apr. 8, 1874.

563. Abram Wilder, b. in Bolton, Mass.; d. in Lawrence, Kansas.

564. Eunice, b. Oct. 29, 1811; d. Nov. 21, 1811.

SIXTH GENERATION.

CHILDREN OF EDMUND (546)

AND

LUCY FLETCHER (545) FLETCHER.

565. Edmund Dix, b. in Dedham, Mass., Oct. 1, 1823; m. Mary Annette Lovejoy (566); Caroline Almeda Hartwell (567).

566. Mary Annette Lovejoy, b. in Wilton, N. H., Apr. 20, 1829; m. Nov. 14, 1850; d. Mar. 31, 1859.

567. Caroline Almeda Hartwell, b. in West Dedham, Mass., Aug. 30, 1827; m. June 20, 1867.

568. Isaac Allen, b. in Boxboro', Apr. 20, 1829; m. Mary E. Rand (569).

569. Mary E. Rand of Barnstead, N. H., b. Aug. 16, 1830.

CHILDREN OF SILAS (548)

AND

SARAH FLETCHER (547) NOURSE.

570. FRANCIS H., b. 1819; m. Harriet Parker (571).
571. HARRIET PARKER of Lowell, b. 1820.
572. CALVIN, b. ——; m. Mary Rebecca Barnard (573); d. ——.
573. MARY REBECCA BARNARD, b. Aug. 29, 1822; m. June 17, 1845.
574. SILAS, b. ——; d. ——.
575. MARY ELIZA, b. ——; m. Joel Barnard (576); d.
576. JOEL BARNARD, b. Aug. 24, 1820; m. Aug. 15, 1852.

CHILDREN OF PETER (550)

AND

BETSEY W. PATCH (551) FLETCHER.

577. JOHN PATCH, b. Feb. 16, 1822; d. March 11, 1825.
578. ISAAC WARREN, b. Jan. 5, 1824; m. Sophia L. Hayward (579); Eliza Josephine Newhall (580).
579. SOPHIA L. HAYWARD, b. Nov. 12, 1826; m. Nov. 27, 1851; d. Sept. 7, 1858.
580. ELIZA JOSEPHINE NEWHALL, b. Jan. 3, 1838.
581. LUCY ANN, b. Jan. 3, 1827; m. Nehemiah Abbot Newhall (582).
582. NEHEMIAH ABBOT NEWHALL, b. in Lincoln, Mass., May 26, 1818; m. Nov. 16, 1848.
583. JOHN SIBLEY, b. Sept. 10, 1833; m. Nancy Bright Tower (584).
584. NANCY BRIGHT TOWER, b. in Concord, Mass., Dec. 31, 1834; m. July 5, 1859.
585. BETSEY MARIA, b. Nov. 16, 1835; d. Jan. 17, 1844.

CHILDREN OF JOHN FLETCHER (554)

BY FIRST WIFE

HULDA T. FLETCHER (555) FLETCHER.

586. Hulda Augusta, b. Nov. 25, 1833; d. March 25, 1844.
587. Rhoda Maria, b. June 3, 1838; d. June 6, 1838.

BY SECOND WIFE

MATILDA BOWKER (556) FLETCHER.

588. Josephine Matilda, b. Nov. 17, 1840.
589. John Herbert, b. Oct. 8, 1842; d. Sept. 19, 1864.
590. Augustine Alford, b. Oct. 19, 1844; m. Maggie Sarah Cheney Boyd (591).
591. Maggie Sarah Cheney Boyd, b. on Mississippi River, opposite Memphis, Tenn., Feb. 17, 1846; m. Jan. 10, 1870.
592. Edwin Dix, b. March 21, 1847; d. Sept. 11, 1850.
593. Elwin Bowker, b. Nov. 25, 1849; m. Sarah H. Redding (594).
594. Sarah H. Redding, b. at Beaver Dam, Wisconsin, March 16, 1850; m. Jan. 18, 1877.

CHILDREN OF DIX (558)

AND

LOUISA PATCH (559) FLETCHER.

595. Mary Louisa, b. ——, 1832; d. ——, 1833.
596. Frances Eliza, b. and d. in Lowell, ——, 1833.
597. Louisa, b. and d. ——, 1835.
598. Georgia Carolina, b. in Savannah, Ga., May 28, 1838; m. Henry G. Cole (599).
599. Henry G. Cole, ——; m. Aug. 25, 1859; d.
600. Eliza Hastings, b. Jan. 29, 1843; m. Lawrence E. Emmons (601).
601. Lawrence E. Emmons, ——; m. May 17, 1866.
602. Louise Eastman, b. Sept. 7, 1848.

CHILDREN OF ABRAM (563)
AND
CYNTHIA FLETCHER (562) WILDER.

603. Lucy Martin, b. May 17, 1837; m. Brinton W. Woodward (604); d. July 25, 1865.
604. Brinton W. Woodward, ——; m. Oct. 29, 1859.
605. Abraham M., of San Francisco, California, b. May 3, 1840; m. Mary E. Jenkins (606).
606. Mary E. Jenkins, b. in Lockport, Ill., Feb. 9, 1842
607. George Peter, b. Dec. 20, 1844; m. Eliza M. Crew (608).
608. Eliza M. Crew, ——; m. Nov. 28, 1867.

SEVENTH GENERATION.

CHILD OF EDMUND DIX (565)
AND
MARY ANNETTE LOVEJOY (566) FLETCHER.

609. Mary Elizabeth, b. Sept. 27, 1854.

CHILD OF ISAAC ALLEN (568)
AND
MARY E. RAND (569) FLETCHER.

610. Anna Dix, b. July 25, 1864.

CHILD OF CALVIN (572)
AND
MARY REBECCA BARNARD (573) NOURSE.

611. Mary Rebecca, b. June 12, 1846; m. Herbert H. Ceiley (612).
612. Herbert H. Ceiley, ——; m. Feb. 12, 1879.

CHILDREN OF ISAAC WARREN FLETCHER (578)

BY FIRST WIFE

SOPHIA L. HAYWARD (579) FLETCHER.

613. George Warren, b. Sept. 2, 1852; d. Aug. 16, 1853.
614. George Hayward, b. Dec. 15, 1854; m. Lizzie Isabella Clapp (615).
615. Lizzie Isabella Clapp, b. in Everett, Mass., June 22, 1856; m. Aug. 30, 1877.

BY SECOND WIFE

ELIZA JOSEPHINE NEWHALL (580) FLETCHER.

616. Caroline Sophia, b. March 28, 1861.
617. Mary Eliza, b. Dec. 12, 1862.
618. Lucy Maria, b. Nov. 27, 1864.
619. Herbert Martin, b. Sept. 12, 1866.
620. Francis Edwin, b. Nov. 22, 1868.
621. Charles Edmund Dix, b. March 15, 1873.
622. Clifton Newhall, b. Sept. 19, 1877.

CHILDREN OF NEHEMIAH ABBOT (582)

AND

LUCY ANN FLETCHER (581) NEWHALL.

623. Sarah Mariah, b. in Ashburnham, Mass., Nov. 26, 1849; d. Jan. 28, 1876.
624. Josephine, b. in Stow, Mass., May 24, 1854.
625. Charles Fletcher, b. in Stow, Sept. 5, 1856; d. Aug. 23, 1858.
626. Ella Frances, b. in Stow, May 9, 1862; d. Apr. 6, 1881.

CHILDREN OF AUGUSTINE ALFORD (590)

AND

MAGGIE SARAH CHENEY BOYD (591) FLETCHER.

627. Matilda Boyd, b. in Marietta, Ga., Sept. 16, 1873; d. Feb, 10, 1874.
628. Mary Louisa, b. Oct. 14, 1875.
629. Maggie Boyd, b. Sept. 8, 1880.

CHILDREN OF ELWYN BOWKER (593)

AND

SARAH H. REDDING (594) FLETCHER.

630. John Herbert, b. March 3, 1878; d. July 8, 1879.
631. Elwyn Redding, b. March 2, 1879.
632. George Elwyn, b. Aug. 22, 1880; d. Jan. 13, 1882.
633. Frederick Dix, b. Oct. 13, 1882.

CHILDREN OF HENRY G. (599)

AND

GEORGIA C. FLETCHER (598) COLE.

634. Mary Warren, b. June 3, 1860.
635. Daniel Webster, b. May 10, 1863.
636. Maude Hastings, b. Jan. 16, 1866.
637. Henry Green, b. May 6, 1869.
638. DeWitt Clinton, b. June 26, 1871.

CHILDREN OF LAWRENCE E. (601)

AND

ELIZA HASTINGS FLETCHER (600) EMMONS.

639. Lawrence Earle, b. Feb. 15, 1867.
640. Lillie Fletcher, b. Feb. 25, 1868.

CHILD OF BRINTON W. (604)

AND

LUCY MARTIN WILDER (603) WOODWARD.

641. Mary, b. Jan. 8, 1862.

CHILD OF GEORGE PETER (607)

AND

ELIZA M. CREW (608) WILDER.

642. Annie, b. Oct. 19, 1868.

CARSHENA WOOD.

Carshena Wood (510), son of Dea. John and Lucy (Martin) Wood, was a man of ability, but had no ambition for public display so far as he was concerned, and avoided, if possible, every public office.

He was an ingenious man, learned the cooper's trade, but was always a farmer. He first settled in Ashby, Mass., but upon the death of his brother John, he sold his estate there, and was settled upon the homestead of his father, grandfather, and great-grandfather, and resided in the house built for his brother John, near the house of his father, the remainder of his life.

He never occupied the fine residence of his father, although it was long in his possession after his parents' decease.

He was a man of strict integrity, was punctiliously exact in all his engagements, and dealt honorably with every one, — was a good neighbor and townsman, an early member and regular attendant of his church.

His descendants are numerous and scattered.

JOHN H. WOOD.

JOHN H. WOOD (658), son of Carshena and Tryphena Lawrence Wood, whose portrait appears in this volume, was born in Littleton, Mass., Dec. 4, 1816. When about fourteen years of age he was engaged with his brother Carshena on the steamer *General Lincoln*, plying between Boston and Hingham.

Afterwards made a brief stay in Lowell, Mass., and attended a seminary in Manchester, Vt.

He then learned the shoemaker's trade, with his brother-in-law, B. W. Priest, and continued in that business until he left the States, in Feb., 1846, the latter part of the time as foreman of John Fletcher's manufactory, Acton, Mass.

In June, 1841, he married Lucy Amanda Priest, daughter of Benj. Priest of Boxboro', Mass., and sister of B. W. Priest, who had previously married John's sister, Eunice Martin Wood.

John's wife died May, 1845, and her three sisters, within a few months, all of consumption. No children by this marriage.

The next year, Feb. 1846, he sailed from Newburyport, Mass., in the Hermaphrodite Brig *Henry*, 155 tons, Capt. Kilborn, bound for Oregon, via Cape Horn and the Sandwich Islands, with a crew of thirteen, including stewardess and cabin boy, eighteen passengers, among whom was his brother, Oral J. R. Wood, W. L. Lee, subsequently Chief Justice and Chancellor of the Hawaiian Kingdom, Charles R. Bishop, now the wealthy banker there.

The passage was very long, tedious, and somewhat eventful. Said the subject of this sketch to the writer:

"South of the Equator, in the Atlantic, our crew mutinied while the Captain was dangerously sick, and were only prevented from throwing the chief mate overboard by my brother,

Respectfully
Jno. H. Wood

myself, and two other passengers, while in the act, with his body over the rail. This necessitated our putting into St. Catherine, Brazil, — part of our crew in irons, where our first mate, wife, child, and a maiden lady passenger, left and returned to the States. We were 46 days off Cape Horn, battling with adverse winds, storms of rain, snow and sleet; at one time with two feet of snow on deck; at another, every block, sheave, rope and sail frozen solid and covered with ice to twice their thickness; at another time, 40 hours, dragged (vessel made fast by long hawsèr to heavy oak plankś, to keep her head to the wind while she rode mountainous waves). We were two weeks without an observation by day or night, — our last was in 62° South; after which were driven south and east until near Palmer's land, and talked of going round Cape of Good Hope.

Passengers had to break out cargo, almost daily, to get wood to cook their food; had to stand watch of mate and men sick and disabled; got out of very many articles of provisions while off the Horn, and were short of wood, water and provisions to port; and, before reaching it had burned all the spare spars, booms and berth material in the vessel. Reached the Sandwich Islands after a passage of 231 days, having sailed in that cockle-shell nearly twenty-five thousand miles, and found we had been preceded by a report from the mate left in Brazil, that passengers and crew had taken money and goods put on board for the missionaries at the Islands, hoisted the black flag, and were gone in pursuit of further booty.

Soon after landing I erected the first brick building in Honolulu, and opened a shoe store in connection with manufacturing with material I brought with me, and such as I could pick up, until I could get orders filled from the United States, which required from 17 to 20 months; continued that business nineteen years and ten months successfully.

Upon the discovery of gold in California, my brother Oral and myself, and six others, formed a company and went to mining there. In August, 1849, I went via Isthmus to Massachusetts, purchased a stock of goods, married in November the only daughter of Jacob Hardy of Salem, Mass., and with her and a cousin, Jacob Hardy, now District Judge on the Island of Kauai, came again around Cape Horn in the good ship

Charles, Capt. Andrews, arriving in Honolulu in May, 1850, after a very pleasant passage.

When I left California for the east, my brother Oral returned to Honolulu and took charge of my business. When I returned he took the situation of Prefect of Police, or Deputy Marshal and Deputy District Attorney, which he held for some years, when he had realized a handsome little fortune.

I bought in 1851, a house lot 200 ft. square, in Honolulu, and ordered a house got out in Boston, sending for a carpenter, Mr. C. E. Williams, who had married my sister Harriet, to attend to its preparation and shipment, and to come out with it if he chose and put it up. This he did, coming with his wife around the Horn, and has since been in the furniture and undertaking business here. In 1856 or '7, I sent for my youngest brother, Henry, who entered my employ as bookkeeper and salesman, and continued with me some eight or nine years, the latter part of the time taking entire charge of my business in town.

My first child, Florence Amanda, was born March 25, 1851, and my daughter, Stella May, was born May 1, 1856. Two sons died in infancy.

In November, 1857, my wife and two daughters took passage in the fine clipper ship *John Gilpin*, bound to Boston, for a visit to home and friends in Massachusetts. Off Cape Horn at 2 A. M., the ship struck an iceberg, springing a leak, and at 4 P. M., next day went down. Fortunately, a large old East Indiaman, British, Capt. Scott, was sighted the morning after the collision, saw the signal of distress, bore down, and though a very heavy sea running, sent boats well manned and took off passengers and crew in safety. Bedding was thrown in the boat and my wife and children tossed from a port on to it, leaving all their clothing, valuables, presents for friends, &c., behind; but very fortunately, through my wife's thoughtfulness, saving $5,000.00 in gold coin I had placed in charge of the Captain as a remittance to my agent in Boston. The English ship *(Herefordshire)*, from Valparaiso for London, on account of so large an addition to her numbers, put into Bahia for supplies, where a part of the Gilpin's passengers took passage, through the American Consul, for New York, while my family and some others continued on in the *Herefordshire* for London. Some days out from Bahia, on a calm day, they fell in with the small clipper ship *Sunny South*, bound to New York. Capt. Scott had his family on board; the ships 'spoke' each other and Mrs. S. requested that the Captain of the *Sunny South* be invited on board to lunch, which was accepted, and during his stay, wrecked passengers were alluded to, which resulted in their being offered a passage to New York. Accepted and arrived in safety.

It had been arranged that I should meet my family in May, via California and the Isthmus, in Boston. While crossing the Isthmus in the cars, and perusing a paper bought in Panama, I saw a notice of the 'wreck off Cape Horn of the *John Gilpin*. No particulars.' You can possibly imagine my feelings and anxiety from that time until I reached New York, where letters awaited me.

After a visit to home and friends, the family returned to Honolulu, where the wife and mother died in January, 1860."

In 1863, Mr. Wood took charge of his sugar plantation, 2 1-2 miles from Honolulu, where he continued the cultivation of cane and the manufacture of sugar until 1871, when he turned it into a stock and dairy farm.

He married third wife, widow Lucy Ann Houghton, *nee* Hobert. He resides upon a portion of his town property in Honolulu, a man of integrity and influence.

His oldest daughter, Florence A., married Pierre Jones, now in mercantile business, and resides at Lahaina, Island of Maui, Hawaiian Islands. He was a graduate of a university, was a teacher of English, French and German for some years, and speaks Italian, Spanish, and Hawaiian. His father, Thomas G. Jones, was principal of a military school at St. Petersburg, married a Russian Princess, by whom he had the one son and two daughters; one residing with her father at Brussels, Belgium; the other, the wife of a banker at Amsterdam, Holland, and mother of four children. John H. Wood remarked: "I had the pleasure of meeting them all at their homes in

1883, and was highly gratified with their refinement and amiability."

The son Pierre, who married Florence A. Wood, has one daughter, born in May, 1883, Mary Nalanialua; the latter name, by request of her godmother, the Queen Dowager Emma, its signification, — there are two in Heaven.

John H. Wood's second daughter, Stella May, married Albert F. Dixon. He entered the Navy as engineer, Oct., 1870. His parents now reside at West Medford, Mass. His father, John A. Dixon, a Naval officer about to be retired.

Albert F. is now located at the Bureau of Engineering, Navy Dept., Washington, D. C. Has one son, born Sept., 1875, named John Albert Wood Dixon.

FIFTH GENERATION.

DESCENDANTS OF CARSHENA (510),

AND

BETSY LAWRENCE (511) WOOD.

643. Elizabeth, b. in Ashby, Mass., Mar. 16, 1803; m. Alvah Mansur (644); Alfred Whittredge (645); Samuel C. Pratt (646); d. Sept. 5, 1862.

644. Alvah Mansur, b. Mar. 25, 1801, in Temple, N. H.; merchant of Lowell, Mass.; d. Nov. 1, 1840.

645. Alfred Whittredge of Lowell; d. in Cuba, W. I.

646. Samuel C. Pratt, b. Aug. 6, 1808, in Marlboro', Vt.; d. July 27, 1872.

647. Lucy, b. in Ashby, Mar. 1, 1805; d. Apr. 23, 1840.

648. Carshena, b. in Ashby, Jan. 6, 1807; d. Nov. 20, 1837.

649. Mary, b. in Ashby, Oct. 26, 1808; m. Francis Wood (650); Hervey Wood (651); d. Apr. 23, 1879; childless.

650. Francis Wood, b. Jan. 1, 1803; d. Feb. 28, 1838.
651. Hervey Wood, b. Feb. 11, 1805; d. Aug. 23, 1884.
652. Maria, b. in Ashby, Sept. 12, 1810; m. Kilburn Smith (653); d. Mar. 19, 1855.
653. Kilburn Smith of Mt. Vernon, N. H.; d. Oct. 13, 1881.

CHILDREN OF CARSHENA (510)

AND

TRYPHENA LAWRENCE (512) WOOD.

654. Betsy, b. June 8, 1812; d. Aug. 30, 1812.
655. Sarah L., b. July 16, 1813; m. Rufus Keyes (656); d. Sept. 20, 1883.
656. Rufus Keyes of West Boylston, Mass., b. Aug. 14, 1804; d. May 11, 1869.
657. Eunice, b. Dec. 18, 1815; d. Jan. 18, 1816.
658. John H., b. in Littleton, Dec. 4, 1816; m. Lucy A. Priest (659); Sarah W. Hardy (660); widow Lucy Ann Houghton (661).
659. Lucy Amanda Priest of Boxboro', b. ——, 1819; d. May 2, 1845.
660. Sarah W. Hardy of Salem, Mass.; d. at Honolulu, Oahu, Hawaiian Islands, Jan., 1860.
661. Mrs. Lucy Ann Houghton, *nee* Hobert.
662. Eunice Martin, b. in Littleton, Mass., Jan. 4, 1819; m. Benjamin Wetherbee Priest (663); has done much to collect the records of her father's family.
663. Benjamin Wetherbee Priest, b. Feb. 12, 1817; residence, Littleton, Mass., near the Wood Homestead.
664. Timothy Lawrence, b. July 9, 1821; m. Mary H. Richardson (665); and Caroline M. Haynes (666); d. Sept. 6, 1874; was a Captain in the Union Army in the Civil War.
665. Mary H. Richardson of Dracut, Mass.; b. Nov. 24, 1825; d. in Illinois.

666. Caroline M. Haynes, b. in Charlestown, Mass., in 1827.

667. Oral J. Reed, b. July 12, 1824; m. Ann Marie Whitcomb (668).

668. Ann Marie Whitcomb, of Boxboro, Mass., b. May 11, 1834.

669. Isaac, b. in Boxboro, Feb. 25, 1827; m. Harriet Maria Benson (670).

670. Harriet Maria Benson, b. Apr. 22, 1826, on Marshall's Island, Maine; d. Nov. 4, 1884.

671. Nathan Henry, b. in Boxboro, May 22, 1828; m. Ella Floretta Nutting (672).

672. Ella Floretta Nutting, of Francestown, N. H.

673. Harriet Augusta, b. in Boxboro, Apr. 1, 1831; m. Charles Edward Williams (674).

674. Charles Edward Williams, b. in Hatley, Canada East, Province of Quebec, of American parents.

SIXTH GENERATION.

CHILDREN OF ELIZABETH WOOD (643)

BY FIRST HUSBAND,

ALVAH MANSUR (644),

ALL BORN IN LOWELL, MASS.

675. Alvah, Jr., b. Dec. 13, 1829; d. Sept. 3, 1832.

676. Warren Wood, b. Oct. 18, 1831; d. Aug. 27, 1832.

677. Alvah, Jr., 3d son, b. Dec. 5, 1833; m. Angeline P. Blackington (678).

678. Angeline P. Blackington; m. Oct. 1, 1863, in Homer, N. Y.; d. Mar. 17, 1870, in Kansas City, Mo.

679. Ellen Elizabeth, b. Oct. 12, 1835; m. Lewis Bates Tebbetts (680).

680. Lewis Bates Tebbetts, b. in Great Falls, N. H., Aug. 30, 1834.

Isaac Wood

681. Charles Warren, b. May 31, 1837; d. July 20, 1838.

682. Joseph, of St. Louis, Mo., b. Sept. 20, 1839.

BY THIRD HUSBAND,

SAMUEL C. PRATT (646).

683. Charles Eddy, of Boston, Mass., b. in Lowell, Mass., May 16, 1852; m. Elmira I. Hale (684).

684. Elmira I. Hale, b. in Haverhill, May 10, 1855.

CHILD OF KILBURN (653)
AND
MARIA WOOD (652) SMITH.

685. Agnes Maria, of Lowell, Mass., b. May 11, 1836.

CHILDREN OF RUFUS (656)
AND
SARAH L. WOOD (655) KEYES.

686. Henry Warren, of Monticello, Ill., b. Dec. 26, 1849, in Littleton, Mass.; m. Agnes Stephens.

687. Agnes Stephens, b. Aug. 10, 1849, in Bristol, England.

688. Ellen Maria, b. May 7, 1851.

689. Charles Herbert, b. Jan. 14, 1854; d. July 22, 1863.

690. Lewis Grafton, b. Mar. 14, 1856; d. July 17, 1863.

691. Sarah Annis, b. Apr. 1, 1858; m. Otis Kittredge (692).

692. Otis Kittredge, b. in Shirley, Mass., Sept. 17, 1852.

CHILDREN OF JOHN H. (658)
AND
SARAH WHEAT HARDY (660) WOOD.

693. Florence Amanda, b. Mar. 25, 1851; m. Pierre Jones (694).

694. PIERRE JONES; res. Lahaina, Island of Maui, Hawaiian Islands.

695. STELLA MAY, b. May 1, 1856; m. Albert Ferman Dixon (696).

696. ALBERT FERMAN DIXON, of U. S. Navy; b. in Kittery, Me.

697. Two sons who died in infancy.

CHILDREN OF BENJAMIN W. (663) AND EUNICE MARTIN WOOD (662) PRIEST.

698. CARSHENA TREVANIAN PRIEST, b. Dec. 2, 1837; d. March 4, 1838.

699. OREN ADELBERT, b. Nov. 16, 1839; m. Mary A. Vanaman (700).

700. MARY A. VANAMAN, b. in Wilmington, N. C.; d. Nov. 26, 1884; aged 43.

701. ARABELLA WOOD, b. June 30, 1841; m. George F. Keyes (702).

702. GEORGE F. KEYES, son of Ivory and Lucy Keyes, b. in Acton, Mass., Jan'y 27, 1838.

CHILDREN OF TIMOTHY LAWRENCE (664) AND MARY HAZELTON RICHARDSON (665) WOOD.

703. NATHAN L., b. Dec. 7, 1847; d. Sept. 13, 1848.

704. ANNETTE E., b. in Boxboro, Jan. 31, 1849; d. Apr. 9, 1874; she m. Henry Howard (705).

705. HENRY HOWARD, b. in New York.

706. MARTHA RHOENAH, b. in Dracut, May 14, 1850; m. Elisha Haven Winters; he was b. July 24, 1834, in Logan Co., Ohio.

707. CARSHENA, b. in Littleton, May 28, 1852; m. Mary A. Doyle; has five children.

708. MARY A. DOYLE, b. Sept. 16, 1854, at Cherry Valley, Ill.

709. Artemas Clinton, b. June 185–; d. 1856, in Illinois.

710. Charles Henry, b. in Byron, Ill., May 8, 1856; d. in West Los Animas, Colorado, Apr. 27, 1881.

BY SECOND WIFE,

CAROLINE M. HAYNES (666).

711. Welma Lawrence, born in Boxboro, Mass., Dec. 21, 18—.

CHILDREN OF ORAL REED (667)

AND

ANN MARIE WHITCOMB (668) WOOD.

712. Arthur Oral, b. in Honolulu, Oahu, Hawaiian Islands, June 19, 1854.

713. Agnes Leora, b. in Honolulu, Oahu, H. I., Nov. 15, 1856; m. Thompson Kossuth White (714).

714. Thompson Kossuth White, b. in N. Y. city, 1852; m. in Stockton, California, June 26, 1884.

715. Charles Oren, b. in Acton, Mass, Oct. 9, 1859.

716. Eugene Austin Carshena, b. in Honolulu, Oahu, H. I., Aug. 7, 1864.

CHILDREN OF NATHAN HENRY (671)

AND

ELLA FLORETTA NUTTING (672) WOOD.

717. Cora Floretta, b. Apr. 27, 1873.

718. Allen Henry, b. May 30, 1881; d. Aug. 7, 1881.

CHILDREN OF CHARLES EDWARD (674)

AND

HARRIET AUGUSTA WOOD (673) WILLIAMS.

719. Edward Austin, b. June 24, 1854, in the town of Maitland, New South Wales, Australia; m. Phœbe A. Hathaway (720).

720. Phœbe A. Hathaway, b. in Springfield, Ill., May 6, 1853.

721. Henry Herbert, b. May 9, 1856, in the township of Castlemain, Victoria, Australia.

722. Lelia Isabel, b. Sept. 18, 1859, in Honolulu, Oahu, Hawaiian Islands.

723. Charles Carshena, b. Aug. 15, 1861, in Honolulu, Oahu, H. I.; d. Sept. 6. 1877, at San Luis Obispo, Cal., U. S. A.

724. Charlotte Augusta, b. Nov. 20, 1863, in Honolulu, Oahu, H. I.

725. Harriet Eloise, b. Jan. 19, 1866, in Honolulu, H. I.; d. in San Francisco, Cal., Nov. 14, 1884.

726. Daisy Lucenia, b. May 6, 1868, in Honolulu, H. I.

727. Ada May Williams, b. Dec. 22, 1873, in Honolulu, H. I.

SEVENTH GENERATION.

CHILD OF ALVAH (677) AND ANGELINE P. BLACKINGTON (678) MANSUR.

728. Nellie Blackington, b. in Nevada, Gilpin Co., Col., July 15, 1864.

CHILDREN OF LEWIS BATES (680) AND ELLEN ELIZABETH MANSUR (679) TEBBETTS.

729. Alice, b. in Lowell, Mass., Aug. 24, 1858.

730. George Stevens, b. in Woodbury, Baltimore Co., Md., Aug. 8, 1863.

731. Ellen Mansur, b. in Woodbury, Md., Nov. 6, 1864.

732. Alvah Mansur, b. in Baltimore, Md., Oct. 16, 1868.

733. Mabel, b. in Baltimore, Md., Nov. 16, 1869.
734. Florence, b. in Baltimore, Md., Feb. 2, 1871; d. July 7, 1871.
735. Rebecca Homer, b. in Baltimore, Md., Nov. 10, 1872.
736. Grace, b. in Baltimore, Md., Aug. 22, 1874; d. June 24, 1875.
737. Lewis Bates, Jr., } twins, b. in St. Louis, Mo., Nov.
738. Joseph Lee, } 22, 1879.
Joseph Lee d. Feb. 19, 1880; Lewis Bates, Jr. d. Mar. 29, 1880.

CHILDREN OF CHARLES EDDY (683)

AND

ELMIRA I. HALE (684) PRATT.

739. Chandler H., b. in Boston, Mass., Apr. 29, 1876.
740. Dana F., b. in Boston, Mass., May 20, 1880.

CHILDREN OF HENRY WARREN (686)

AND

AGNES STEPHENS (687) KEYES.

Harry Mayo, b. Oct. 26, 1875, in Chicago, Ill.; d. Oct. 17, 1876.
741. Frank Mayo, b. Aug. 17, 1877, in Chicago, Ill.
742. Ida Florence, b. Sept. 12, 1879, in Chicago, Ill.
Mildred Agnes, b. Aug. 1, 1884, in Monticello, Ill.

CHILD OF OTIS (692)

AND

SARA ANNIS KEYES (691) KITTREDGE.

743. Forrest Eugene, b. Sept. 21, 1883.

CHILD OF PIERRE (694)
AND
FLORENCE AMANDA WOOD (693) JONES.

744. MARIE NALANIALUA, b. May 28, 1883.

CHILD OF ALBERT FERMAN (696)
AND
STELLA MAY WOOD (695) DIXON.

745. JOHN ALBERT WOOD, b. Sept. 11, 1875.

CHILD OF OREN ADELBERT (699)
AND
MARY A. VANAMAN (700) PRIEST.

746. CHARLES AUSTIN, b. Oct. 22, 1865.

CHILDREN OF GEORGE F. (702)
AND
ARABELLA WOOD PRIEST (701) KEYES.

747. GEORGE SCOTT WINSLOW, b. June 20, 1870.
748. MATTIE BELL, b. Nov. 13, 1873.

CHILDREN OF EDWARD AUSTIN (719)
AND
PHŒBE A. HATHAWAY (720) WILLIAMS.

749. RENA ALICE, b. in Honolulu, H. I., Oct. 24, 1877.
750. CHARLES EDWARD, b. in Honolulu, H. I., Oct. 8, 1878.
751. FRANCIS WILLIAM, b. in Honolulu, H. I., June 12, 1881.

CHILDREN OF HENRY (705)

AND

ANNETTE E. WOOD (704) HOWARD.

752. A Daughter, b. Nov. 25, 1866; d. Dec. 10, 1866.
753. Monroe E., b. Feb. 7, 1869.

CHILD OF ELISHA H. (707)

AND

MARTHA R. WOOD (706) WINTERS.

754. Janie Winters, b. Aug. 15, 1882, at Eureka Springs, Carroll Co., Arkansas.

CHILDREN OF CARSHENA (708)

AND

MARY A. DOYLE (709) WOOD.

755. Oral James, b. Feb. 16, 1875, in Seward, Winnebago Co., Ill.
756. Mary Ellen, b. Aug. 13, 1877, in Byron, Ogle Co., Ill.
757. Rosie Jane, b. July 20, 1879, in Byron, Ogle Co., Ill.
758. Lawrence Clinton, b. Aug. 29, 1880, in Pomeroy, Pocahontas Co., Iowa.
759. Maggie Roena, b. May 17, 1882, in Pomeroy, Pocahontas Co., Iowa.

FIFTH GENERATION.

DESCENDANTS OF ABEL (506)

AND

SARAH WOOD (505) WHITE.

CHILDREN.

ALL BORN IN PHILLIPSTON, MASS.

760. Two Sons and two Daughters, died in infancy.
761. John, b. Oct. 17, 1799; m. Amelia Metcalf (762); d. Oct. 29, 1852.

762. Amelia Metcalf, of Providence, R. I., b. Nov. 18, 1804; d. Sept. 27, 1868.

763. Asa, b. Sept. 12, 1800; m. Mary Ann Spooner (764); d. Dec. 28, 1874.

764. Mary Ann Spooner, b. in Templeton, Mass., Nov. 13, 1807; d. June 13, 1865.

765. Lucy Martin, b. Sept. 24, 1801; m. William Miller (766); d. Feb. 15, 1879.

766. William Miller, of Provincetown, Mass., b. May 4, 1799; d. March 19, 1865.

767. Polly, b. Aug. 16, 1804; m. Daniel Parker (768); d. Feb. 13, 1866.

768. Daniel Parker, of Hubbardston, b. in Westboro, Mass., March 23, 1799.

769. Sally, b. Nov. 2, 1806; m. Col. George W. Sawyer (770); d. Jan. 8, 1874.

770. George W. Sawyer, of Phillipston, Mass., b. July 18, 1807.

771. Nancy, b. May 19, 1808; m. Baxter Swan (772); b. Sept. 6, 1872.

772. Baxter Swan, of Phillipston, Mass., b. Aug. 16, 1806; d. Apr. 12, 1873.

773. Thomas, b. Oct. 19, 1809; m. Rosina Lovering (774); Eliza Stone (775); Mary Tooley (776); d. Dec. 27, 1884.

774. Rosina Lovering, b. in Phillipston, Mass., Mar. 27, 1810; d. May 21, 1856.

775. Eliza Stone, of Barre, Mass., b. Sept. 10, 1819; d. Sept. 6, 1871.

776. Mary Jane Tooley, of Barre, Mass., b. in New Salem, Sept. 8, 1821; d. Feb. 11, 1883.

777. Antrim, b. May 13, 1811; m. Lucy A. Baker (778); Rebecca M. Howe (779); d. Dec. 14, 1878.

778. Lucy A. Baker, of Phillipston, d. Sept. 10, 1843.

779. Rebecca M. Howe, b. in Petersham, Mass., Sept. 4, 1810.

780. Abel Hanson, b. Nov. 2, 1814; m. Nancy R. Beidoman (781).

781. Nancy R. Beidoman, b. in Highland Co., O., Feb. 9, 1817; no children.

782. William, b. July 3, 1816; m. Rebecca Evelyn Newton (783); Edna Caroline Keightley (784); d. Nov. 14, 1868.

783. Rebecca Evelyn Newton, of Phillipston, b. Oct. 19, 1818; d. Aug. 1, 1864.

784. Edna Caroline Keightley, b. in Boston, England, August 7, 1826.

SIXTH GENERATION.

CHILDREN OF JOHN (761)

AND

AMELIA METCALF (762) WHITE.

785. Samuel M., b. in Providence, R. I., Aug. 6, 1829; m. Elizabeth A. Easton (786).

786. Elizabeth A. Easton, of Morristown, N. J., b. Jan. 27, 1832.

787. John A., b. in Willoughby, O., Oct. 10, 1831; m. Mary J. Anderson (788).

788. Mary J. Anderson, of Lexington, Ky., b. Jan. 27, 1832.

789. Mary R., b. in Cuyahoga Co., Ohio, May 10, 1834; m. Benjamin F. Smith (790); G. H. Redfield (791).

790. Benjamin F. Smith, of Muskingum Co., O., b. May 22, 1829; d. June 23, 1865, in U. S. service, 20th Illinois Regiment.

791. G. H. Redfield, of Orange Co., N. Y., b. Jan. 7, 1819.

792. Sarah, b. in Lafayette, Stark Co., Ill., Nov. 21, 1839; m. Thomas D. Church (793).

793. Thomas D. Church, of St. Lawrence, Jefferson Co., N. Y., b. Apr. 11, 1836.

CHILDREN OF ASA (763)
AND
MARY ANN SPOONER (764) WHITE.

794. MARY ANN MASON, b. in Boston, Mass., Feb. 20, 1834.
795. SARAH LOUISA, b. in Boston, Mass., Jan. 12, 1843; m. Thomas H. Gaut (796); d. Aug. 13, 1880.
796. THOMAS H. Gaut, of Hartford, Conn.

CHILDREN OF WILLIAM (766)
AND
LUCY MARTIN WHITE (765) MILLER.

ALL BORN IN PHILLIPSTON, MASS.

797. LUCY WHITE, b. July 29, 1823.
798. WILLIAM ATKINS, b. Aug. 18, 1824; d. May 12, 1849.
799. SARAH, b. Apr. 11, 1826; m. Nathaniel Y. Lord (800); d. Sept. 16, 1854.
800. NATHANIEL Y. LORD, of Athol, b. Sept. 22, 1819; d. Apr. 29, 1876.
801. ELIZABETH ISABELLA, b. Oct. 20, 1827; m. Robert M. Miller (802); d. Apr. 28, 1849.
802. ROBERT M. MILLER, of Provincetown, Mass., b. Sept. 22, 1822.
803. JOHN, b. March 7, 1829; m. Roena Cheney (804).
804. ROENA CHENEY, of Phillipston, Mass., b. Nov. 12, 1827.
805. THEODORE THOMAS, b. Aug. 24, 1830; m. Harriet G. Goodspeed (806); d. Apr. 16, 1862.
806. HARRIET G. GOODSPEED, b. in Hubbardston, Mass., May 16, 1831; d. Nov. 3, 1865.
807. EMILY JANNETTE, b. June 29, 1832; m. Merrill Gage, of Athol; d. Aug. 22, 1861.
808. BENJAMIN EDWARD, b. Feb. 8, 1835; d. June 3, 1858.
809. FRANCES ALMIRA, b. Nov. 19, 1836; m. Merrill Gage (810); Gurdon E. Beates (811).

810. MERRILL GAGE, of Athol, Mass., d. Oct. 28, 1865.
811. GURDON E. BEATES, of Junction City, Kansas, b. Dec. 4, 1832, in Andes, Delaware Co., N. Y.
812. ROBERT SOPER, of Tucson, Arizona, b. Oct. 18, 1838; m. Georgie Warner (813).
813. GEORGIE WARNER, of Warnersville, N. Y.
814. CHARLES HENRY, b. June 12, 1840; m. Virginia A. Bigelow (815).
815. VIRGINIA A. BIGELOW, b. in Belleville, Jefferson Co., N. Y., July 10, 1837.
816. STEPHEN HARRISON, b. Aug. 18, 1842.
817. ABBIE MARIA, b. June 7, 1844; m. Theodore A. Reynolds (818).
818. THEODORE A. REYNOLDS, of Junction City, Kansas, b. in Orange, Mass., Nov. 7, 1843.

CHILDREN OF DANIEL (768)
AND
POLLY WHITE (767) PARKER.

ALL BORN IN HUBBARDSTON, MASS.

819. SUSAN, b. Feb. 18, 1831; d. Sept. 5, 1863.
820. MARY, b. Jan. 27, 1833; m. Henry T. Sears (821); Samuel Estey (822).
821. HENRY T. SEARS, of Greenwich, Mass.; d. Oct. 3, 1866.
822. SAMUEL ESTEY, of Greenwich, Mass.
823. MELISSA, b. Aug. 7, 1834; d. Dec. 9, 1855.
824. SARAH, b. Oct. 15, 1835; m. Henry C. Work (825); d. Oct. 2, 1882.
825. HENRY C. WORK, of Chicago, Ill.; d.
826. DANIEL WEBSTER, b. Sept. 26, 1837; d. July 24, 1840.
827. ISAAC, b. Sept. 12, 1839; d. July 29, 1840.
828. DANIEL WEBSTER, b. June 13, 1841; m. Fanny E. Morse (829); d. Oct. 10, 1875.
829. FANNY E. MORSE, of Greenwich, Mass.

830. Lucy Augusta, b. Oct. 30, 1843.
831. Hattie Elizabeth, b. May 9, 1845.
832. Abel Otis, b. Dec. 20, 1847; m. widow Fannie E. M. Parker, of Greenwich, Mass.

CHILDREN OF GEORGE W. (770)

AND

SALLY WHITE (769) SAWYER,

OF PHILLIPSTON, MASS.

833. Henrietta, b. Dec. 10, 1829.
834. Sereno, b. Apr. 11, 1832; d. Dec. 31, 1861, in U. S. service, in 21st Regiment Massachusetts Volunteers.
835. Christopher, b. Mar. 17, 1834; Capt. Co. H, 36th Regt. Massachusetts Volunteers; m. Mary S. Underhill (836).
836. Mary S. Underhill, b. in Indianapolis, Ind., June 20, 1844.
837. Betsey Berdille, b. Aug. 27, 1836; m. Ephraim Wyman Stone (838).
838. Ephraim Wyman Stone, b. in Templeton, Mass., Dec. 5, 1830. He was in U. S. service, in the Civil War, in 21st Regt. Mass. Volunteers.
839. Sarah White, b. May 21, 1839; d. Nov. 12, 1841.
840. Dorathy, b. May 21, 1841; m. Eliphalet W. Clark (841).
841. Eliphalet W. Clark, b. in Rockport, Cuyahoga Co., O., Feb. 12, 1831.
842. Abner Washington, b. June 18, 1843; m. Olive Ward (843)
843. Olive Ward, of Orange, Mass.
844. George Sawyer, b. May 11, 1845.
845. Sarah White, b. Oct. 16, 1847; m. Albert G. Bushnell (846).
846. Albert G. Bushnell, b. in Phillipston, Wor. Co., Mass., Oct. 17, 1843. Was in U. S. service, in 53d Regt. Mass. Volunteers, in Civil War.

847. Julia Louisa, b. Mar. 8, 1850; m. Thomas E. Ryan (848).

848. Thomas E. Ryan, of Templeton, Mass., b. Apr. 2, 1848; d. July 27, 1876.

CHILDREN OF BAXTER (772) AND NANCY WHITE (771) SWAN.

849. Baxter C., b. Mar. 30, 1834; m. Caroline E. King (850).

850. Caroline E. King, b. Feb. 8, 1835, in Barre, Mass.

851. Abel Estin, b. Mar. 7, 1842; m. Bloomy Holden (852).

852. Bloomy Holden, b. in Rutland, Mar. 22, 1845.

CHILDREN OF THOMAS WHITE (773) AND ROSINA LOVERING (774) WHITE.

BY FIRST WIFE.

853. Helen, b. Mar. 14, 1836; m. George B. Lynde (854).

854. George B. Lynde, b. in Guilford, Vt., Oct. 23, 1830; d. Dec. 31, 1864.

855. Thomas Hanson, b. Nov. 28, 1842; was in U. S. service in Civil War, 42nd Mass. Infantry; Sergt. 2nd Vt. Battery, and afterwards Capt. of Militia organized at Barre, Mass.; m. Mary E. Marsh (856).

856. Mary E. Marsh, b. in Petersham, Mass., March 25, 1840.

857. William Howard, b. July 14, 1848; m. Mary Ada Peese (858).

858. Mary Ada Peese, of Barre, Mass.

859. Emma Rosina, b. Apr. 27, 1850; m. Lewis Sabin Manning (860).

860. Lewis Sabin Manning, b. in Templeton, Mass., May 2, 1853.

BY SECOND WIFE,

ELIZA STONE (775) WHITE.

861. Charles Asa, b. June 15, 1859; d. Oct. 18, 1861.

CHILDREN OF WILLIAM (782)
AND
REBECCA EVELYN NEWTON (783) WHITE.

862. Victor Franklin, b. in Barre, Mass., Sept. 16, 1839; m. Emily Yearly (863); Mrs. Louise Ann F. Rosenfeltd (864).

863. Emily Yearly, b. in New Canton, Pike Co., Ill., Aug. 23, 1843; d. Jan. 22, 1875.

864. Mrs. Louise Ann F. Rosenfeltd, of Barry, Pike Co., Ill.

865. Lucy Annetta, b. in Phillipston, Mass., Dec. 13, 1843; m. Charles Morehouse Caldwell (866).

866. Charles Morehouse Caldwell, b. in Margeretta, Erie Co., Ohio, Sept. 10, 1840.

867. Evelyn Rebecca, b. in Warren, Mass., Nov. 6, 1849; m. Randolph Randall Keightley (868).

868. Randolph Randall Keightley, b. in Columbus, Ohio, Sept. 15, 1839.

869. William Newton, b. in Griggsville, Pike Co., Ill., Oct. 12, 1862.

SEVENTH GENERATION.

CHILDREN OF SAMUEL M. (785)
AND
ELIZABETH A. EASTON (786) WHITE.

ALL BORN IN LAFAYETTE, STARK CO., ILL.

870. Abel H., b. Sept. 2, 1855; m. Mary E. Redfield (871).

871. MARY E. REDFIELD, b. at Rockaway, Morris Co., N. J., March 17, 1856.
872. S. MARIA, b. July 29, 1857; m. John Hilliard (873).
873. JOHN HILLIARD, b. in Chicago, Ill., May 8, 1856.
874. PHEBE J., b. Jan. 13, 1860; d. Apr. 11, 1864.
875. STEPHEN E., b. Dec. 11, 1862.
876. SAMUEL A., b. Dec. 13, 1866; d. Sept. 3, 1868.
877. WILLIE R., b. Aug. 7, 1869.
878. MABEL V., b. July 23, 1874.

CHILDREN OF JOHN A. (787)
AND
MARY J. ANDERSON (788) WHITE.

879. JOHN HANSON, b. July 9, 1855; m. Della E. Jones (880).
880. DELLA E. JONES, b. in Lafayette, Stark Co., Ill., July 22, 1857.
881. SARAH EMMA, b. Nov. 17, 1856; m. Charles Abbott (882).
882. CHARLES ABBOTT, b. near Iatan, Platte Co., Mo., Oct. 26, 1857.
883. MINNIE E., b. Apr. 11, 1858; m. L. V. Snyder (884).
884. L. V. SNYDER, b. in Lafayette, Ill., July 26, 1858.
885. M. VIOLA, b. Sept. 10, 1860; m. Charles Dunbar (886).
886. CHARLES DUNBAR, b. near Lafayette, Ill., Oct. 16, 1859.
887. AMELIA A., b. Dec. 18, 1861.
888. HARRIET E., b. Dec. 5, 1865; d. Oct. 14, 1867.
889. CHARLES F., b. Mar. 24, 1867.
890. LUNA J., b. Jan. 14, 1869.
891. GEORGE A., b. Apr. 26, 1871.
892. PHEBE P., b. July 13, 1872.
893. ASA G., b. Apr. 13, 1874.
894. LUCY B., b. Jan. 16, 1877.
895. FRANCIS L., b. Oct. 18, 1879.

896. FRANK, b. Sept. 12, 1881.
897. LUNA MAY, b. Feb. 3, 1883.
898. LIZZIE MAY, b. Nov. 25, 1884.

CHILDREN OF MARY R. WHITE (789)

AND

BENJAMIN F. SMITH (790).

BY FIRST HUSBAND.

899. J. FRANKLIN, b. Oct. 21, 1855; m. Carrie M. Tracy (900).
900. CARRIE M. TRACY, b. in Macon City, Macon Co., Mo., Aug. 20, 1860.

THE FOLLOWING BORN IN LAFAYETTE, ILL.

901. AMELIA L., b. Apr. 12, 1857.
992. CARRIE M., b. July 22, 1859.
903. JESSIE E., b. Dec. 28, 1861.

BY SECOND HUSBAND,

G. H. REDFIELD (791)

904. JAMES ARTHUR, b. Aug. 2, 1868.
905. MARY A., b. Dec. 29, 1871.

CHILDREN OF THOMAS D. (793)

AND

SARAH WHITE (792) CHURCH.

ALL BORN IN LAFAYETTE, ILL.

906. CHARLES C., b. Nov. 16, 1859; m. Dec. 8, 1880, Lydia Hoff (907).
907. LYDIA HOFF, b. in Marietta, O., Mar. 15, 1859.
908. WALLACE H., b. May 5, 1861.
909. ELMER E., b. Aug. 9, 1862.
910. ELLA A., b. Aug. 19, 1864; d. Sept. 2, 1866.
911. NELLIE V., b. Mar. 8, 1866.
912. WILLIE O., b. Apr. 11, 1868.
913. MARY J., b. Nov. 13, 1869.
914. SARAH H., b. Mar. 24, 1870.

CHILDREN OF THOMAS H. (796)

AND

SARAH LOUISA WHITE (795) GAUT.

ALL BORN IN CHICAGO, ILL.

915. Mary Spooner, b. May 12, 1868.
916. Mattie Louisa, b. Aug. 15, 1869; d. Mar. 21, 1874.
917. Anna Evelina, b. Jan. 26, 1871.

CHILD OF ROBERT M. (802)

AND

ELIZABETH ISABELLA MILLER (801) MILLER.

918. Robert William, b. Aug., 1848, in Phillipston; d. Sept. 3, 1848.

CHILDREN OF JOHN (803)

AND

ROENA CHENEY (804) MILLER.

919. William, b. May 17, 1855; d. 1855.
920. Sara Isabella, b. Dec. 22, 1856.
921. John Edward, b. Oct. 9, 1858; m. Anna A. Powers (922).
922. Anna A. Powers, b. in Phillipston; m. Sept. 27, 1883.

CHILDREN OF THEODORE THOMAS (805)

AND

HARRIET G. GOODSPEED (806) MILLER.

923. Frank Thomas, b. Aug. 15, 1854.
924. William Theodore, b. Aug. 12, 1856.
925. Marion Louise, b. May 13, 1862.

CHILDREN OF MERRILL
AND
EMILY JANNETTE MILLER (807) GAGE.

926. WILLIE, b. and d. Apr. 13, 1857.
927. ROBERT MERRILL, b. June 16, 1859.

CHILDREN OF ROBERT SOPER (812)
AND
GEORGIE WARNER (813) MILLER.

928. ROBERT WILLIAM, b. Aug. 19, 1867.
929. MAUD, b. Feb. 28, 1869.
930. MAY LOUISE, b. Jan. 2, 1872.

CHILDREN OF GURDON E. (811)
AND
FRANCES ALMIRA MILLER (809) BEATES.

931. MARY LUCY, b. Apr. 26, 1872.
932. JAMES WILLIAM, b. May 25, 1874.
933. EMMA FRANCES, b. Sept. 13, 1880.

CHILD OF CHARLES HENRY (814)
AND
VIRGINIA A. BIGELOW (815) MILLER.

934. ANNA VIRGINIA, b. Dec. 22, 1865; graduated in Junction City, Kansas, 1882.

CHILDREN OF THEODORE A. (818)
AND
ABBIE MARIA MILLER (817) REYNOLDS.

935. LENORA ALICE MILLER, b. Jan. 10, 1871.
936. ALBERT THEODORE, b. Mar. 28, 1878.

CHILD OF HENRY T. (821)
AND
MARY PARKER (820) SEARS.

937. Nellie M., b. Apr. 28, 1865.

CHILDREN OF HENRY C. (825)
AND
SARAH PARKER (824) WORK.

938. Waldo F., b. Oct. 2, 1859; d. July 2. 1871.
939. Helen L., b. Oct. 9, 1863.
940. Willie L., b. Dec. 10, 1861 or 2; d. July 22, 1864.
941. Clara Etta, b. Apr. 13, 1868; d. Aug. —, 1868.

CHILDREN OF DANIEL WEBSTER (828)
AND
FANNY E. MORSE (829) PARKER.

942. Frank L., b. Oct. 1, 1868.
943. Charles M., b. Jan. 28, 1871; d. May 14, 1871.

CHILD OF ABEL OTIS (832)
AND
MRS. FANNY E. M. PARKER PARKER.

944. Webster M., b. July 4, 1883.

CHILDREN OF E. WYMAN (838)
AND
BETSEY BERDILLE SAWYER (837) STONE.

945. Abby Cook, b. July 4, 1859; m. James Mason Maynard (946).
946. James Mason Maynard, b. in Templeton, Mass., July 19, 1853.
947. Helen Margaret, b. Sept. 24, 1863; graduate of State Normal School, Framingham, Mass.

948. GEORGE SAWYER, b. Feb. 3, 1866.
949. EVERETT WYMAN, b. Sept. 22, 1868.
950. LYDIA RICHARDSON, b. Aug. 14, 1871; d. Aug. 19, 1873.
951. RALPH BUSHNELL, b. June 4, 1882.

CHILD OF ELIPHALET W. (841) AND DORATHY SAWYER (840) CLARK.

952. ELIPHALET WILLIAM, b. in Middleburgh, Cuyahoga Co., Ohio, Feb. 8, 1882.

CHILDREN OF ABNER WASHINGTON (842) AND OLIVE WARD (843) SAWYER.

953. JULIA WARD, b. Apr. 18, 1869.
954. CARRIE ELIZA, b. Nov. 30, 1871.
955. SALLIE WHITE, b. June —, 18—.
956. OLIVE ———, b. Sept. —, 1878.

CHILD OF ALBERT G. (846) AND SARAH WHITE SAWYER (845) BUSHNELL.

957. JULIA SAWYER, b. Apr. 13, 1872.

CHILD OF THOMAS E. (848) AND JULIA LOUISA SAWYER (847) RYAN.

958. EDWARD SAWYER, b. Mar. 4, 1875.

CHILDREN OF BAXTER C. (849) AND CAROLINE E. KING (850) SWAN.

959. ANNA BELLE, b. Apr. 3, 1862; m.
960. GEORGE DINSMORE, b. Aug. 17, 1866.

CHILDREN OF ABEL ESTIN (851)
AND
BLOOMY HOLDEN (852) SWAN.

961. Ethel May, b. May 29, 1877.
962. Lizzie Florence, b. Apr. 4, 1880; d. Sept. 5, 1882.
963. Leon Baxter, b. Jan. 19, 1884.

CHILDREN OF GEORGE B. (854)
AND
HELEN WHITE (853) LYNDE.

964. John Herbert, b. in Gardner, Feb. 15, 1859; d. Sept. 17, 1861.
965. William Henry, b. in Gardner, Apr. 25, 1860; d. Sept. 8, 1860.
966. Helen Maria, b. in Brattleboro, Vt., Sept. 17, 1861; d. Aug. 3, 1862.

CHILDREN OF THOMAS HANSON (855)
AND
MARY E. MARSH (856) WHITE.

967. Mary E., b. Jan. 7, 1861; m. Frederic A. Brigham (968).
968. Frederic A. Brigham, of Brockton, Mass., b. in Barre, Mass.
969. Helen Rosina, b. May 12, 1863; m. Daniel H. Rice (970).
970. Daniel H. Rice, of Chicago, Ill., b. in Barre, Mass.
971. Everett Hanson, b. May 26, 1872.
972. Ada Maud Emily, b. Nov. 11, 1877.

CHILDREN OF LEWIS SABIN (860)
AND
EMMA ROSINA WHITE (859) MANNING.

973. Herbert Asa, b. in Vineland, N. J., Nov. 3, 1875.
974. Mabel, b. in Vineland, N. J., June 2, 1877; d. July 10, 1883.

CHILDREN OF VICTOR FRANKLIN (862) AND EMILY YEARLY (863) WHITE.

975. George Franklin, b. in Griggsville, Pike Co., Ill., Nov. 13, 1862; d. March 18, 1864.
976. Charles William, b. in Griggsville, Ill., Aug. 22, 1864.
977. Linnie May, b. in Atlas, Pike Co., Ill., Jan. 31, 1866.
978. Lucette Rebecca, b. in Atlas, Ill., Jan. 10, 1868.
979. Michael Gard, b. in Atlas, Ill., Sept. 19, 1869.
980. Lagrange, b. in Atlas, Ill., Nov. 22, 1871.

CHILDREN OF CHARLES MOREHOUSE (866) AND LUCY ANNETTE WHITE (865) CALDWELL.

981. Evelyn Eliza, b. in Griggsville, Ill., Aug. 2, 1867.
982. Jay Charles, b. in Decatur, Ill., Sept. 27, 1877; d. Oct. 8, 1883.

CHILDREN OF RANDOLPH RANDALL (868) AND EVELINE REBECCA WHITE (867) KEIGHTLEY.

983. Beulah Blanche, b. in Belleview, Calhoun Co., Ill., Sept. 6, 1872.
984. Olive Ethel, b. in Clarksville, Pike Co., Mo., Oct. 29, 1874.

EIGHTH GENERATION.

CHILDREN OF ABEL H. (870) AND MARY E. REDFIELD (871) WHITE.

985. Samuel Clyde, b. May 8, 1879.
986. Victor Easton, b. May 22, 1882.

CHILDREN OF JOHN (873)
AND
S. MARIA WHITE (872) HILLIARD.

987. Stephen Earle, b. in Lafayette, Ill., Dec. 11, 1879.
988 Grace, b. in Lafayette, Ill., Oct. 27, 1882.

CHILDREN OF JAMES M. (946)
AND
ABBY COOK STONE (945) MAYNARD.

989. Helen Janette, b. Aug 16, 1881.
990. Elsie Agnes, b. Jan. 13, 1884.

CHILDREN OF J. FRANKLIN (899)
AND
CARRIE M. TRACY (900) SMITH.

991. Stewart Arthur, b. in Lafayette, Ill., Dec. 17, 1880.
992. Charles Gilbert, b. in Lafayette, Ill., Sept. 17, 1883.

CHILD OF CHARLES C. (906)
AND
LYDIA HOFF (907) CHURCH.

993. Ella Leota, b. Aug 7, 1882, in Lafayette, Ill.

CHILD OF JOHN HANSON (879)
AND
DELLA E. JONES (880) WHITE.

994. Ella Mary, b. in Lafayette, Ill., Aug. 16, 1884.

CHILDREN OF CHARLES (882)

AND

SARAH EMMA WHITE (881) ABBOTT.

995. INEZ VIOLA, b. in Iatan, Platte Co., Mo., Aug. 28, 1880.

996. GERTRUDE LAURENA, b. in Iatan, Platte Co., Mo., Sept. 5, 1881.

CHILD OF L. V. (884)

AND

MINNIE E. WHITE (883) SNYDER.

997. NELLIE T., b. Aug. 29, 1881, in Lafayette, Stark Co., Ill.

FIFTH GENERATION.

CHILDREN OF JOHN WOOD, JR. (513)

AND

MARY HAYWARD (514) WOOD.

998. JOHN HAYWARD, b. in Littleton, Mass., Aug. 19, 1805; m. Roxana Sawyer (999); d. Sept. 21, 1859.

999. ROXANA SAWYER of Bolton, Mass.; d. Nov. 16, 1877, aged 65 yr. 10 mo. 3 da.; no children.

1000. MARY ANN, b. in Littleton, Oct. 31, 1806; m. Wm. P. Trask (1001); d. Oct. 7, 1854, aged 47 yr. 11 mo.

1001. WM. P. TRASK, of Bolton, Mass.; d. Dec. 29, 1856, aged 51 years; no children.

JAMES HAYWARD.

JAMES HAYWARD (516), was born in Boxboro', Mass., Jan. 2, 1779; lived there with the exception of years 1804 and 5, during his life; was named for his uncle, James Hayward, of Acton, Mass., who fell at Lexington, April 19, 1775, the day of the Concord fight, beginning of the Revolutionary war. He was a successful farmer and one of the largest cultivators of hops in the State for many years. Frequently held positions of trust in town affairs. Always ready to lend a helping hand to the sick or needy. He married Eunice, daughter of Dea. John Wood, of Littleton, Mass., April 29, 1806. They had nine children, and in 1884 their descendants were as follows: Children dead 6, living 3; grandchildren, 7 dead, 21 living; great grandchildren, 10 dead and 32 living; whole number dead 23, living 56, total 79.

I copy from the *Boston Recorder* of Dec. 10, 1846:

"DEATH OF A WHOLE FAMILY IN BOXBOROUGH.

"On the 28th of September, Paul Hayward, youngest son of Mr. James Hayward, of Boxborough, and then a member of Phillips Academy, at Andover, came home sick with the typhoid fever. He was very sick three weeks, and died at the age of 20 years and 10 months, greatly lamented.

"About a week before he died his father and mother, Mr. James and Mrs. Eunice Hayward, were both taken sick with the same disease. Mrs. Hayward died October 30, ten days after her son, aged 65, and her husband died Nov. 11, twelve days after his wife, aged 68. These parents left children who are all married and settled, but themselves and the above named son constituted their whole present family, and are all cut off by death in the short space of twenty-two days."

They were all professors of religion, and were exemplary and respected. The *Lowell Journal* said:

"Mr. Hayward was an excellent man and universally esteemed by those who knew him."

Less than five years before, their highly respected son, John Hayward, died at the age of twenty-six.

James Wood Hayward, son of James and Eunice (Wood) Hayward, resides in West Acton, Mass. He has been an active and enterprising man. He worked for his father, or attended school, until he was 24 years of age, taught school three terms where he went to school in his youth, then for ten years marketed farmers' produce, and for twelve years following was an extensive contractor of milk which he took into Boston in R. R. cars prepared for that purpose. Since then has been engaged in farming. Is a prominent man in his town. He was a Captain of Infantry, commissioned by Gov. Levi Lincoln; also served in the Cavalry. He has done much to prepare the records of his branch for this volume.

Stevens Hayward, son of James and Eunice Wood Hayward, after an academic education, taught school in his native town, and in Acton; but he was settled on his father's homestead, and has lived there most of his life. A substantial and honorable citizen.

Lucy Ann Hayward, sister of the above, married Thomas Burbeck, who was in the dry goods and grocery business, and flouring-mill, at Racine, Wisconsin, at the time of his death, Sept. 21, 1870. His widow, in 1877, returned to Massachusetts, and is now living near her old home.

Should be pleased to mention more of the grandchildren than space will permit. Several have been very successful in business pursuits.

Rev. Joel Francis Fairbanks, son of Emory and Eunice (Hayward) Fairbanks, graduate of Amherst College, 1862; Princeton Theological Seminary, 1863; Union Theological Seminary, 1864. Ordained pastor Congregational Church in 1864. Since 1877, pastor Congregational Church, West Boylston, Mass.

Joseph Whitcomb Fairbanks, A. M., Ph. D., son of Emory and Eunice Hayward Fairbanks. Grad. of Amherst College, 1866; Principal of High School, So. Hadley Falls, '66–'68; of Centre School, Norwalk, Conn., '68–'74; of Dix Street Grammar School, Worcester, Mass., '74–'75; of High School, Worcester, '75–'78; of Williston Seminary, Easthampton, Mass., since '78. Ph. D., Amherst, 1879; visited Europe in '82.

John Quincy Hayward, son of Stevens and Charlotte (Conant) Hayward. Graduate of Amherst College, 1882; Principal of the High School, Bolton, Mass.

FIFTH GENERATION.

DESCENDANTS OF JAMES (516) AND EUNICE WOOD (515) HAYWARD.

CHILDREN.

ALL BORN IN BOXBORO, MASS.

1002. EUNICE, b. Mar. 10, 1807; m. Emory Fairbanks (1003); d. Sept. 21, 1865.

1003. EMORY FAIRBANKS, b. in Gardner, Mass., May 15, 1800; d. Mar. 3, 1871.

1004. SUSANNAH, b. Apr. 13, 1808; m. Sewel Fairbanks (1005); John Wetherbee (1006).

1005. SEWEL FAIRBANKS, b. in Gardner, Mass., Mar. 4, 1804; d. Jan. 12, 1834.

1006. JOHN WETHERBEE, b. in Boxboro, Mass., Nov. 7, 1800; d. July 31, 1858.

1007. JAMES WOOD, b. May 31, 1810; m. Hannah Elizabeth Conant (1008).

1008. HANNAH ELIZABETH CONANT, dau. of Joel Conant of Acton, Mass., b. in Acton, Mass., May 15, 1818.

1009. ANDREW, b. Nov. 22, 1811, d. June 21, 1818.
1010. JOHN, b. July 9, 1815; d. Feb. 19, 1842.
1011. STEVENS, b. Aug. 25, 1817; m. Charlotte Conant (1012).
1012. CHARLOTTE CONANT, dau. of Dea. Abraham and Eunice (Jones) Conant of Acton, Mass., b. in Acton, Mass., May 26, 1820.
1013. ANDREW, b. Sept. 19, 1819; d. Oct. 5, 1824.
1014. LUCY ANNA, b. July 7, 1821; m. Thomas Burbeck (1015).
1015. THOMAS BURBECK, b. July 14, 1815, at Campton, N. H.; d. Sept. 21, 1870.
1016. PAUL, b. Dec. 11, 1825; d. Oct. 20, 1846.

SIXTH GENERATION.

CHILDREN OF EMORY (1003) AND EUNICE HAYWARD (1002) FAIRBANKS.

1017. EMORY HAYWARD, b. Oct. 30, 1829, in Boxboro, Mass.; jewelry business, Jamaica Plain, Boston, Mass.; m. Julia Maria Bacon (1018); Laura Ann Cooledge (1019).
1018. JULIA MARIA BACON, b. Nov. 8, 1836; d. Nov. 8, 1857.
1019. LAURA ANN COOLEDGE, b. in Sherborn, Mass., Dec. 9, 1839.
1020. ANDREW STEVENS, b. Jan. 30, 1832; d. Aug. 12, 1835, in Ashburnham, Mass.
1021. JOEL FRANCIS, REV., b. in Ashburnham, Mass., Sept. 8, 1835; m. Abbie Smith Russell (1022).
1022. ABBIE SMITH RUSSELL, b. Oct., 1837, in Ashburnham.
1023. JAMES HENRY, b. in Ashburnham, May 16, 1837; m. Josephine Brewer (1024); successful jeweller, Fitchburg, Mass.

1024. Josephine Brewer, b. June 28, 1836.

1025. Eunice Elizabeth, b. in Ashburnham, Feb. 14, 1835; m. Hosea Foster Lane (1026).

1026. Hosea Foster Lane, b. Feb. 7, 1831, in Ashburnham; m. Aug. 16, 1858. Since 1856, Principal of the Templeton, Mass., High School.

1027. Joseph Whitcomb, A. M., Ph. D., b. in Ashburnham, Mar. 26, 1841; m. Ellen Maria Cutting (1028).

1028. Ellen Maria Cutting, b. in Templeton, Mass., June 11, 1846.

1029. Susan Augusta, b. in Ashburnham, Apr. 14, 1843; m. Charles Edward Woodward (1030).

1030. Charles Edward Woodward, b. in Ashburnham, Apr. 23, 1842.

1031. Lucy Ann, b. in Ashburnham, Dec. 8, 1846; m. George Nelson Ells (1032); she grad. State Normal School, Framingham, Mass., 1865.

1032. George Nelson Ells, b. in Norwalk, Conn., Nov. 24, 1837; in book, stationery, and periodical business, Waterbury, Conn.; he was for twenty-five years one of the editors and proprietors of the Norwalk (Conn.) *Gazette*.

1033. Laura Amelia, b. in Ashburham, Oct. 30, 1848; d. Apr. 29, 1855.

CHILDREN OF SUSANNAH HAYWARD (1004)

BY FIRST HUSBAND,

SEWEL FAIRBANKS (1005).

1034. James Hayward, b. in Gardner, Mass., Nov. 1, 1830; m. Anna Mehitable Gibbs (1035).

1035. Anna Mehitable Gibbs, b. in Boston, Mass.

1036. Sewel Whitcomb, b. in Gardner, Oct. 21, 1832; jewelry business, Boston, Mass.; m. Caroline Blood (1037); Mrs. Carrie J. Brown Boyt (1038).

1037. Caroline Blood, b. in Auburn, N. Y.; m. Nov. 29, 1860; d. in Boston, Feb. 15, 1875.

1038. Mrs. Carrie J. Brown Boyt, b. in Groton, Mass.; m. in Boston, Jan. 12, 1881.

BY SECOND HUSBAND,

JOHN WETHERBEE (1006).

1039. Ellen Augusta, b. in Boxboro, Nov. 17, 1843.
1040. Susan Ann, b. in Boxboro, Apr. 8, 1846; m. Delette Haynes Hall (1041).
1041. Delette Haynes Hall, b. in Bolton, Mass., Mar. 20, 1843. Large manufacturer of churns, tubs and pails.
1042. Emmaetta Frances, b. in Boxboro, June 27, 1850.

CHILDREN OF JAMES WOOD (1007)

AND

HANNAH ELIZABETH CONANT (1008) HAYWARD.

ALL BORN IN ACTON, MASS.

1043. Henry Stevens, b. May 5, 1841; d. Mar. 2, 1842.
1044. Elizabeth, b. Jan. 18, 1843; m. Henry Hanson (1045).
1045. Henry Hanson, b. in Birmingham, England, July 30, 1838; m. Sept. 14, 1865, in Acton, Mass.
1046. Abba Malvina, b. May 17, 1845; d. Oct. 2, 1846.
1047. Ella Augusta, b. July 8, 1847; m. Samuel Rogers Burrough (1048).
1048. Samuel Rogers Burrough, b. in Acton, Mar. 25, 1843; m. in Acton, Feb. 14, 1866. Served through the Civil War in 6th Mass. Infantry.
1049. Miron, b. June 5, 1850; d. Aug. 16, 1850.
1050. Frank Conant, b. Mar. 22, 1852; a prosperous merchant and manufacturer, South Abington, Mass.
1051. James Webster, b. Nov. 15, 1854; m. Jennie Gillespie (1052).
1052. Jennie Gillespie, b. in Belleville, Ont., July 11, 1854; m. in Richmond, Ill., Aug. 21, 1883.

1053. Charles Sumner, of Vinton, Iowa, b. July 8, 1857; in company with his brother Jas. W. in retail and jobbing shoe trade; m. Abbie Chamberlain Jones (1054).

1054. Abbie Chamberlain Jones, b. in Cambridge, Mass., Apr. 18, 1856; m. Aug. 21, 1884.

1055. Edward Ellsworth, of South Abington, Mass., b. Dec. 12, 1860; interested with his brother Frank C. in South Abington, Mass.; m. Eldora Rickard (1056), May 14, 1884.

1056. Eldora Rickard, b. in North Carver, Mass., Jan. 10, 1854.

CHILDREN OF STEVENS (1011)

AND

CHARLOTTE CONANT (1012) HAYWARD.

ALL BORN IN BOXBORO, MASS.

1057. Charles Henry, b. May 25, 1851; d. Jan. 12, 1852.

1058. Herbert Nelson, b. Feb. 21, 1853; m. Sarah Preble Baldwin (1059).

1059. Sarah Preble Baldwin, b. in Waltham, Mass., July 9, 1854; m. Aug. 12, 1875.

1060. John Quincy, b. Sept. 25, 1855. Graduate of Amherst College.

1061. Clara Sophia, b. Dec. 21, 1857; m. Charles Lysander Woodward (1062).

1062. Charles Lysander Woodward, b. in Landsgrove, Vt., Apr. 9, 1858; m. Mar. 25, 1884; res. Boxboro, Mass.

1063. Charlotte Maria, b. Apr. 5, 1862; m. June 19, 1884, Charles Volney McClenathan (1064).

1064. Charles V. McClenathan, b. in New York, July 4, 1858.

SEVENTH GENERATION.

CHILDREN OF EMORY HAYWARD FAIRBANKS (1017)

BY FIRST WIFE,

JULIA MARIA BACON (1018).

1065. Francis Bacon, b. in Holliston, Mass., Oct. 26. 1856.

BY SECOND WIFE,

LAURA ANN COOLEDGE (1019).

1066. Annie Maria, b. in Sherborn, Oct. 19, 1863.
1067. Edith, b. at Jamaica Plain, Mass., Dec. 9, 1868; d. Dec. 2, 1876.
1068. Herbert, b. at Jamaica Plain, July 19, 1870; d. Dec. 4, 1876.
1069. Laura, b. at Jamaica Plain, Nov. 29, 1874; d. July 26, 1875.
1070. Emory, b. at Jamaica Plain, Mar. 27, 1876; d. Dec. 12, 1876.
1071. Helen, b. at Jamaica Plain, May 29, 1883.

CHILDREN OF JOEL FRANCIS (1021)

AND

ABBIE SMITH RUSSELL (1022) FAIRBANKS.

1072. Ernest Hayward, b. in Westminster, Vt., Dec. 30, 1866.
1073. Francis Joel, b. in Westminster, Vt., Mar. 20, 1869; d. Apr. 9, 1874.
1074. Alice Russell, b. in Westminster, Vt., Apr. 20, 1871.
1075. George Stevens, b. in Ayer, Mass., Aug. 2, 1873.
1076. Herbert Stockwell, b. in Paxton, Mass., Oct. 20, 1875.

CHILDREN OF JAMES HENRY (1023) AND JOSEPHINE BREWER (1024) FAIRBANKS.

FIRST THREE BORN IN FRAMINGHAM, MASS.; NEXT SIX IN FITCHBURG, MASS.

1077. Mary Eunice, b. Feb. 2, 1862.
1078. Arthur Brewer, b. June 22, 1865.
1079. Carrie Fay, b. June 22, 1867.
1080. Emma Josephine, b. Feb. 10, 1869; d. May 3, 1869.
1081. Freddie Hayward, b. Aug. 22, 1870; d. July 15, 1872.
1082. Emma Josephine, b. July 30, 1872.
1083. Bertie, b. Feb. 27, 1874; d. May 7, 1874.
1084. Alice May, b. June 13, 1875.
1085. Florence Louise, b. Feb. 5, 1877.

CHILDREN OF HOSEA FOSTER (1026) AND EUNICE ELIZABETH FAIRBANKS (1025) LANE.

1086. Charles Hosea, b. in Templeton, Mass., Sept. 14, 1859. He collected the records of the Abel White descendants for this volume.
1087. Arthur Francis, b. in Templeton, Mass., July 17, 1861; d. Oct. 17, 1862.

CHILDREN OF JOSEPH WHITCOMB (1027) AND ELLEN MARIA CUTTING (1028) FAIRBANKS.

1088. Gertrude Maria, b. in Norwalk, Conn., Oct. 28, 1869.
1089. Helen Louise, b. in Templeton, Mass., Aug. 31, 1871.
1090. Joseph Whitcomb, b. in Worcester, Mass., Dec. 17, 1874.

CHILD OF CHARLES EDWARD (1030) AND SUSAN AUGUSTA FAIRBANKS (1029) WOODWARD.

1091. ADELLA FAIRBANKS, b. in Ashburnham, Mass., Nov. 29, 1876.

CHILD OF GEORGE NELSON (1032) AND LUCY ANN FAIRBANKS (1031) ELLS.

1092. ARTHUR FAIRBANKS, b. in Norwalk, Conn., Dec. 17, 1879.

CHILD OF JAMES HAYWARD (1034) AND ANN MEHITABLE GIBBS (1035) FAIRBANKS.

1093. JAMES HAYWARD, b. in Natick, Mass., Dec. 17, 1858; d. Aug. 23, 1865.

CHILDREN OF SEWEL WHITCOMB (1036) AND CAROLINE BLOOD (1037) FAIRBANKS.

ALL BORN IN BOSTON, MASS.

1094. FRANCES BLOOD, b. Sept. 2, 1864.
1095. JAMES LINCOLN, b. June 12, 1866.
1096. CARRIE ISABEL, b. June 29, 1868.
1097. EMMA FLORENCE, b. July 16, 1870; d. Apr. 20. 1872.
1098. BERTHA MAY, b. May 4, 1874; d. June 30, 1875.

CHILDREN OF DELETTE HAYNES (1041)

AND

SUSAN ANN WETHERBEE (1040) HALL.

1099. Eugene Lazelle, b. in Acton, Mass., Sept. 13, 1869.

1100. Bertram Delette, b. in Acton, Mass., Oct. 3, 1871.

1101. Etta Roxana, b. in Acton, Mass., May 27, 1874.

CHILDREN OF HENRY (1045)

AND

ELIZABETH HAYWARD (1044) HANSON.

1102. Alice May, b. in Arlington, Mass., June 12, 1867; d. Mar. 13, 1870.

1103. Carrie Field, b. in Arlington, Mass., Dec. 6, 1869.

1104. Alice May, b. in Arlington, Mass., July 9, 1873.

CHILD OF SAMUEL ROGERS (1048)

AND

ELLA AUGUSTA HAYWARD (1047) BURROUGH.

1105. Mabel Ella, b. in Reading, Mass., July 20, 1874.

CHILD OF HERBERT NELSON (1058)

AND

SARAH PREBLE BALDWIN (1059) HAYWARD.

1106. William Baldwin, b. in Waltham, Mass., Aug. 24, 1876.

AMARIAH WOOD.

Amariah Wood was a son of Dea. John Wood of Littleton, Mass., who was the son of John, son of Jeremiah.

He thoroughly learned the trades of tanner and currier, and carried on that business about a quarter of a century in Bolton, Massachusetts.

He married and had a large family of children by his first wife; he had no children by his second wife.

Amariah Wood was an honored citizen, having held civil offices of trust. I also have before me a commission as Lieutenant, given him by Gov. Caleb Strong of Massachusetts, and a commission as Captain. To the former office he was elected Nov. 27, 1812, and the latter May 3, 1814, and was Captain of an independent company later.

He was a conscientious and upright man, of marked ability and scholarly attainments,—was a persistent student all his life, and was always ready for research in science and metaphysics,—was a close student of the Bible and was guided by it. He was skilled in musical composition, and took much pleasure in it. Selections from his manuscripts were published long after his decease. He often had original music to use at the meetings of the family.

His conversations in later years were masterly, having accurate knowledge and a clear logical mind, thoroughly disciplined.

In his last days he purchased a home near Worcester, Mass., where some of his children had settled.

Here he, and the able and estimable wife of his early and maturer years and the mother of all his children, rested from their labors.

Amariah Wood

He was born in Littleton, Mass., Sept. 9, 1785,—one century ago.

His portrait, from a copy of a daguerreotype, is bound in this volume.

FIFTH GENERATION.

DESCENDANTS OF AMARIAH (519) AND HANNAH SMITH (520) WOOD.

CHILDREN.

1107. George Hobbs, b. in Littleton, Mass., Dec. 5, 1805; m. Relief Doane (1108); d. Nov. 7, 1878.

1108. Relief Doane, b. Apr. 28, 1803; d. Aug. 13, 1848.

1109. Amariah Martin, b. in Bolton, Mass., May 6, 1807; m. Rachel Atherton (1110); residence Sublette, Lee Co., Illinois.

1110. Rachel Atherton, b. in Harvard, Mass., Feb. 4, 1811; dau. of Philemon and Elizabeth (Patterson) Atherton, and granddaughter of Oliver Atherton.

1111. Mary Elvira, b. in Bolton, Mass., Dec. 5, 1808; d. June 12, 1815.

1112. Hannah Amanda, b. in Bolton, May 31, 1810; m. Alvin Babcock (1113); res. Clinton, Mass.

1113. Alvin Babcock, son of Ephraim and Eunice (Sawyer), b. in Berlin, Nov. 9, 1808; d. Apr. 7, 1881.

1114. John, b. in Bolton, Sept. 8, 1811; m. Eliza Atherton (1115); res. Rockport, Cuyahoga Co., Ohio.

1115. Eliza Atherton, b. in Harvard, Mass., Oct. 6, 1814; dau. of Philemon and Elizabeth (Patterson) Atherton, and granddaughter of Oliver Atherton.

1116. Lucy, b. in Bolton, Jan. 8, 1813; m. James Lawrence Estey (1117).

1117. JAMES LAWRENCE ESTEY, b. in Middleton, Mass., May 28, 1814; m. Oct. 16, 1838; res. Worcester, Mass.

1118. CHARLES, b. in Bolton, Feb. 14, 1814; d. Jan. 19, 1816.

1119. MARY ELVIRA, b. in Bolton, Dec. 3, 1815; d. Feb. 11, 1816.

1120. LUCIUS FRANCIS, b. in Bolton, Nov. 9, 1816; m. Harriet Newell Ball (1121); Sarah Isabelle Gerry (1122); Harriet Ellen Davis (1123).

1121. HARRIET NEWELL BALL, b. in Townsend, Mass., Apr. 25, 1817; d. May 23, 1860.

1122. SARAH ISABELLE GERRY, b. in Harvard, Mass., Dec. 4, 1830; d. Oct. 4, 1872.

1123. HARRIET ELLEN DAVIS, b. in Lunenburg, Mass., Mar. 16, 1838.

1124. SUSANNAH WRIGHT, b. in Bolton, Nov. 28, 1818; m. Henry Edward Warren (1125); res. Worcester, Mass.

1125. HENRY EDWARD WARREN, son of Timothy and Hannah Warren, b. in Northboro, Mass., Jan. 4, 1817; d. July 25, 1869.

1126. AUGUSTINE WASHINGTON, b. in Bolton, Feb. 7, 1820; m. Permelia Adelaide Trim (1127).

1127. PERMELIA ADELAIDE TRIM, b. in Northport, Maine, July 1, 1825.

1128. LOWELL MILTON, b. in Bolton, Sept. 3, 1821; m. Sarah W. Gilley (1129); Martha Bunker (1130); d. Dec. 13, 1875.

1129. SARAH W. GILLEY, b. in Maine; d. Nov. 2, 1859.

1130. MARTHA BUNKER, b. at Cranberry Isles, Maine, June 30, 1835.

1131. SARAH ELIZABETH, b. in Bolton, Apr. 18, 1823; m. John Farwell (1132); George Farwell (1133).

1132. JOHN FARWELL, b. in Harvard, Mass., July 27, 1816; d. Aug. 21, 1878.

1133. GEORGE FARWELL, b. in Westford, Mass., May 14, 1821.

1134. ELIZA ANN, b. in Bolton, Nov. 20, 1824; d. Dec. 3, 1830.

1135. CHRISTOPHER, b. in Bolton, May 15, 1826; probably lost at sea several years ago.

1136. SAMPSON WILDER, b. in Bolton, Aug. 1, 1828; was a non-commissioned officer in Col. Caleb Cushing's Massachusetts Regt. in the "Mexican War"; m. Sylvia Hovey (1137); Mrs. Ann M. (Emerson) Wade (1138).

1137. SYLVIA HOVEY, b. in Troy, Vt., Aug. 12, 1830; d. Sept. 16, 1867.

1138. MRS. ANN M. (EMERSON) WADE, b. in Millbury, Mass., April 17, 1833.

1139. WILLIAM SMITH WOOD, b. in Boxboro, Mass., Feb. 18, 1832; Superintendent of city schools, Seymour, Indiana; Compiler and publisher of this volume; an educator for twenty-nine years; was Captain of Co. D, 34th Illinois Veteran Volunteer Infantry, in the U. S. service in the Civil War; m. Sarah S. Knowlton (1140); Louisa Hamilton Anderson (1141).

1140. SARAH S. KNOWLTON, b. in Massachusetts, Sept. 19, 1836; m. Aug. 18, 1856; d. Feb. 2, 1860.

1141. LOUISA HAMILTON ANDERSON, b. in Geneva, N. Y., Dec. 9, 1845; m. May 4, 1863.

GEORGE HOBBS WOOD.

GEORGE H. WOOD, of Providence, R. I., eldest son of Amariah and Hannah Wood, was for more than forty years foreman, or otherwise connected with the manufacturing establishment of Wm. Chase & Sons, of Providence. He was a student in Harvard University, — he did not graduate on account of sickness, but never lost his interest in literary pursuits and scientific investigation. He was a man of intelligence and good judgment, and his opinions with reference to business and other matters were sought by very many of his fellow-citizens.

He held offices of honor and trust, but always refused when he could consistently do so. He was respected and greatly beloved by all who knew him.

The following message to his children was written by him in his latest account book which was found after his decease :—

"How can I attempt to write, feeling as I do at the present time, — this mortal body has almost performed its last task, — my earthly career is nearly ended; disease has already attacked my body and fatal will be the result.

"I would address a few words, dear children, to you, that after this hand that now writes is cold and stiff or mingled with the mother earth, and this spirit that now prompts the hand what to write shall have departed, you may read, reflect and soberly consider what may be advantageous in your short journey of life.

"I hope you will read the Sacred Scriptures, particularly the New Testament, — that you will pay particular attention to the commands of Jesus Christ, and that these you will follow.

"In all your dealings, in whatever you say or do, keep in remembrance this command, and follow it as far as in you is possible:

"'Do unto others as ye would that others should do unto you;' be patient, be charitable, love one another, and prepare for death. The time will soon come when you must also be laid with me in the silent tomb, when the time of your probation will expire. Improve the time in doing good, and may your reward be great when you are called at the judgment.

GEORGE H. WOOD."

A beautiful monument marks his resting-place and that of members of his family, in North End Cemetery, Providence, Rhode Island.

AMARIAH M. AND JOHN WOOD.

The brothers Amariah Martin and John Wood married sisters.

For many years they were in the tanning and currying business, under the firm name of A. M. & J. Wood.

Later in life both were interested in farming in Illinois. John was also in the real estate business in Cleveland, Ohio, where his daughter, Abbie Eliza, before her marriage was a successful teacher for about ten years.

Amariah M. had three sons in the Union Army during the great Civil War: George Patterson, who was killed in the battle before Vicksburg, Miss.; Frank Amariah, who died in hospital at Nashville, Tenn.; and Oliver Atherton, who was severely wounded at the battle of Perryville, Ky. The latter is married, has a family, and is settled on the home place of his father.

JAMES LAWRENCE ESTEY.

JAMES LAWRENCE ESTEY and family have long resided in Worcester, Massachusetts; he went there in March, 1829, as an apprentice to the printing business, and has followed that occupation constantly from that time until the present year, 1885, and he is still in the establishment of Charles Hamilton, the printer of this book, where he has been constantly employed since 1862.

From 1840 to 1853 he was employed on the Worcester *Spy*. Although in the same business for himself elsewhere, for a time, he returned with pleasure to Worcester where he has a pleasant home, and is a most genial and worthy husband, brother, father and friend.

His son, George L. Estey, also resides in Worcester, which has been his home the most of his life, excepting a year in Minnesota and Illinois, and two or three in California.

LUCIUS FRANCIS WOOD.

Lucius Francis Wood is a deacon in the Baptist Church and has been for more than a score of years,—has written many hymns; is engaged in the manufacture and sale of medicines, &c.; has accomplished much good; residence West Townsend, Mass.

His son, Francis Warren, was a great sufferer in consequence of a long imprisonment in the rebel prison at Salisbury, North Carolina, during the war of the rebellion.

HENRY EDWARD WARREN.

Henry Edward Warren was a man beloved by all who knew him.

He was remarkably active in his business, which he continued successfully until his death.

He was buried in his family lot in the Shrewsbury, Mass., cemetery, where he had previously laid to rest five of his children, viz: Lucius Henry, Charlotte Eliza, Edward Marshall, Frank Wilder, and Annah Elizabeth.

His widow lives in Worcester, Mass.; her son, Edgar William Warren and family, residing with her.

LOWELL MILTON WOOD.

From sixteen years of age, with the exception of three years at the Worcester Academy, Worcester, Mass., and a brief stay in Europe, Lowell M. Wood was a resident of Boston, Mass., where he was in business for more than a quarter of a century. He died there, and lies buried in Mount Hope Cemetery.

A man of ability, strict integrity and honor.

His widow, and daughter Josephine M. Wood reside upon the old homestead in Boston.

JOHN FARWELL.

JOHN FARWELL was *a friend* of the poor and unfortunate and cared for such for many years. He was Superintendent of the City Farm and Almshouse of the City of Worcester for nearly twenty years, and had other experience. No better evidence of his capacity and energy, as well as that of his wife, can be given than the oft-repeated commendations of the city authorities as published in the City Documents during the many years he held the position of Superintendent in Worcester.

He resigned in the spring of 1878, and removed to a farm owned by him in the westerly part of Hubbardston, Mass., which overlooks the village and the surrounding towns towards Worcester, and has a magnificent view of Wachusett mountain. His thoughts were led upwards by his surroundings, and August 21, 1878, his spirit was free; his body was buried in the beautiful cemetery at New Worcester, Mass.

His son, Henry A. Farwell, Esq., and family, have since occupied the home place.

SIXTH GENERATION.

CHILDREN OF GEORGE HOBBS (1107) AND RELIEF DOANE (1108) WOOD.

ALL BORN IN NORTH PROVIDENCE, R. I.

1142. SARAH AUGUSTA, b. May 24, 1826; m. Nathaniel G. Totten; she died April 20, 1847.

1143. GEORGE LEONARD, b. Oct. 23, 1828; m. Frances Potter Kenyon (1144); residence Providence, R. I.

1144. FRANCES POTTER KENYON, b. in Richmond, R. I., Jan. 13, 1828; d. May 30, 1884.

1145. Ann Sophia, b. Nov. 30, 1830; d. Apr. 10, 1839.

1146. Henry Franklin, b. Feb. 26, 1833; d. Mar. 23, 1833.

1147. Franklin Henry, b. Apr. 19, 1834.

1148. Edwin Harrison, b. Feb. 9, 1836.

1149. Ann Olive, b. Apr. 4, 1844; m. Charles Prestwich (1150); residence Providence, R. I.

1150. Charles Prestwich, b. in Hudson, N. Y., Nov. 27, 1837.

CHILDREN OF AMARIAH MARTIN (1109) AND RACHEL ATHERTON (1110) WOOD.

1151. Oliver Atherton, b. in Bolton, Mass., June 22, 1833; was in Union Army, 75th Illinois Infantry; severely wounded at battle of Perryville, Ky.; m. Climena Hubbard (1152); res. Sublette, Ill.

1152. Climena Hubbard, b. in Princeton, Ill., July 5, 1842; dau. of Royal Prescott and Mary (Boring) Hubbard, and granddau. of Moses Hubbard.

1153. Adeline Eliza, b. in Northboro, Mass., Aug. 2, 1837; d. Feb. 4, 1844.

1154. George Patterson, b. in Stow, Mass., Feb. 16, 1839; d. Dec. 28, 1862; was in Union Army, 13th Illinois Infantry; was instantly killed in a charge before Vicksburg, Miss.

1155. Francis Amariah, b. in Stow, Mass., Jan. 17, 1841; d. Jan. 3, 1864; was in Union Army, 13th Illinois Infantry; Sergeant Co. C; died in hospital at Nashville, Tenn.

1156. Annah Caroline, b. in Stow, Apr. 6, 1843; d. Aug. 19, 1844.

1157. Ella Adelaide, b. in Fitzwilliam, N. H., Dec. 15, 1844; d. Aug. 29, 1847.

1158. Galen Milton, b. in Sublette, Ill., June 23, 1853; d. May 16, 1854.

CHILDREN OF ALVIN (1113)
AND
HANNAH AMANDA WOOD (1112) BABCOCK.

1159. HANNAH AMANDA, b. Sept. 20, 1831; m. George Edward Colburn (1160); residence Clinton, Mass.

1160. GEORGE EDWARD COLBURN, b. in Leominster, Mass., Jan. 3, 1829.

1161. ALVIN WALDO, b. Nov. 10, 1835; d. May 12, 1845.

CHILD OF JOHN (1114)
AND
ELIZA ATHERTON (1115) WOOD.

1162. ABBIE ELIZA, b. in Stow, Mass., Aug. 24, 1837; m. James Howard Gleason (1163); res. Rockport, Ohio.

1163. JAMES HOWARD GLEASON, b. in Sandisfield, Berkshire Co., Mass., Nov. 28, 1836.

CHILDREN OF JAMES LAWRENCE (1117)
AND
LUCY WOOD (1116) ESTEY.

1164. SARAH ADELAIDE, b. in Worcester, Mass., Dec. 29, 1840; d. Sept. 7, 1841, aged 8 mo. and 9 da.

1165. GEORGE LAWRENCE, b. in Worcester, Jan. 23, 1848; m. Charlotte Hill Gates (1166); res. Worcester, Mass.

1166. CHARLOTTE HILL GATES, b. in Hubbardston, Mass., Feb. 8, 1851.

CHILDREN OF LUCIUS FRANCIS WOOD (1120)
BY FIRST WIFE,
HARRIET NEWELL BALL (1121).

1167. HARRIET FRANCENA, b. in Leominster, Mass., Apr. 22, 1841; m. David Haselton (1168); d. Jan. 6, 1882.

1168. DAVID HASELTON, b. in Hudson, N. H., July 31, 1827; d. July 7, 1880.

1169. FRANCIS WARREN, b. in Pepperell, Mass., Oct. 28, 1844; was in the Union Army, and mustered out June 9, 1865; he had an eventful career during his service; m. Isabella Catherine Torrey (1170); Hannah Maria Thurston (1171); residence West Bridgewater, Mass.

1170. ISABELLA CATHERINE TORREY, of Groton, Mass., b. Apr. 17, 1846; d. May 28, 1870.

1171. HANNAH MARIA THURSTON, b. in Somerset, Mass., Mar. 28, 1847.

BY SECOND WIFE,

SARAH ISABELLE GERRY (1122).

1172. GEORGE GERRY, b. in West Townsend, Mass., Aug. 20, 1867; d. Aug. 26, 1868.

1173. EDWARD HARTSHORN, b. in West Townsend, Mass., Dec. 20, 1871; d. July 23, 1872.

BY THIRD WIFE,

HARRIET ELLEN DAVIS (1123).

1174. EDITH ISABELLE, b. in West Townsend, Dec. 20, 1873.

1175. ETHEL ROXANA, b. in West Townsend, Apr. 3, 1878.

CHILDREN OF HENRY EDWARD (1125) AND SUSANNAH W. WOOD (1124) WARREN.

ALL BORN IN SHREWSBURY, MASS.

1176. LUCIUS HENRY, b. Nov. 23, 1843; d. Mar. 3, 1844.

1177. CHARLOTTE ELIZA, b. Feb. 26, 1845; d. May 8, 1847.

1178. EDWARD MARSHALL, b. May 11, 1847; d. Oct. 14, 1847.

1179. FRANK WILDER, b. Aug. 1, 1848; d. July 7, 1857.

1180. Annah Elizabeth, b. June 15, 1850; d. Dec. 31, 1851.

1181. Edgar William, b. Oct. 4, 1853; of the firm of C. C. Houghton & Co., boot manufacturers, Worcester, Mass.; m. Delia Harriet Prentice (1182)

1182. Delia Harriet Prentice, b. in Grafton, Mass., June 3, 1854.

1183. Herbert Walter, orphan nephew, adopted, b. June 15, 1855, son of Timothy W. and Elizabeth H. Warren; m. Fannie Louise Kendall (1184); res. Worcester, Mass.

1184. Fannie Louise Kendall, b. in Sterling, Mass., July 26, 1857.

CHILDREN OF AUGUSTINE W. (1126) AND PERMELIA A. TRIM (1127) WOOD.

1185. Mary Augusta, b. in Boston, Mass., Jan. 4, 1846; m. Edward Noyes (1186).

1186. Edward Noyes, b. June 27, 1844, in Goldsboro, Me.; residence East Sullivan, Maine.

1187. Augustine Washington, b. in Boston, Feb. 22, 1848; served in band of 11th U. S. Infantry, U. S. Post band, Richmond, Va.; fifteen years in band of 17th U. S. Infantry, — more than ten years of his last service as principal musician; m. Rena Armundson (1188).

1188. Rena Armundson, b. Oct, 16, 1860, at Gudbansdal, Norway.

1189. Susie Elizabeth, b. in Boston, Mass., Dec. 18, 1849; m. William A. Searle (1190); she d. Sept. 21, 1876; no children.

1190. William A. Searle.

CHILD OF LOWELL MILTON (1128) AND MARTHA BUNKER (1130) WOOD.

1191. Josephine Martha, b. in Boston, Mass., Nov. 25, 1863; residence Boston, Mass.

CHILDREN OF JOHN (1132)

AND

SARAH ELIZABETH WOOD (1131) FARWELL.

1192. Henry Augustus, b. in Worcester, Mass., June 27, 1841; student in Yale College and Harvard Law School; studied law with Davis & Stoddard, Worcester, Mass.; was Principal of High School, Illinois; Supt. City Schools, Ohio; Trial Justice, &c., Massachusetts; m. Alice Adeline Benneson (1193).

1193. Alice Adeline Benneson, b. in Quincy, Illinois, Apr. 8, 1844.

1194. Charles Alfred, b. in Worcester, Mass., June 23, 1843; d. Sept. 23, 1844.

1195. Sarah Elizabeth, b. in Worcester, July 27, 1845; d. Sept. 13, 1847.

CHILD OF SAMPSON WILDER (1136)

AND

SYLVIA HOVEY (1137) WOOD.

1196. George Amariah, b. in Shrewsbury, Mass., May 8, 1853; m. Chloe Maria Cudworth (1197); res. Winchendon, Mass.

1197. Chloe Maria Cudworth, b. June 3, 1855.

CHILDREN OF WILLIAM SMITH WOOD (1139)

BY FIRST WIFE,

SARAH S. KNOWLTON (1140).

1198. William Charles, b. in North Attleboro, Mass., Nov. 18, 1857; graduate of Salem, Ohio, High school; m. Lizzie A. Buchan (1199); res. Cleveland, Ohio.

1199. Lizzie A. Buchan, b. in Cleveland, Ohio, Jan. 18, 1860; graduate of Cleveland, Ohio, High school.

William C Wood

John A Wood

Walter M Wood.

Orville F. Wood.

BY SECOND WIFE,

LOUISA HAMILTON ANDERSON (1141).

1200. JOHN ANDERSON, b. in Cleveland, Ohio, Aug. 14, 1865; graduate of Seymour, Indiana, High school, 1883.

1201. WALTER MABIE, b. in Findlay, Ohio, Jan. 19, 1871.

1202. ORVILLE FISK, b. in Salem, Ohio, Dec. 15, 1876.

SEVENTH GENERATION.

CHILDREN OF GEORGE LEONARD (1143)

AND

FRANCES P. KENYON (1144) WOOD.

1203. ADELINE FRANCES BLAISDELL, b. in North Providence, R. I., Apr. 15, 1850; m. George Henry Peters (1204).

1204. GEORGE HENRY PETERS, b. in Providence, R. I., Sept. 29, 1838; general freight agent of Grand Trunk railroad in Boston, Mass.

1205. GEORGE WASHINGTON FREMONT, b. in North Providence, R. I., May 22, 1856; d. Apr. 5, 1880.

CHILD OF CHARLES (1150)

AND

ANN OLIVE WOOD (1149) PRESTWICH.

1206. GRACE WOOD, b. in North Providence, Aug. 6, 1871.

CHILDREN OF OLIVER ATHERTON (1151)

AND

CLIMENA HUBBARD (1152) WOOD.

ALL BORN IN SUBLETTE, LEE CO., ILL.

1207. GEORGE FRANK, b. Oct. 20, 1865.

1208. Leon. Atherton, b. Oct. 23, 1869.
1209. Minnie Gertrude, b. May 19, 1871; d. Aug. 15, 1872.
1210. Abbie Eliza, b. June 9, 1879; d. Mar. 16, 1880.
1211. Oliver Prescott, b. Nov. 29, 1881.

CHILD OF GEORGE EDWARD (1160) AND HANNAH AMANDA BABCOCK (1159) COLBURN.

1212. Albert Waldo, b. Dec. 2, 1870, in Boylston, Mass.

CHILD OF DAVID (1168) AND HARRIET FRANCENA WOOD (1167) HASELTON.

1213. William Clifford, b. in West Townsend, Mass., Jan. 18, 1869.

CHILD OF FRANCIS W. (1169) AND HANNAH MARIA THURSTON (1171) WOOD.

1214. Ida Frances, b. at Fishkill Landing, N. Y., Dec. 31, 1872.

CHILDREN OF EDGAR WILLIAM (1181) AND DELIA HARRIET PRENTICE (1182) WARREN.

1215. Bertha Carrie, b. in Worcester, Mass., Nov. 6, 1877; d. Jan. 3, 1882.
1216. Henry Edward, b. in Worcester, Aug. 3, 1882.
1217. Bessie Leland, b. in Worcester, Aug. 2, 1884.

CHILDREN OF EDWARD (1186)

AND

MARY AUGUSTA WOOD (1185) NOYES.

1218. Edward Augustine, b. Dec. 31, 1867, in Cutler, Maine; d. Feb. 1, 1868.
1219. Addie Villa, b. Nov. 27, 1868, in Cutler, Me.
1220. Susie May, b. Jan. 22, 1871, in Sullivan, Me.
1221. Edward Raymond, b. Dec. 30, 1873, in Sullivan, Me.
1222. John Farwell, b. Feb. 19, 1875, in Sullivan, Me.; d. Apr. 4, 1884; accidentally hanged while playing with a roller towel.
1223. George Taft, b. Aug. 25, 1879, in Sullivan, Me.
1224. William Wood, b. May 22, 1882, in Sullivan, Me.

CHILDREN OF AUGUSTINE WASHINGTON WOOD, JR. (1187)

AND

RENA ARMUNDSON (1188) WOOD.

1225. Alfred Lester, b. in Fort Yates, Dakota Territory, Jan. 31, 1878.
1226. Susie Adelaide, b. in Fort Yates, Dakota Territory, Sept. 23, 1879.
1227. Annie Irene, b. in Rothsay, Minnesota, Jan. 18, 1882.

CHILDREN OF HENRY AUGUSTUS (1192)

AND

ALICE ADELINE BENNESON (1193) FARWELL.

1228. Robert Benneson, b. in Quincy, Ill., Mar. 25, 1871.
1229. Seymour Allston, b. in Norwalk, O., Dec. 8, 1872.
1230. Oscar John, b. in Ironton, O., Jan. 24, 1875.

1231. Theodore Channing, b. in Hubbardston, Mass., Jan. 24, 1877.

1232. Henry Warren, b. in Hubbardston, Mass., Nov. 29, 1878; d. Apr. 21, 1880.

1233. Clarence Gilbert, b. Oct. 16, 1880, in Hubbardston, Mass.

1234. Everett Lawrence, b. July 15, 1883, in Hubbardston, Mass.

CHILDREN OF GEORGE AMARIAH (1196) AND CHLOE MARIA CUDWORTH (1197) WOOD.

1235. Clara May, b. in Worcester, Mass., Feb. 5, 1875.

1236. John Wilder, b. in Worcester, Mass., Mar. 6, 1876.

1237. Florence Pamelia, b. in Worcester, Mass., Mar. 18, 1881.

CHILD OF WILLIAM CHARLES (1198) AND LIZZIE A. BUCHAN (1199) WOOD.

1238. John Buchan, b. in Cleveland, Ohio, Dec. 13, 1884.

EIGHTH GENERATION.

CHILD OF GEORGE HENRY (1204) AND ADALINE FRANCES BLAISDELL WOOD (1203) PETERS.

1239. Lillian Westcott, b. in Chelsea, Mass., June 23, 1878.

FIFTH GENERATION.

DESCENDANTS OF FRANK (523) AND MARY WOOD (522) PRIEST.

CHILDREN.

1240. JOHN WOOD, b. in Pomfret, Vt., Oct. 18, 1809; m. Olive Wakefield (1241); Lucinda Stafford (1242); Katherine E. Wright (1243); Mrs. Phœbe Eggleston (1244). Has been Mayor of Springfield, Illinois, three terms, and has been prominent there as a man of wealth and enterprise.

1241. OLIVE WAKEFIELD, of Parishville, N. Y.; d. 1842.

1242. LUCINDA STAFFORD, of Springfield, Ill.; d. Sept. 10, 1851.

1243. KATHERINE E. WRIGHT, of St. Lawrence Co., N. Y.; deceased.

1244. MRS. PHŒBE EGGLESTON, of Rochester, Ill.

1245. NIANA JONES, b. in Pomfret, Vt., Nov. 27, 1810; m. Henry Converse (1246); d. Aug. 17, 1882.

1246. HENRY CONVERSE, b. in Lyme, Grafton Co., N. H., June 7, 1806. He has been an active, energetic citizen, and has accumulated a handsome property. Himself and wife have always been interested in the care of orphans, having furnished a home for 16 in number. They celebrated their golden wedding, Feb. 4, 1880, and had lived together over fifty-two years when she was killed by a runaway team.

1247. MARIA, b. in Pomfret, Vt., Apr. 26, 1812; m. Charles B. Smythe (1248); d. Aug. 9, 1856.

1248. CHARLES B. SMYTHE; m. in 1834; d. Apr. 1, 1859.

1249. MARY, b. in Pomfret, Vt., Mar. 14, 1814; m. George B. Pease (1250); d. Feb. 11, 1844.

1250. George B. Pease, m. Sept. 21, 1834.

1251. Lucy, b. in Parishville, N. Y., Nov. 5, 1816; m. J. H. Currier (1252); d. Apr. 9, 1858.

1252. J. H. Currier; m. Feb. 16, 1848.

1253. Benjamin Franklin, who always writes his name Franklin Priest, has been prominently connected with the important enterprises in Decatur, Illinois, and has twice been Mayor of that city; b. in Parishville, N. Y., Feb. 20, 1818; m. Adeline Pike (1254); Abigail Jane Priest (1255).

1254. Adeline Pike; m. in Painesville, Ohio; d. Sept. 23, 1854.

1255. Abigail Jane Priest, of Littleton, Mass.; d. Mar. 22, 1883.

1256. Miranda, b. Oct. 22, 1819; m. J. H. Currier, Mar. 26, 1846; d. May 1, 1847.

1257. Luther, b. in Parishville, N. Y., Mar. 31, 1821. Capt. Co. E, 106th Regt. N. Y. Vol. in Civil War; m. Barbara Rose (1258); Elizabeth F. Rose (1259); d. Mar. 14, 1863, at Martinsburg, Va.; buried at Parishville, N. Y.

1258. Barbara Rose; d. Mar. 27, 1849; she left no children.

1259. Elizabeth F. Rose; m. Jan. 21, 1852.

1260. Frederick W. L., b. Apr. 28, 1823; m. Eveline E. Parker (1261); Susan Cassidy (1262); Sarah Johnson (1263).

1261. Eveline E. Parker, b. Sept. 6, 1825; d. 1866.

1262. Susan Cassidy; m. Feb. 25, 1868; d. Jan. 14, 1870.

1263. Sarah Johnson, 3d wife; m. June 28, 1871.

1264. Valentine Thomas, b. in Parishville, N. Y., June 16, 1831; m. Celestia B. Sanford (1265); residence for past seventeen years, Helena, Montana Territory.

1265. Celestia B. Sanford, b. in St. Lawrence Co., N. Y., Mar. 29, 1833.

SIXTH GENERATION.

CHILDREN OF JOHN WOOD PRIEST (1240)

BY FIRST WIFE,

OLIVE WAKEFIELD (1241) PRIEST.

1266. FRANKLIN G., b. in Parishville, N. Y., Jan. 7, 1839; d. Feb. 19, 1842.

BY SECOND WIFE,

LUCINDA STAFFORD (1242) PRIEST.

1267. OLIVE LUCINDA, b. Feb. 24, 1846, in Springfield, Ill.; m. George Clayton Latham (1268).
1268. GEORGE CLAYTON LATHAM, b. in Springfield, Ill., Sept. 18, 1842.
1269. JOHN ORSON, b. in Springfield, Ill., Oct. 6, 1847; d. Dec. 22, 1847.
1270. MARY ELIZA, b. in Springfield, Ill., Nov. 2, 1848; m. Silas W. Currier (1271).
1271. SILAS W. CURRIER; m. July 15, 1878.
1272. EMMA REBECCA, b. in Springfield, Ill., Sept. 28, 1850; d. Sept. 1, 1851.

CHILDREN OF HENRY (1246)

AND

NIANA JONES PRIEST (1245) CONVERSE.

1273. HENRY FRANKLIN, b. in Parishville, N. Y., Dec. 26, 1830; d. May 14, 1851. (Killed by an Indian in California).
1274. WILLIAM OTIS, b. in Painesville, O., June 30, 1840; m. Ella Little (1275).
1275. ELLA LITTLE, b. in Springfield, Ill., Dec. 14, 1847.
1276. ALBERT LUTHER, b. in Painesville, O., June 29, 1842; graduated in medicine March 4, 1864, and is a prominent citizen of Springfield, Ill.; m. Henrietta Thompson (1277), Sept. 6, 1864.

1277. HENRIETTA THOMPSON, b. in Louisville, Ky., Mar. 16, 1844.

CHILDREN OF CHARLES B. (1248)

AND

MARIA PRIEST (1247) SMYTHE.

1278. AGNES, b. July 6, 1835; m. Oscar E. Dowe (1279).
1279. OSCAR E. DOWE.
1280. INEZ, b. May 28, 1837; d. Dec. 1, 1845.
1281. CHARLES, b. Sept. 18, 1843; m. Marcella Greer (1282); d. Apr. 21, 1868.
1282. MARCELLA GREER.
1283. LUCY, b. Dec. 20, 1845; d. Aug. 6, 1855.
1284. JAMES, b. July 9, 1847; m. Elizabeth Testament (1285).
1285. ELIZABETH TESTAMENT.
1286. FRANK H., b. Aug. 20, 1850; m. Annis Glick (1287).
1287. ANNIS GLICK.
1288. JOHN HUSTED, b. May 21, 1852; m. Matilda Field (1289).
1289. MATILDA FIELD.

CHILDREN OF GEORGE B. (1250)

AND

MARY PRIEST (1249) PEASE.

1290. GEORGE L., b. in Painesville, O., June 26, 1835; m. J. Frances Gregory (1291).
1291. J. FRANCES GREGORY, b. in Brooklyn, N. Y., Feb. 6, 1866.
1292. MARY MIRANDA, b. in Parishville, N. Y., Aug. 20, 1837; m. Newton Bliss Burnap (1293); d. July 24, 1863.
1293. NEWTON BLISS BURNAP; m. Sept. 6, 1860; d. Sept. 10, 1882.

CHILDREN OF BENJAMIN FRANKLIN PRIEST (1253).

BY FIRST WIFE,

ADELINE PIKE (1254) PRIEST.

1294. JOSEPH FRANKLIN, b. in Painesville. O., Sept. 3, 1846.

1295. MARY ADELINE, b. in Springfield, Ill., Feb. 25, 1848; m. John O'Neal (1296).

1296. JOHN O'NEAL; m. in Decatur, Ill.

1297. GEORGE ROGERS, b. in Springfield, Ill., Nov. 18, 1849; m. Julia McNamara (1298); d. Jan. 13, 1884.

1298. JULIA MCNAMARA; m. in Decatur, Ill., June 8, 1879.

BY SECOND WIFE,

ABIGAIL JANE PRIEST (1255) PRIEST.

1299. HATTIE, b. in Decatur, Ill., Jan. 3, 1860; d. July 25, 1860.

1300. ATTIE L., b. Oct. 9, 1862, in Decatur, Ill.; d. July 1, 1876.

CHILD OF J. H.

AND

MIRANDA PRIEST (1256) CURRIER.

1301. AZRO, b. Jan. 15, 1847; d. July 28, 1864.

CHILDREN OF LUTHER (1257)

AND

ELIZABETH F. ROSE (1259) PRIEST.

1302. ADDIE BARBARA, b. Dec. 27, 1854; m. Edgar A. Newell (1303), Nov. 19, 1879.

1303. EDGAR A. NEWELL.

1304. CYNTHIA ELIZABETH, b. Dec. 2, 1858; d. Aug. 29, 1877.

1305. LUCY ROSE, b. June 1, 1861.

CHILDREN OF FREDERICK W. L. PRIEST (1260)

BY FIRST WIFE,

EVELINE E. PARKER (1261) PRIEST.

1306. Clarissa Mary, b. Oct. 26, 1846; m. Harrison McDaniel (1307); d. Aug. 3, 1879.
1307. Harrison McDaniel; m. Feb., 1868; d. 1882.
1308. Orville F., b. May 22, 1848; m. Jennie Taylor (1309), in 1881; have two daughters.
1309. Jennie Taylor.
1310. Frank L., b. Aug. 1, 1850.
1311. Lucy D., b. Feb. 20, 1852; m. Peter Lanham (1312), in 1883.
1312. Peter Lanham.
1313. Niana M., b. Sept. 20, 1855;
1314. Ina E., b. Oct. 1857; d. Jan. 1859.
1315. Harriet E., b. Dec. 27, 1859; m. —— Russell (1316); have two daughters.
1316. —— Russell.
1317. Frederick F., b. Sept. 18, 1861.

BY SECOND WIFE,

SUSAN CASSIDY (1262) PRIEST.

1318. Susan A., b. Jan. 2, 1870; d. Aug. 7, 1870.

BY THIRD WIFE,

SARAH JOHNSON (1263) PRIEST.

1319. John W., b. June 5, 1872.
1320. Thomas W., b. Oct. 21, 1879.

CHILDREN OF VALENTINE THOMAS (1264)

AND

CELESTIA B. SANFORD (1265) PRIEST.

1321. Celestia Abba, b. in Taylorsville, Ill., Oct. 25, 1855; d. June 11, 1856.
1322. Permelia Clarinda, b. in Taylorsville, Ill., Aug. 10, 1859; m. Clarence M. Goodale (1323).

1323. Clarence M. Goodale; m. in Helena, Montana Territory, Aug. 15, 1880.

1324. Mary Abba, b. in Taylorsville, Ill., June 28, 1861; d. Jan. 15, 1865.

1325. Celestia Sanford, b. in Taylorsville, Ill., Aug. 13, 1863; d. Jan. 28, 1865.

1326. Alice Sanford, b. in Taylorsville, Ill., Jan. 10, 1868.

SEVENTH GENERATION.

CHILDREN OF GEORGE CLAYTON (1268) AND OLIVE LUCINDA PRIEST (1267) LATHAM.

ALL BORN IN SPRINGFIELD, ILL.

1327. Olive Priest, b. Sept. 2, 1868.

1328. Mary Magruder, b. Sept. 6, 1870.

1329. John Priest, b. Jan. 31, 1875.

1330. Georgia Clayton, b. Sept. 8, 1882.

CHILD OF SILAS W. (1271) AND MARY ELIZA PRIEST (1270) CURRIER.

1331. Mary Lucinda, b. in Springfield, Ill., June 19, 1880.

CHILDREN OF WILLIAM OTIS (1274) AND ELLA LITTLE (1275) CONVERSE.

ALL BORN IN SPRINGFIELD, ILL.

1332. Nina Little, b. Aug. 1, 1874.

1333. Elsie May, b. Apr. 1, 1876.

1334. Nellie, b. Aug. 5, 1880.

CHILDREN OF ALBERT LUTHER (1276)
AND
HENRIETTA THOMPSON (1277) CONVERSE.

ALL BORN IN SPRINGFIELD, ILL.

1335. Florence Niana, b. Aug. 24, 1865; d. Sept. 27, 1882.
1336. Anais D., b. July 24, 1867.
1337. Olive Thompson, b. June 27, 1870; d. Feb. 6, 1872.
1338. Henry Aaron, b. Sept. 9, 1875.
1339. Albert Edward, b. Feb. 26, 1881.

CHILDREN OF OSCAR E. (1279)
AND
AGNES SMYTHE (1278) DOWE.

1340. Inez Lucy, b. Sept. 11, 1855; d. Dec. 11, 1855.
1341. Charles Eugene, b. July 25, 1857.
1342. Mary Isabelle, b. Nov. 4, 1860; d. June 29, 1882.
1343. Grace W., b. June 12, 1871; d. Aug. 24, 1875.
1344. Georgia Agnes, b. Sept. 9, 1874; d. Aug. 24, 1875.
1345. Paul LaBaron, b. July 1, 1877.

CHILD OF CHARLES (1281)
AND
MARCELLA GREER (1282) SMYTHE.

1346. Charles G.; d. Sept., 1869, aged 1 yr.

CHILDREN OF JAMES (1284)
AND
ELIZABETH TESTAMENT (1285) SMYTHE.

1347. John Herbert, b. May, 1870.
1348. Charles, b. Dec., 1872.

1349. Oscar, b. Aug., 1875.
1350. Henry, b. Nov., 1879.
1351. Son, b. July 1883; d. 1884.

CHILDREN OF FRANK H. (1286) AND ANNIS GLICK (1287) SMYTHE.

1352. Inez, b. 1871.
1353. Henry, b. 1873.
1354. Walter, b. 1875; d. Mar. 1884.
1355. Frank, b. 1877.
1356. Charles, b. 1880.
1357. Gladys, b. May, 1882.

CHILDREN OF JOHN HUSTED (1288) AND MATILDA FIELD (1289) SMYTHE.

1358. Florence Bertie, b. Nov. 5, 1879.
1359. James Luther, b. Mar. 31, 1881.

CHILD OF GEORGE L. (1290) AND J. FRANCES GREGORY (1291) PEASE

1360. Gertrude G., b. Nov. 3, 1866.

CHILD OF NEWTON BLISS (1293) AND MARY MIRANDA PEASE (1292) BURNAP.

1361. Frank P., b. Aug. 6, 1861.

CHILD OF JOHN (1296)
AND
MARY ADELINE PRIEST (1295) O'NEAL.

1362. Georgie O'Neal.

CHILD OF GEORGE ROGERS (1297)
AND
JULIA McNAMARA (1298) PRIEST.

1363. Mary Ethel Georgia, b. Sept. 28, 1881.

CHILDREN OF EDGAR A. (1303)
AND
ADDIE BARBARA PRIEST (1302) NEWELL.

1364. Albert Priest, b. Jan. 3, 1882.
1365. William Allan, b. Apr. 22, 1883.

CHILD OF HARRISON (1307)
AND
CLARISSA MARY PRIEST (1306) McDANIEL.

1366. Robert Priest, b. in 1873.

LYDIA WOOD.

OLIVER AND LYDIA (WOOD) (492) DAVIS

AND

THEIR DESCENDANTS.

LYDIA WOOD married Oliver Davis, Dec. 8, 1763. She was the daughter of John Wood, who was son of Jeremiah Wood. She was a sister of Dea. John Wood, Timothy, Ebenezer, and Salmon. Oliver Davis was the son of Eleazer and Sarah Davis of Harvard, Mass. Eleazer Davis came to this country from England; he was a soldier in the French and Indian War. His son Oliver was one of the minute-men in the beginning of the Revolutionary War, and was present at the battle of Bunker Hill. He had by wife, Lydia Wood, five children; two daughters and three sons:

1901. SARAH, b. in Harvard, Mass, Mar. 8, 1765.
1902. OLIVER, b. in Harvard, Mass., May 12, 1767.
1903. DAVID.
1904. JONAS.
1905. MARY, or perhaps HEPSIBAH or otherwise, as my informers do not agree upon the name, and I have not an official record.

Sarah may have been the Sarah Gary mentioned on page 58. Oliver, David and Jonas went to Hancock, N. H., in 1794 or 5, and settled near their uncle Salmon Wood, who had previously located there. Oliver and David settled near each other, and built houses on the land they bought, which are still owned and occupied by their descendants, having always retained the Davis name.

Oliver sold and moved to Acworth, N. H., in 1822, where he died in 1851.

David remained on his old place in Hancock till his death.

Jonas died in Dublin, N. H., leaving no children.

The youngest daughter settled in Vermont.

Their mother, Lydia (Wood) Davis, d. in Harvard, Mass., after which their father married again and had Jonathan, Eleazer, Ephraim, Lydia and Ann. He died in Harvard, Mass.

Oliver Davis (1902), son of Oliver and Lydia (Wood) Davis, first m. in 1790, Sally Pollard of Harvard or Leominster, Mass., before he settled in Hancock, N. H. Had by Sally Pollard seven children, six girls and one boy, viz: Sally, Lydia, Lucy, Betsy, John, Lucinda (died young), and Lucinda. He m. 2nd, Relief Heath, by whom he had seven children, viz: Levi, Thomas J., Oliver, Nancy, Joseph, Emeline and Samuel.

I.

1930. SALLY DAVIS, the eldest, born 1791; m. Joshua Greenwood; settled in Dublin, N. H.; had one girl and five boys.

The girl Sarah, m. Wm. Dickerson and settled in Keene, N. H.

Charles m. Adeline McGilvary. He was a Methodist preacher.

Curtis lived in Woburn, Mass.

Henry, clerk in Boston; unmarried.

Monroe, settled in San Francisco; principal officer of Telegraph and Telephone Co. there.

II.

1931. LYDIA DAVIS, b. 1793; m. Jonathan Sleeper; 2nd, m. Edward Savage; settled first in Unity, N. H., and afterwards in Acworth, N. H.; no children; she d. 1878.

III.

1932. Lucy Davis, b. 1795; d. 1861; m. Benj. Winship; settled in Hancock, N. H.; had eleven children, viz: George, John, Elizabeth Ann, Abel, Brown, Oliver, Lydia, Mark, Relief, Sarah, Horace; all but two living, John and Lydia; of the others, most of them reside in Boston, Mass., or vicinity.

IV.

1933. Betsy Davis, b. 1798; m. Reid Richardson; settled in Peterboro', N. H.; had seven children, viz: Lydia Jane, Charles, Betsey, Eliza, Nancy Emeline and Joshua; Charles, Nancy and Betsey deceased.

V.

1934. John Davis, b. 1800; m. Catherine E. Houghton; settled in Acworth, N. H., where he has always lived. A successful farmer; had four children: Charles J., Nancy, Henry and Josephine. All deceased but Charles J., who lives with his father on the farm in Acworth.

VI.

1935. Lucinda Davis, b. 1802; died young.

VII.

1936. Lucinda Davis, b. 1804; d. 1881; m. 1st, George Clark; had one son, John Clark. She m. 2nd, Benj. Fletcher; settled in Nashua, N. H., and had seven children, Mary E. Fletcher, Lydia, Benjamin, Cooledge, Lucius C., Joseph and Lucinda. All living but Joseph, who died in the army, and Lucinda, who died young. Benjamin Fletcher was one of the overseers in Forge Shop, Nashua, N. H., and was two terms Mayor of that city.

VIII.

1937. Levi Davis, b. 1805; d. 1880; m. Susan Parsons; settled in Acworth, N. H.; had Sarah F., and Josephine, deceased.

IX.

1938. Thomas J. Davis, b. 1807; m. Calista Newton; settled in Acworth, N. H.; had Joab N., Hubbard L. and Miranda C.; sons now living, daughter died young. The father m. 2nd, Mrs. Polly Washburn; had no children.

X.

1939. Oliver Davis, son of Oliver and Relief (Heath) Davis, b. 1809; d. 1882; he m. Elizabeth Moore; settled in Lempster, N. H.; had eight children, viz: Henry J., George E., Jefferson T., Charles B., Lucy, William, Benjamin F. and Lizzie.

XI.

1940. Nancy Davis, b. 1811; d. 1883. She m. 1st, John Adams; settled in New York; had one child, Ronie C.; she m. 2nd, Eldad Butler; settled in Manchester, N. H.; had two children, Imogene and Josephine.

XII.

1941. Joseph Davis, b. 1813; m. Mrs. Eliza B. Wallace, widow of Dr. John Wallace, of Milford, N. H., by whom she had one son, John J. Wallace, railroad clerk in J. Gould's office, Peoria, Illinois. She had two children by Joseph Davis: Charles J. and Emma C.; the latter died Sept. 24, 1851, aged two years. The son, Charles J., b. Apr. 11, 1841, m. Sarah Twiss, of Antrim, N. H., May, 1865; his wife died Jan. 20, 1870, leaving three children, Emma C., b. July 2, 1867; Edward J., b. Oct. 26, 1868; Frank T., b. Jan. 13, 1870. Charles J., their father, d. July 2, 1883.

Joseph Davis settled in Hancock, N. H., where he has since resided. He attended academies in Cavendish, Vt. and Hancock, N. H., and taught school every year from three to nine months for over thirty years; married in 1840. In 1841 opened a store in Hancock, and continued in trade until about 1850, never relinquishing his school work. He was Superintending School Committee fifteen to twenty years, Town Clerk some twelve years, Town Treasurer eight years, Representative to the General Court two years, Chairman of the Board of Selectmen three years. An influential man.

XIII.

1942. EMELINE DAVIS, b. 1815; m. Henry Gould; settled in Acworth; afterwards removed to Peterborough, N. H.; had three children, Emma L., Lillian V., Albina. Lillian deceased.

XIV.

1943. SAMUEL DAVIS, b. 1816; m. Cassandra Marshall; settled in Unity, N. H.; had two children, Ellen M. and Sabrina; m. 2nd, Rowena Keyes; had by her two children, Martin and Emma. Obtained an education and taught school many years, after which engaged in farming in Unity, N. H.

David (1903), son of Oliver and Lydia (Wood) Davis, had one son and four daughters; one died young. Hannah, David, Polly and Melvina married and had famliles.

I.

1944. HANNAH; m. Amos Knight and had four children.

II.

1945. DAVID DAVIS, JR., b. Apr. 26, 1795; m. Sally Hayward; d. Feb. 5, 1858.

CHILDREN:

PRESTON R., b. Nov. 21, 1820.
CHARLES H., b. Feb. 21, 1825.
GEORGE D., b. July 13, 1833.
MILAN E., b. Sept. 30, 1839.

Preston R. lives in Peterboro, N. H. He has two sons in clothing house there, "E. G. Davis & Co."

Charles H., d. George D. is married and lives in Orange, Mass.

Milan E. Davis m. Ellen M. Jenkins and had Wilfred M., Frank R., d. aged about 3 yrs., Nellie L., Emma S., Alice M., and George F.

Milan E. Davis resides upon the homestead of his grandfather, David Davis, in Hancock, N. H. A good citizen.

III.

1946. POLLY DAVIS, m. Reed Washburn for her first husband who died. She afterwards m. Jefferson Davis.

IV.

1947. MELVINA DAVIS, m. William Lakin and had five children, all girls, three now living, viz: Ellen H., m. Hon. Adolphus G. Foster, of Hancock, N. H.; Ann, m. John Little, and Mary, m. Charles Little, brothers; residence of both in California.

TIMOTHY WOOD.

TIMOTHY (494) AND ELIZABETH (CHENEY) WOOD AND DESCENDANTS.

TIMOTHY, son of John and Lydia (Davis) Wood, lived for a time in Rindge, N. H., but finally settled in Harvard, Mass., the home of his grandparents, Ebenezer and Sarah Davis, and died there July 18, 1801, aged 51 years, 11 months and 9 days; his wife, Elizabeth (Cheney) Wood, d. Sept. 10, 1796, aged 49 years, 11 months, 25 days. They had three children:

1948. JOHN, b. March 24, 1772.
1949. BETSEY, b. in Rindge, N. H., June 7, 1777.
1950. SUSANNA, b. in Rindge, N. H., Sept. 2, 1779.

John (1948), son of Timothy, m. Lois Humphries, dau. of John Humphries, of Scituate. The husband died July 19, 1832. The wife Lois, b. Sept. 13, 1773; d. March 24, 1838. They had:

1951. FRANCIS, b. Jan. 1, 1803; d. Feb. 28, 1838.
1952. HARVEY, b. Feb. 11, 1805; d. Aug. 23, 1884.
1953. JOHN HARRISON, b. Oct. 13, 1811; d. Mar. 26, 1824.

Francis m. his second cousin, Mary Wood, dau. of Carshena and Betsy (Lawrence) Wood. She was b. Oct. 26, 1808.

Francis died. After a time his brother Harvey m. his widow, and she died April 23, 1879. No children by either marriage.

Timothy Wood and wife, their son John Wood and wife, John's sons, Francis and Harvey Wood and wife are buried in the Harvard cemetery, Mass., near the Congregational Church edifice, to which church Harvey Wood left several thousand dollars at his decease in 1884.

Eliphalet Wood, an uncle of Timothy, and several of his descendants are buried in this cemetery.

DESCENDANTS OF BETSEY WOOD (1949)

AND

BENJAMIN JEWETT.

Betsey Wood was b. at Rindge, N. H., June 7, 1777; moved to Harvard, Mass., and was there married, May 6, 1802, to Benjamin Jewett, of Littleton, Mass., who was b. Mar. 1, 1773. Had:

1954. Benjamin, Jr., b. July 10, 1803.
1955. Betsey, b. Sept. 4, 1804.
1956. Louisa, b. Feb. 7. 1806.
1957. A Daughter, b. and d. March 15, 1807.
1958. Clarinda, b. Mar. 11, 1808; d. aged 1 yr. 9 mo.
1959. Aquilla, b. Dec. 2, 1810; d. aged 1 yr. 2 mo.
1960. George A., b. Feb. 25, 1813.
1961. Susannah, b. Mar. 1, 1815.
1962. Timothy, b. Oct. 23, 1817.
1963. George H., b. Aug. 31, 1820; d. aged 2 yrs.

Jan. 29, 1823, Benjamin Jewett, husband of Betsey (Wood) Jewett, died and was buried at Littleton. All their children were b. in Littleton, excepting Louisa and a dau. not named, who were b. in Petersham, Mass.

April 2, 1828, Betsey Wood Jewett m. Dea. David Chatterton, of Mount Holly, Vermont. He died Oct. 12, 1837; no children by this marriage.

Dea. Chatterton was, for over twenty years immediately preceding his death, a deacon and an active member of the Baptist church of his town. He was a successful farmer, acquiring considerable property. He reared a family of five children.

Betsey Wood Jewett Chatterton, on the 10th day of March, 1844, m. Levi Bailey, of Redding, Vt., and he d. Oct. 21, 1850. No children by this marriage.

Mr. Bailey was what might be called in his day "a rich man," owning and operating a large woollen factory, employing over one hundred hands; he was extensively engaged in mercantile pursuits and kept a large hotel.

Nov. 6, 1853, Betsey (Wood) Jewett Chatterton Bailey died at Harvard, Mass., and was buried in the Harvard cemetery.

Her grandson, Judge Mason D. Chatterton of Mason, Ingham County, Michigan, has furnished many of the records of her descendants.

I.

Benjamin Jewett (1954), son of Benjamin and Betsey (Wood) Jewett, was m. at Harvard, Mass., Dec. 27, 1827, to Clarissa Emerson. Had:

1964. Maria E., b. in Harvard, Mass., Sept. 17, 1833.
1965. Clarissa L., b. in Harvard, July 26, 1843. Both of whom are married and now living, but have no children.

Benjamin resided for more than thirty years on his farm in Harvard, Mass., and then changed his residence, taking with him his wife, two daughters and their husbands to Gilbert's Mills, Oswego Co., N. Y.

Oct. 22, 1878, Benjamin Jewett died and was buried at Gilbert's Mills.

This family has always been noted for its refinement, culture and social standing. Their early education at

Harvard, and the high social standing of the community in which they lived, helped to mould their lives for the high christian walks of life, in which their feet ever tread.

II.

Betsey Jewett (1955) remained in Littleton until the year 1828, when she went to Mount Holly, Vt., where, on the 9th day of October, 1831, she married Daniel Chatterton of the same place.

Daniel was the youngest son of David, and after the death of his father he purchased from the heirs the old homestead where he was born, and resided there until June, 1851, when he, with his family, consisting of a wife and four children, moved to the township of Meridian, Michigan, and purchased a new farm four miles east of Lansing, the capital of the State, it being near the village of Okemos, and resided there in a log house with his family for several years.

All of the four children of this marriage were born in Mount Holly, Vt., as follows:

1966. George A., b. Aug. 13, 1832.
1967. Sarah E., b. Sept. 4, 1833.
1968. Mason D., b. Aug. 3, 1838.
1969. Jewett E., b. Dec. 7, 1840.

Daniel Chatterton d. Apr. 9, 1866, and his wife Betsey (Jewett) Chatterton Feb. 8, 1877; both died and were buried in the township of Meridian.

Daniel and Betsey Chatterton owned a large farm; lived lives of christian piety,—died respected and regretted.

George A. Chatterton (1966), the oldest son of Daniel and Betsey, m. Jane Thompson Dec. 24, 1854, and have two children, both married—Watts, married and has one child; Elva L., a physician, and has no children.

George A., wife and daughter, live at Hubbardston, Mich.

George A. is a prominent member of the Congregational Church, and General Insurance Agent of the State.

Sarah E. Chatterton (1967), m. Nov. 11, 1852, Augustus L. Sturges, of Meridian, Mich., and have had three children, Eva E. (Watson), Wallace A. Sturges, and Clara B. (Hewett).

These children are all living near Okemos. Wallace, unmarried; the other two have one child each, while Augustus L., and wife Sarah E., are living in Virginia.

Augustus L. is devotedly attached to Sabbath school interests, and is a successful farmer, owning a large plantation (the "Hopewell Farm"), on the bank of the James river, eight miles from the city of Richmond.

Mason D. Chatterton (1968) was married June 2, 1865, to Mary A. Morrison, of Okemos, and has one child, Floyd M., who is unmarried. Mason D. graduated at the Michigan State University, March 27, 1861, receiving the degree of LL.B. He was admitted to practice law in Michigan, March 23, 1861, and in the U. S. courts, Sept. 2, 1875. He held the office of Judge of Probate for Ingham Co. for eight years; spent the year 1882 in Europe, sight seeing, and was elected a delegate to the National Republican Convention of 1884. Financially, the rumor is that "he is rich." He with his family now reside in Mason, Michigan.

Jewett E. Chatterton (1969), married Elizabeth A. Adams, Apr. 29, 1867, and has two children, Howard E., and Harry J., both unmarried.

Jewett E. graduated at Eastman's Business College, in Poughkeepsie, N. Y., and since then he has spent his whole time in mercantile pursuits, with good success. He now resides, with his family, at Mount Pleasant, Michigan.

III.

Louisa Jewett (1956), died Dec. 1, 1825; unmarried, and was buried in Littleton, Mass.

IV.

George A. Jewett (1960), m. Lucy Colver, Sept. 19, 1841, at Mount Holly, Vt., and had two children, viz.:

1970. George H., b. in Mount Holly, May 17, 1844, and lived three years.

1971. Edson, b. at Mount Holly in 1863; is unmarried and living with his mother in Winchendon, Mass.; he is the only living descendant of Benjamin Jewett, Sr., who bears the family name.

George A. Jewett d. in Winchendon, in the fall of 1883, and was buried there; he was a mechanic by occupation in the earlier part of his life, but later he studied medicine and became quite a skilful physician.

V.

Susannah Jewett (1961), m. Varnum C. Dexter at Mount Holly on the 7th day of March, 1835, and there were born the following children:

1972. Maria L., b. Dec. 24, 1835.
1973. Mary E. A., b. Apr. 17, 1837.
1974. Melissa S., b. Apr. 10, 1839.
1975. Jonathan C., b. Sept. 12, 1842.

Jonathan C. was never married; he enlisted in the war of 1861, in a Michigan regiment, and was killed in the battle of Chicamauga.

The daughters were married and each had children.

Maria L. was killed in a railroad accident at Pontiac, Mich., in the winter of 1884, and was buried in Franklin, Mich. The other two children are still living.

Susannah Jewett Dexter d. and was buried at Franklin, Mich., Nov. 13, 1857.

Varnum C. Dexter chose the occupation of a school teacher and was educated accordingly. He followed his profession for several years with great success.

He moved with his family to Michigan, about 1842, bought a farm and became a farmer.

His children were especially noticeable for their intelligence.

VI.

Timothy Jewett (1962) was never married; he was a professional school teacher; died at Springfield, Mass., and was buried there Jan. 30, 1864.

DESCENDANTS OF SUSANNA WOOD (1950) AND ISRAEL HOUGHTON JEWETT.

Susanna Wood was b. in Rindge, N. H., Sept. 2, 1779; was married to Israel Houghton Jewett at Harvard, Mass., Sept., 1796. He was born in Littleton, Mass., Dec. 21, 1768, and died at Alstead, N. H., Feb. 2, 1813. She afterwards married Hoxxey Barber, of Mount Holly, Vt., Apr. 18, 1822, where she resided until her death, July 16, 1855. Mr. Barber died May 27, 1837, in his 71st year. She had seven children by her first husband, Israel Houghton Jewett, viz:

1976. Elizabeth.
1977. Aquilla.
1978. Eli.
1979. Susan.
1980. Harriet.
1981. Mary.
1982. Lois.

I.

Elizabeth (1976) was b. in Littleton, Mass., Oct, 15, 1797; was m. to Joel Newton, of Alstead, N. H., 1827; she d. Oct. 4, 1858. Had three daughters born in Worcester, Vt.:

1983. Mary L., b. Aug. 14, 1829; d. Apr. 12, 1847.
1984. Susan E., b. Feb. 8, 1833; m. Henry F. Partridge, Dec. 15, 1864.
1985. Calista A., b. Nov. 1, 1835; m. Alfred W. Partridge, Aug. 15, 1852; have two daughters born in Alstead, N. H.:

Charlotte L., b. July 30, 1853.
Agnes E., b. Nov. 30, 1864.

II.

Aquilla Jewett (1977), b. Oct. 11, 1799; d. Mar. 1, 1800.

III.

Eli Jewett (1978), b. June 20, 1801; d. in Alstead, N. H., Aug. 9, 1883.; left a wife and one adopted daughter.

IV.

Susan Jewett (1979), b. in Alstead, Oct. 15, 1803; m. Alvin Sherman, of Mt. Holly, Vt., Dec. 22, 1840; she died Jan. 2, 1865, leaving no children.

V.

Harriet Jewett (1980), b. in Alstead, N. H., Mar. 9, 1806; m. David B. Johnson Dec. 7, 1825. He was born in Putney, Vt., July 3, 1804, and his death occurred Dec. 27, 1872. Their children and descendants are as follows:

1986. Alvin Jewett Johnson, b. in Wallingford, Vt., Sept. 23, 1827; m. Lucia Helena Warner, of Sunderland, Mass. He died April 22, 1884, leaving a widow, two daughters and one son.

The son William W., after going through Columbia College, graduated 1874, degree of A. M. 1877; his father took him into the publishing business with himself, and he is carrying it on now, 1885. He is married and has two sons, William Alvin and Robert Pierce Johnson.

The two daughters of A. J. Johnson are Virginia Helena and Minnie Augusta Johnson.

I quote from an article published in the *Boston Herald:*

"[*Boston Herald*, Tuesday, April 22, 1884.]

THE HAND OF DEATH.

SKETCH OF THE CAREER OF A. J. JOHNSON, THE WELL-KNOWN PUBLISHER.

The telegraph announces the death, which occurred this morning at his residence in New York, of Mr. A. J. Johnson, the publisher of 'Johnson's Atlas of the World,' 'Johnson's Universal Cyclopædia,' and of other well-known works. Mr. Johnson was born in Wallingford, Vermont, Sept. 23, 1827. The only educational advantages which he enjoyed in his early youth were such as the common schools of his native State then afforded, supplemented by those of a brief course at the country academy. Thrown at length upon his own resources and obliged to earn his own living, he began active life as a teacher. This profession taught him many valuable lessons, which availed him much in his subsequent career; but it was not a profession which satisfied his restless spirit or even his ambition. The 'subscription plan' of selling books had already come into vogue, and as it promised success and good rewards to all active and energetic workers, Mr. Johnson was induced to leave his school and go into the field as a book canvasser. It was for him a fortunate move. One success led to and was followed by another, until at last he became enrolled in the guild of publishers, and found himself at the head of the greatest map-publishing house in the world, and 'Johnson's Atlas' became an authority whenever or wherever an atlas was to be consulted. In 1877 Mr. Johnson planned the greatest undertaking of his life—namely: his 'Universal Cyclopædia of Useful knowledge,' which was first put upon the market complete in four large volumes. In the preparation of this gigantic work upwards of a quarter of a million of dollars was paid to authors, the list of which included the ablest men in every walk of life. The undertaking has proved a most brilliant success, and brought increased wealth and reputation to its projector. Mr. Johnson was a marked man among men; of regular habits, untiring industry, and marvellous perseverance. He always sought out gentlemen as his employés, and would accept no other. Honest and honorable in all his dealings, fearless when he believed himself in the right, an unflinching antagonist when assailed, unselfish, modest, and unassuming, the best of friends, the most tender in his domestic relations — such is his record. He was in every sense of the word a self-made man, and by his energy and well-directed efforts was rewarded bounteously."

Horace Greeley was an intimate friend of Alvin Jewett Johnson, and was frequently a member of Mr. Johnson's family. Upon the anniversary of Mr. Greeley's sixty-first birthday, his family being absent in Europe, I find that a very large party was given to the literary friends of Horace Greeley by A. J. Johnson, at his fine residence in New York City. Their friendship was never broken.

The establishment of A. J. Johnson & Co., Publishers, is at 11 Great Jones street (near Broadway), New York.

Johnson's New Illustrated family Atlas of the World, with a New Treatise on Physical Geography, by Prof. A. Guyot, LL.D., was awarded the *First Prize Medal* at both

Universal Expositions in Paris. This is the largest, most finely executed, and only illustrated Township Atlas of the World ever published.

Of "Johnson's Universal Cyclopædia" the greatest institutions of learning speak loudly in its favor, viz: Harvard University, Yale, Brown University, Dartmouth, Williams, Cornell University, Columbia, Amherst, Hamilton, Rochester University, Richmond, &c. I quote:

"From the Faculty of Yale and other distinguished Gentlemen of New Haven.

"Johnson's Universal Cyclopædia, a work in four volumes, of nearly 1700 pages each, or about 6800 closely-printed pages, presents the following important features:

"It is convenient for ready reference; its most important articles are original productions, prepared for this work by men who are well known to be distinguished in the several departments of learning which they represent, each article being signed by the writer; it embraces a wide range of subjects—about 20,000 in each volume—and is especially adapted to the needs of American readers.

"An examination of it must convince any one that, as a table-book for the homes of the people and for the use of professional men, merchants, and manufacturers, it will prove to be a work of great usefulness.

"It is practically a geographical gazetteer, a biographical dictionary, a medical and legal manual, and a scientific repertory. The treatment of the subjects is thorough and comprehensive, and at the same time simple and judiciously adapted to the requirements of general readers.

"A fortunate combination of circumstances has, under the energetic and persevering efforts of the chief editors, contributed to the securing of the co-operation of a large number of eminent writers, whose names will be recognized as among the best in the country in their respective branches of learning.

"The work contains a vast amount of useful knowledge, presented in a popular and convenient form, and at moderate price.

THE FACULTY.

"THEODORE D. WOOLSEY, Ex-President of Yale College.
NOAH PORTER, President.
WM. P. TROWBRIDGE, Prof. of Dynamical Engineering.
W. A. NORTON, Prof. of Civil Engineering.
LEONARD BACON, Kent Prof. of Law.
SAMUEL W. JOHNSON, Prof. of Theoretical and Agricultural Chemistry.
A. E. VERRILL, Prof. of Zoology.
JOHNSON T. PLATT, Prof. of Pleading and Equity Jurisprudence.
B. SILLIMAN, Prof. of Chemistry.
J. H. HOPPIN, Prof. of Homiletics.
GEORGE P. FISHER, Prof. of Ecclesiastical History.
STEPHEN G. HUBBARD, Prof. of Obstetrics.
THOMAS A. THATCHER, Prof. of Latin.
LEONARD J. SANFORD, Prof. of Anatomy and Physiology.
H. A. NEWTON, Prof. of Mathematics.
HENRY B. HARRISON, Fellow of Yale College.

REV. S. R. DENNIN, Pastor Third Congregational Church.
B. G. NORTHROP, Sec. Connecticut Board of Education.
JAMES E. ENGLISH, Ex-Governor of Connecticut.
CHAS. R. INGERSOLL, Governor of Connecticut."

"The amount of valuable information is wonderful, etc.

RT. HON. W. E. GLADSTONE, LL.D."

Johnson's General Cyclopædia, containing 1600 pages (2 vols.); Johnson's Natural History (2 vols.); Johnson's Household Treasury, &c., &c., are among their publications.

1987. ELI H. JOHNSON, second son of D. B. and Harriet (Jewett) Johnson, b. in Rutland, Vt., Dec. 7, 1828; m. Nov. 21, 1848, Lovica B. Cole, of Mt. Holly, Vt.; he was in the 16th Vermont Infantry during the Rebellion and served three years. He died June 2, 1880, leaving Edwynah Iowne Johnson; had buried two children; residence Mechanicsville, Vt.

1988. WILLARD R. F. JOHNSON, 3d son of D. B. and H. J., b. in Wallingford, Vt., Dec. 24, 1830; m. July 4, 1851, Martha E. Graves, of Mt. Holly, Vt.; 2nd, m. Oct. 21, 1866, Mary Ellen Jaquith, of Weston, Vt.; he was in the 2nd Regt. Vermont Vol. Infantry; served three years during the Rebellion. He has two sons, Charles S. and George A., both married; no children; residence, Putney, Vt.

1989. GEORGE B. JOHNSON, 4th son of D. B. and H. J., b. in Wallingford, Vt., Oct. 5, 1832; m. Mar. 13, 1864, Laura Fisher, of Newfane, Vt.; no children; residence Newfane, Vt.

1990. LAURA M., dau. of D. B. & Harriet J. Johnson, b. in Clarendon, Vt., May 23, 1834; m. Oct. 21, 1855, Merrill Graves, of Lowell, Mass.; she d. Oct. 10, 1856, leaving one child, Jane L., who m. Mr. Benson and has one child, Lillie M.

1991. HENRY C. Johnson, son of D. B. and H. J., b. in Clarendon, Vt., July 14, 1836; m. Jan. 16, 1862, Bernice A. Perry, of Michigan; he died June 8, 1883; left one adopted daughter, Bernice May Johnson. He was Supt. in Adams, Blackmer & Lyon Publishing Co., Chicago, Ill.; residence Berlin, Wisconsin.

1992. SUSANNAH L. JOHNSON, dau. of D. B. and H. J., b. in Shrewsbury, Vt., Feb. 26, 1838; m. Nov. 27, 1869, M. H. Shipley, of Berlin, Wisconsin; res. Forest Grove, Oregon; no children.

1993. ADELIA M. JOHNSON, dau. of D. B. and H. J., was b. in Shrewsbury, Vt., Dec. 2, 1840; m. July 3, 1859, Alonzo W. Dickerman, of Mechanicsville, Vt.; he died April 7, 1879, in his 36th year. Had five children, four living, John A., Bernice A., George H., and Harley M. John A. married and has two children, Dwight and John A., Jr.; residence, Rutland, Vt.

1994. CYNTHIA C. JOHNSON, dau. of D. B. and H. J., b. in Wallingford, Vt., July 4, 1843; m. Charles Stowe, of Hubbardston, Mass., Dec. 10, 1864. She died Aug. 24, 1882; had three children, two living, William L. and Hattie M.; both unmarried; residence, Boston, Mass.

1995. HATTIE L. JOHNSON, dau. of D. B. and H. J., b. in Mechanicsville, Vt., Apr. 27, 1845; m. Oct. 9, 1872, A. Tyler, Berlin, Wisconsin; no children; residence, Forest Grove, Oregon.

1996. MARY J. JOHNSON, dau. of D. B. and H. J., b. in Wallingford, Vt., Mar. 15, 1847; m. Nov. 20, 1871, Fred. O. Pierce, of East Putney, Vt. Has one son, Jewett Johnson Pierce; residence, East Putney, Vt.

1997. WILLIAM E. JOHNSON, son of D. B. and H. J., b. in Mechanicsville, Vt., Mar. 14, 1849; m May 1, 1873, Etta Dyer, in Portland, Me.; no children. Supt. Hudson River State Hospital; residence, Poughkeepsie, N. Y.

VI.

MARY JEWETT (1981), dau. of Israel H. and Susanna (Wood) Jewett, b. in Alstead, N. H., Feb. 4, 1809; m. Russell Barber, of Mt. Holly, Vt., May 15, 1837; moved in 1866 to Danby, Vt., where she buried her husband, in 1878; then moved to Weston, Vt., with her only daughter, d. Mar. 13, 1884.

1998. CELESTE S. BARBER, now Mrs. John Mattocks, of Weston, Vt.

VII.

LOIS JEWETT (1982), dau. of Israel H. and Susanna (Wood) Jewett, b. Jan. 5, 1813; m. Charles L. Earl, of Mt. Holly, Vt.; she died in Rutland, Dec. 18, 1878. Had a family of nine children, six living in 1885, viz: Maria Maynard, Clarinda Snow, Marsella Allen, Lucina unmarried, Ellen m., and Charles.

EBENEZER WOOD.

EBENEZER (496) AND PHEBE (BROOKS) WOOD AND THEIR DESCENDANTS.

EBENEZER WOOD, son of John and Lydia (Davis) Wood, was born Jan. 20, 1754, in Littleton, Mass.; m. Phebe Brooks, Apr. 7, 1776; d. Dec. 28, 1840, in Washington, N. H.

Phebe Brooks, b. Sept. 29, 1751; d. Jan. 2, 1844, in Washington, N. H.

Ebenezer Wood first settled in Littleton, Mass., where his first three children were born, but in 1781 he emigrated to Washington, N. H., and settled on a farm in the valley near Lovell's Mountain.

At that time there were only a few settlers in town and no roads excepting for travellers on horseback, and these were indicated by marked trees.

He lived on the farm where he settled, about two miles from Washington village, until his death.

He was a Lieutenant in the Revolutionary War; he afterwards received a pension of ninety-six dollars a year; was a cooper by trade as well as a farmer.

Ebenezer and Phebe (Brooks) Wood had eleven children; four sons and seven daughters, as follows:

2301. LYDIA, b. in Littleton, Mass., May 9, 1777.
2302. EBENEZER, b. in Littleton, Mass., Sept. 29, 1778.
2303. JONAS D., b. Sept. 13, 1780; d. Oct. 1, 1867, in Washington; unmarried.
2304. ASA, b. July 18, 1782.
2305. MARY, b. in Washington, Apr., 1784; d. Apr. 17, 1784.
2306. PHEBE, b. in Washington, May 4, 1787.
2307. SOPHIA, b. in Washington, Dec. 27, 1788.

2308. LOIS B., b. in Washington, Feb. 17, 1791; d. Mar. 20, 1834; unmarried.
2309. BETSEY, b. in Washington, Feb. 17, 1793.
2310. MARY, b. in Washington, Mar. 16, 1796.
2311. TIMOTHY, b. in Washington, Mar. 18, 1798.

Of the above named children:

I.

LYDIA WOOD (2301), m. Luther Whitney, of Heniker, N. H.; afterwards lived at Washington, and a small village near Saratoga, N. Y., where she died. Had three children:

2312. HANNAH.
2313. ORPHA; m. Wm. Wood, son of Asa, of Washington, N. H.
2314. MARTIN. Lives in Michigan.

II.

EBENEZER WOOD (2302), m. Lydia Davis, Feb. 7, 1805, dau. of Major Ephraim Davis, of Harvard, Mass. They resided in Washington, N. H., with the exception of one year in Lowell, Mass. He was a carpenter by trade. They had seven children, as follows:

2315. DANIEL, b. in Washington, N. H., Oct. 4, 1805.
2316. ELSINA, b. in Washington, N. H., Aug. 27, 1808.
2317. EBENEZER, b. Dec. 9, 1810.
2318. LYDIA, b. in Washington, N. H., Apr. 5, 1813.
2319. PHEBE, b. May 2, 1816.
2320. HORACE, b. Jan. 10, 1820.
2321. JOHN, b. in Washington, N. H., June 23, 1826.

Daniel Wood (2315), m. Permelia Chatman of Nobleboro', Maine. He lived most of the time in Lowell, Mass., and died there in 1862. Had several children; only three lived to grow up, viz:

2322. PERMELIA; m. Wm. Hamman, of Boston, Mass.
2323. ROYAL; m. and lives in Somerville; no children.
2324. LUELLA; m. Lon. Hoyt; residence Charlestown, Mass.

Permelia (2322), has one son, Wm. B. Hamman. She died about 1870.

Luella (2324), has two children, George and Eddie P. Hoyt.

Elsina Wood (2316), residence Washington, N. H., with her brother John.

Ebenezer Wood (2317), m. Esther Lawrence of Guttenberg, Iowa, 1852. She d. in 1883. He has five children living, viz:

2325. Horace.
2326. Elsina.
2327. Emery.
2328. Willie.
2329. Warren.

The date of birth of these children is not at hand but their ages (1884) are 30, 26, 23, 17, 12, in the order named. They all reside in Glen Haven, Wisconsin, where the father has a large farm and is called a successful farmer. He was a merchant in Boston many years ago.

Lydia Wood (2318), d. in Washington, N. H., Nov. 13, 1857. For some time she resided in Lowell and Lawrence, Mass.

Phebe Wood (2319), m. Charles Scott, of Newton Upper Falls, Nov. 5, 1837, where she died Dec. 28, 1860. They had three children:

2330. Harriet P.; m. Caleb Hollis, of Cambridge.
2331. Charles E.; d. about three years old.
2332. Mary Sophia; d. about three months old.

Harriet P. Scott (2330) and Caleb Hollis reside in Chicago, Ill., and have two children, Henry and Fanny.

Horace Wood (2320), was in a factory at Nashua, N. H.; he was drowned in Nashua river, Nashua, in 1842, while bathing.

John Wood (2321), m. Julia A. Crane, of East Washington, Jan. 4, 1853.

He was named for Dea. John Wood, of Littleton, Mass., his grandfather's brother, who died May 4, 1826, the month before John's birth. His father, Ebenezer Wood, lived in sight of his own father's farm, and John now lives on the adjoining farm, which contains about four hundred acres on the bank of a large brook named "Wood Brook," for his grandfather, Ebenezer Wood. Both of his grandfathers were in the War of the Revolution, and his uncle Jonas, and his father, Ebenezer, volunteered as minute-men in 1812, but were never called into action.

Ebenezer Wood, 1st, was a Whig, and all of this branch were Whigs or Republicans but two.

John lived fifteen years in Newton Upper Falls; he was a mason by trade; he went home and took care of his father and mother, and it has been a home to the family. He is an honored citizen; is generous to his relatives and friends and looks well after his own family and their highest good. He has five children, all born in Washington, N. H.:

2333. JULIA M., b. Sept. 22, 1856.
2334. PHEBE E., b. Jan. 25, 1862.
2335. EMILY J., b. Feb. 8, 1864.
2336. JOHN W., b. July 29, 1869.
2337. LYDIA A., b. Dec. 14, 1871.

Two of the above are teachers in the public schools of the State.

III.

Asa Wood (2304), m. Mary Ware, of Hancock, and resided in Washington until his death. They had eight children, viz:

2338. ASA; married.
2339. ELVIRA; d. unmarried.

2340. SARAH; m. Ahial Tandy, of Lempster.
2341. William; m. Orpha Whitney, of N. Y.; he is not living.
2342. NATHANIEL W.; m. widow —— Beard; res. Hillsboro, N. H.
2343. SYLVESTER; m. three times; has four children.
2344. MARIETTA; d. unmarried.
2345. TIMOTHY DEXTER; m.; had son Herbert; d.

Sylvester and Timothy D. Wood, sons of Asa (2304), were in the Union Army in the Rebellion. Sylvester was in the Cavalry from N. H.; he had one son killed in the war, another son was in the Regular Army, at Fort Comfort, after the war. Timothy D. Wood enlisted from Massachusetts.

IV.

Phebe Wood (2306), m. Daniel Jaquith, of Washington, and afterwards of Stillwater, N. Y., where she died. They had three children:

2346. EBENEZER.
2347. RUTH; d.
2348. STEPHEN.

V.

Sophia Wood (2307), m. Mason W. Putnam, of Boston, Mass.; she died Oct. 29, 1879; no children.

VI.

Betsey Wood (2309), m. Benajah Sabin, of Lempster, N. H. They had three children.

2349. BETSEY.
2350. PERMELIA; m. Carroll C. Churchill, of Vermont.
2351. BENAJAH.

Permelia (2350) and C. C. Churchill have two children, viz:

2352. DORA; m. Charles Leland, of Mass.
2353. CHANCY.

VII.

Mary Wood (2310), m. Dea. Joseph Crane, of East Washington, Oct. 18, 1840. She died Sept. 4, 1866. No children.

VIII.

Timothy Wood (2311), m. Lucy Sweet, of Washington. He died May 2, 1871; no children.

SALMON WOOD.

SALMON (497) AND SIBYL (WHETTEMORE) WOOD AND THEIR DESCENDANTS.

Salmon Wood, youngest son of John and Lydia (Davis) Wood, was b. in Littleton, Mass., Aug. 15, 1757. His father d. in 1758; his mother afterward m. Dea. David Goodridge, of Fitchburg, Mass., where Salmon lived until he m. Sibyl Whettemore, of New Ipswich, N. H., 1780; she was born Sept. 21, 1762, and d. Mar. 19, 1845. Salmon d. Feb. 25, 1823.

They lived at Rindge a short time, then settled in Hancock, N. H., 1784, where some of the descendants still reside. They were two of the sixteen original members of the first church organized in Hancock. Bought several hundred acres of land. In 1784 he built a part of the house and in 1801 he built the rest. In addition to his extensive farm, he kept a hotel, run a saw-mill and a blacksmith shop. This farm is now owned and occupied by his descendants. A view of the old homestead which is the Skatutahkee Valley Farm, is now being prepared for their town history. Salmon Wood was out three times in the war of the Revolution. He was an upright, honorable citizen, accomplished much in his time, and was ably assisted by his wife, a woman of great ability and personal worth. Their children were:

2501. David Wood, b. Feb. 9, 1782; d. Jan. 23, 1784.

2502. Sibyl Wood, b. in Rindge, N. H., Dec. 19, 1783; m. Benj. Estabrook in 1804; d. in Manchester, Vt., Oct. 1, 1851. He was b. Oct. 28, 1774; d. in Worcester, Vt., June 29, 1833.

2503. Salmon Wood, Jr., b. Apr. 16, 1786; m. Achsa Mason, of Dublin, N. H., settled there; died Dec. 30, 1842. Wife died Aug. 4, 1856.

2504. Daniel Wood, b. in Hancock, N. H., Apr. 19, 1788; m. Anna Wood, of Hancock, N. H., Dec. 23, 1817; b. May 24, 1795. She d. Jan. 19, 1829. He is now living July, 1885, in his 98th year.

2505. Sally Wood, b. Apr. 18, 1790; m. Earl Stone; he died June 12, 1846; no children. Living in her 96th year.

2506. Betsy Wood, b. Apr. 30, 1793; m. James Boutelle, of Hancock; after some years removed to Nashua, N. H., where they died. She died Aug. 6, 1852.

2507. Nathan Wood, b. July 24, 1795; d. Aug. 12, 1800.

2508. Lucy Wood, b. May 8, 1797; m. Benjamin P. Stone, who died Jan. 6, 1839; she died Oct. 27, 1867.

2509. Stephen Wood, b. Jan. 11, 1800; m. Maria Foster (page 50), in Stoddard, N. H., Nov. 4, 1823; she was b. Apr. 29, 1804. He d. Apr. 30, 1874. Was a deacon of the Congregational Church in Hancock, N. H., for 48 years. Portraits of both appear in this volume taken from old pictures.

2510. Nathan Wood, b. Dec. 5, 1802; m. Abigail C. Fuller; 2nd, Hannah J. Silsby; was b. Jan. 14, 1812; d. Nov. 15, 1879. He d. Oct. 1, 1869, in Illinois.

CHILDREN OF BENJAMIN

AND

SIBYL WOOD (2502) ESTABROOK.

2511. David W., b. June 30, 1805; m. Mary Clogstone, Oct. 10, 1839; Strafford, Vt.; d. Feb., 1843; m. 2nd, Lucy Benedict, Thetford, Vt., June, 1844; d.; m. 3d, Mary Walters, Fairfield, Ill., in 1864.

2512. Levi Daniel, b. June 15, 1807; d. Nov. 15, 1823.

Stephen Wood

2513. Elvira Calista, b. July 17, 1810; m. Jacob Baldwin, Mar. 13, 1828, in Worcester, Vt., she d. in Manchester, Vt., Aug. 31, 1841. Residence, Yorktown, Ill.

2514. Salmon W., b. Apr. 1, 1812; moved to the State of Georgia; probably deceased.

2515. Joel Anson, b. Mar. 6, 1819; supposed to be lost at sea about the year 1840.

2516. Sarah Maria, b. Mar. 31, 1821; m. Sept. 4, 1842, to Noah J. Hogeboom, Manchester, Vt.; res. Tampico, Ill.

2517. Stephen Monroe, b. Mar. 31, 1821; m. Apr. 28, 1845, Roselta Howe, Manchester, Vt.; d. In 1863, m. Frances Rice, Springfield, Ill.; res. Plumb Creek, Nebraska.

CHILDREN OF SALMON, Jr. (2503)

AND

ACHSA MASON WOOD.

2518. Emily Wood, b. Apr. 15, 1810; d. June 18, 1859.

2519. Augustine Wood, b. Feb. 7, 1812; m. Elizabeth Richardson, of Dublin, N. H.; residence Dublin, N. H.; homestead of his father.

2520. George Wood, b. Nov. 28, 1815, in Dublin, N. H.; m. in Philadelphia, Penn., Feb. 23, 1843, Sarah Stott; residence Harrisville, N. H.

2521. Curtis Wood, b. Dec. 18, 1818; d. Dec. 30, 1845.

CHILDREN OF DANIEL (2504)

AND

ANNA (WOOD) WOOD.

BORN IN HANCOCK, N. H.

2522. David A. Wood, b. June 11, 1819; m. Sarah L. Stanley, Apr. 4, 1843; b. July 5, 1822; she d. Mar. 14, 1879; m. Mar. 28, 1880; Mrs. Susannah P. (Rowell) Corning, b. in Jefferson, Me., Sept. 10, 1828; res. Boston Highlands, Mass.

2523. Horace A. Wood, b. June 1, 1821; d. Aug. 23, 1835.

2524. Salmon F. Wood, b. Mar. 27, 1824; d. Mar. 30, 1824.

2525. George C. Wood, b. Mar. 29, 1826; d. June 22, 1877; never married.

CHILDREN OF JAMES AND BETSY WOOD (2506) BOUTELLE.

2526. James E., b. in Hancock, N. H., 1816; m. 1st, Joanna Sprague, of Hudson, N. H.; b. 1818; d. Feb. 16, 1856; 2nd, Mrs. Eliza Eddy, of Boston, Mass.; 3rd, Angie R. Ripley, of Londonderry, Vt.; he d. in Concord, Nov. 24, 1876. He was in 1st Regiment, Mass. Vol. Cavalry, in Civil War.

2527. Stephen; died; unmarried.

2528. Moses; m. and d.; had Moses G.; res. Burlington, Vt., and James I., res. Springfield, Mass.

2529. Dexter; m. and died; had Charles; res. Cambridgeport, Mass.

CHILDREN OF BENJAMIN P. AND LUCY WOOD (2508) STONE.

2530. Julia Ann, b. in Hancock, N. H., Feb. 10, 1820; d. May 30, 1867; unmarried.

2531. Sibyl J., b. in Lempster, N. H., Apr. 9, 1882; m. James Wilson, b. in Peterborough, N. H., Feb. 11, 1816; no children.

2532. George S., b. in Lempster, Aug. 7, 1823; m. Mary Wilson; had one child, Ella, b. in Peterborough, N. H.

Maria F. Wood

2533. Ella Lucetta, b. in Hancock, Mar. 2, 1828; m. William Parker; no children. She died Sept. 28, 1850.

2534. Charles H., b. in Peterborough, N. H., Mar. 2, 1834; m. Martha Clark, b. in Londonderry, N. H.; had one son, Frederick S. Stone, b. in Nashua, N. H., Nov. 27, 1853.

CHILDREN OF STEPHEN (2509) AND MARIA (FOSTER) (page 50) WOOD.

2535. Franklin Salmon Wood, b. in Hancock, N. H., Jan. 8, 1825; m. Margaret Jane Coe, b. in Benton, Yates Co., N. Y., May 24, 1828.

2536. Sabrina Wood, b. Feb. 9, 1830; m. Dea. Alfred Hardy, in Hancock, N. H., Sept. 21, 1869; residence, Greenfield, N. H.

2537. Oren Stearns Wood, b. Oct. 13, 1837; d. Mar. 30, 1839.

2538. Alden Samuel Wood, b. Jan. 30, 1840.

He was in the Union Army in the Civil War. Residence, Hancock, N. H. Occupies the old homestead of his father and of his grandfather, Salmon Wood.

CHILDREN OF NATHAN (2510) AND ABIGAIL C. (FULLER) WOOD.

2539. Frances, b. in Hancock, N. H., Dec. 26, 1827; m. A. C. Quinn, of N. H.; she d. May, 1870; had six children, four now living in Maine.

2540. Eveline L., b. Oct. 21, 1831; d. June 17, 1833.

2541. Eveline Augusta, b. Oct. 18, 1835, in Hancock; married; d. in Newton, Mar. 22, 1861; no children.

2541*a*. George (adopted) son of Nathan, lives upon the homestead of his father in New Rutland, Ill.

CHILDREN OF DAVID W. (2511)

AND

MARY (CLOGSTONE) ESTABROOK.

2542. George T., b. May, 1842; m. Henrietta Curby, Feb. 24, 1880; had Henry L., b. Feb. 2, 1881; res. Tampico, Ill.

BY WIFE LUCY, HAD:

2543. Martin B., b. Apr. 2, 1845; lives in New Bedford, Ill.

2544. Mary A., b. Feb. 17, 1847; m. William More, 1873; had Burchen, b. Aug. 24, 1874; Charles M., b. Aug. 6, 1876; William, b. July 27, 1878; David, b. July, 1880.

2545. Hannah M., b. Apr. 4, 1849; m. Daniel Woodard, of Morrison, Ill., Sept. 24, 1872; had Ida M., b. July 27, 1873; Lucy M., b. Nov. 14, 1874; Luther B., b. Dec. 24, 1876.

2546. Roselta Elvira, b. Apr. 26, 1851; m. May, 1877, Stephen McPherson; had Myrtle, b. 1883; res. Plum Creek, Nebraska.

2547. Rosella Elmira, b. Apr. 26, 1851; m. Wm. C. Hodkins, Jan., 1874; had Lillian, b. 1876; Marian Lane, b. 1879; res. Bureau Creek, Ill.

2548. Daniel M., b. Aug. 26, 1854, in Manchester, Vt.

2549. Sarah M., dau. of David W. and Mary Walters Estabrook, b. in Fairfield, Ill., May 5, 1865; m. John Stewart, Dec. 18, 1882; had Mary Alice, b. Dec. 21, 1883.

CHILDREN OF ELVIRA CALISTA (ESTABROOK) (2513)

AND

JACOB BALDWIN.

2550. Maria Calista, b. Aug. 20, 1831; m. Almon F. Reynolds, May 22, 1849, in Manchester, Vt.; d. Sept. 11, 1864.

2551. Mary Eliza, b. Feb. 26, 1833; m. Francis M. Lane, Nov. 16, 1857, in Princeton, Ill.; res. Yorktown, Ill.

2552. Joel Manning, b. May 5, 1834; m. Orpha Jane Bigelow, Sept. 17, 1853, in Halifax, Vt.; had Mary Jane, b. May 20, 1856; J. William, b. Mar. 20, 1859; Frank H., b. Jan. 20, 1861; Lizzie Maria, b. Oct. 24, 1871; res. Evans Mills, N. Y.

2553. Lucy Jane, b. July 31, 1838, in Worcester, Vt.; m. Feb. 6, 1859, Harvey Bird Laflin, son of E. and Almira Grover Laflin; res. La Crosse, Wisconsin. A practicing physician; he was born in Pine Grove, Pa., July 27, 1834; adopted dau., Nellie, m. J. A. Raymond, of La Crosse.

CHILDREN OF SARAH MARIA (ESTABROOK) (2516)

AND

NOAH J. HOGEBOOM.

2554. John N., b. June 28, 1843, in Manchester, Vt.; m. in Princeton, Ill., Anna Woodard Kedzie, b. in Elkhart, Indiana, Nov. 26, 1843; had Lillian, b. Nov. 28, 1867, d. Aug. 14, 1882; Minnie M., b. Feb. 19, 1869; John W., b. May 23, 1872, d. Sept. 28, 1872; Daisey Dean, b. Apr. 19, 1874; James Henry, b. June, 27, 1875; Fanny Cynthia, b. Dec. 7, 1877; Nellie A., b. Feb. 15, 1883; res. near Tampico, Ill.

2555. Highland Henry, b. Nov. 12, 1845, in Manchester, Vt.; m. Jennetta Sykes, of Dorset, Vt.; had Jennie Maria, b. June 23, 1880; Emma Lavina, b. Aug. 21, 1882, d. Nov. 27, 1883; Edwin Sykes, b. Apr. 5, 1884; res. near Tampico, Ill.

2556. Elvira Maria, b. Sept. 13, 1848, in Manchester, Vt.; d. Jan. 8, 1863.

2557. Fanny Amelia, b. Nov. 2, 1853, in Manchester, Vt.; d. Apr. 13, 1875.

CHILD OF STEPHEN MONROE (2517)

AND

ROSELTA (HOWE) ESTABROOK.

2558. Rocelia, b. in Manchester, Vt., 1852; m. Luther Scott; had four daughters.

CHILDREN OF AUGUSTINE (2519)

AND

ELIZABETH (RICHARDSON) WOOD.

2559. Curtis A. Wood, b. Apr. 7, 1846; graduate of Dartmouth Medical College, Hanover, N. H.; practicing physician, Greenville, N. H.; m. Ida S. Benson, b. in Maine.

2560. Samuel R. Wood, b. June 10, 1850; d. May 14, 1875.

CHILDREN OF GEORGE (2520)

AND

SARAH (STOTT) WOOD.

2561. George W. Wood, b. July 31, 1844, in Philadelphia, Pa.; m. Elnora Tenny, of Marlboro', N. H., Nov. 21, 1869; had Clarence W. Wood, b. Sept. 5, 1870; Arthur E. Wood, b. Oct. 29, 1874; res. Marlboro', N. H.

2562. Curtis S. Wood, b. May 24, 1846, in Reading, Pa.; m. Kate A. Desler, of Canton, Ohio, Oct. 10, 1872; res. Canton, Ohio.

2563. Theodore A. Wood, b. Jan. 10, 1849, in Reading, Pa.; m. Martha Varner, of Harrisville, N. H., Jan., 1879; res. Harrisville, N. H.

2564. Clara E. Wood, b. Feb. 25, 1856, in Harrisville, N. H.

2565. Harriet E. Wood, b. Feb. 27, 1858, in Harrisville, N. H.; m. Charles L. Yardly, Feb. 15, 1879; res. Harrisville, N. H.

CHILDREN OF DAVID A. (2522)

AND

SARAH L. (STANLEY) WOOD.

2566. TWIN BOYS, b. and d. Mar. 4, 1844, in Hancock, N. H.

2567. DAUGHTER, b. and d. May 4, 1845, in Hancock, N. H.

2568. EDWIN M. WOOD, b. in Hancock, N. H., Feb. 22, 1846; m. Sylvia R. Sawtell, b. in Jaffrey, N. H., June 29, 1848. They were m. Sept. 20, 1868; had Laurice A. F. Wood, b. at Gill, Mass., Nov. 16, 1872; Herbert A. Wood, b. in Gill, Mass., June 30, 1874; res. Boston Highlands, Mass.

2569. MARY ANNA WOOD, b. Nov. 1, 1848; d. Feb. 13, 1850.

2570. GEORGE HENRY WOOD, b. Jan. 13, 1851; d. Feb. 14, 1851.

CHILDREN OF JAMES E. (2526)

AND

JOANNA (SPRAGUE) BOUTELLE.

2571. ADELBERT D., b. May 4, 1842; m. Augusta S. Marston, b. in Pittsfield, N. H., 1841; res. Worcester, Mass. Has one child, Mabel Amelia, b. May 1, 1874; he was in 8th Regt. N. H. Vol. Infantry, in Civil War.

2572. ALBERT L., b. in South Chelmsford, Mass., Aug. 21, 1843; m. Lucy A. Huggins, Dec. 7, 1869, b. in Claremont, N. H., Nov. 11, 1846; had William A., b. Aug. 21, 1872; Chas. R., b. Feb. 20, 1875; Louis W., b. Dec. 21, 1883. Was in 1st N. H. Heavy Artillery in Civil War.

2573. LANDON H., b. in Nashua, N. H., June 4, 1846; m. Nov. 5, 1868, Mary A. Williams, b. in Manchester, N. H., Jan. 21, 1844; had George W., b. Apr. 25, 1870; Charles E., b. June 5, 1872; d.

Jan. 9, 1875; Johanna Day, b. July 2, 1880, Landon H. was in 1st N. H. Heavy Artillery in Civil War.

2574. WILLIAM L., b. in Nashua, N. H., May 25, 1848; m. Aug. 16, 1871, Almira L. Damon, b. in Salisbury, Vt., July 14, 1850; no children. Was in 1st N. H. Heavy Artillery in Civil War.

2575. JOHN S., b. in Nashua, Apr. 29, 1850; m. Jan. 11, 1872, Nellie F. Knowlton, b. in Boscawen, N. H., July 29, 1854.

2576. AMELIA ANTOINETTE, b. 1852; d. Aug., 1856.

2577. LLEWELLYN W., b. in Nashua, Jan. 22, 1853; m. Apr. 30, 1879, Annette J. Sisson, b. in Buckland, Mass., May 11, 1857; had Percy L., b. in Springfield, Mass., May 12, 1881.

The 3d and 9th died in infancy.

CHILDREN OF FRANKLIN S. (2535)

AND

MARGARET JANE (COE) WOOD.

2578. LELIA J. WOOD, b. in Hancock, N. H., May 14, 1850.

2579. EUGENE F. WOOD, b. in Hancock, Oct. 17, 1851; lives in Warren, Mass.

2580. CARRIE M. WOOD, b. in Gaines, Orleans Co., N. Y., Dec. 5, 1853; d. in Keene, N. H., Nov. 18, 1876.

2581. FRED. C. WOOD, b. in Albion, Orleans Co., N. Y., Dec. 31, 1857; m. in May, 1882; res. Springfield, Mass.

JEREMIAH WOOD (9),

SEVENTH CHILD OF

JEREMIAH AND DORATHY WOOD.

The writer copied the following from his gravestone in Littleton, Mass.:

"Here lies buried
the body of
JEREMIAH WOOD,
ye son of
MR. JEREMIAH WOOD
and
MRS. DORATHY WOOD,
who deceased,
Oct. 21, 1736,
Age ye 14 years 10 m. & 20 days."

He was born in Littleton, Dec. 1, 1721.

In the distribution of the property of his father, a portion of the real estate was set to him which, after his decease, was mostly purchased from his heirs by his brother Bennet.—Recorded at Cambridge, Mass.

SARAH WOOD (10)

EIGHTH CHILD OF

JEREMIAH AND DORATHY WOOD.

Was b. in Littleton, Feb. 7, 1724; m. Joseph Chase, of Littleton, Oct. 13, 1743.

CHILDREN:

JOSEPH, b. Sept. 13, 1744; d. July 10, 1745.
BENJAMIN, b. Aug. 9, 1745.
SARAH, b. Oct. 7, 1746.
DOLLY, b. May 8, 1748.
JOSEPH, b. March 8, 1750.

—[Littleton Town Records.]

This family removed to Groton, where other children may be recorded. Inventory of Joseph's estate taken May 14, 1785, a part of which was sold to Thomas Wood, son of Bennet.

JONATHAN WOOD.

JONATHAN WOOD (11)

AND

DESCENDANTS.

JONATHAN WOOD, ninth child of Jeremiah and Dorathy Wood, was b. Aug. 3, 1727, in Littleton, Mass. He married Abigail Daby, in Sudbury, Mass., Mar. 8, 1749; settled in Stow, Mass.; had by first wife, Abigail, Sarah and Jonathan. The wife, Abigail Daby Wood, d. Dec. 26, 1764, aged 31 yrs. 11 mo. 26 da., and was buried in Stow beside Joseph Daby, the pioneer, who died Feb. 22, 1734, aged about 80 years. The Dabys were descendants of the ancestor Derby, in England; pronounced Derbi, or Darbi. Jonathan, Senior, m. second wife, Katherine Gardner, Dec. 18, 1765, by whom he had Katherine, Mary, Charlotte and Joseph. Katherine Gardner was a daughter of Rev. John Gardner and Mary Baxter, his wife. Her father graduated at Harvard College in 1715; ordained Nov. 18, 1720, and was minister of Stow, Mass., fifty-five years. Her brother Henry graduated at Harvard College in 1750, and was a member of the first Provincial Congress which met in Salem, Mass., Oct., 1774. Subsequently he was chosen Treasurer of the Province, by the first Congress. He was a member of the Academy of Arts and Sciences, and was considered a learned man, as well as an earnest and zealous patriot. His residence was the "Old Province House," Boston, Mass.

Mrs. Katherine Wood's aunt, Sarah Baxter, married Thomas Buckminster, of Framingham.

John Wood, the uncle of Katherine's husband, married Elizabeth Buckminster, a sister of Thomas, thus connecting the Buckminsters and Baxters with both the Jeremiah and John branches of the Wood family.

Mary Baxter, who married the Rev. John Gardner, was a dau. of the Rev. Joseph Baxter, of Medford, who was b. June 4, 1676, and his first wife, who was a dau. of Rev. John Fiske. The latter was of a family which begins on the records five generations earlier with Simon, lord of the Manor of Stradhaugh, Laxfield, Suffolk, England, in the time of Henry VI.

It was Mary's grandfather who first came to America.

Jonathan Wood, Esq., died Oct. 18, 1797. He was a prominent and honored man in public affairs, both military and civil. His second wife, Katherine, was b. in Stow, Sept. 9, 1729; d. Oct. 5, 1803.

Jonathan Wood, son of Jeremiah, had by wife Abigail (Daby) Wood:

2601. ABIGAIL, b. Mar. 25, 1750.
2602. SARAH, b. Apr. 15, 1752.
2603. JONATHAN, b. 1761.

BY WIFE,

KATHERINE (GARDNER) WOOD.

2604. KATHERINE, b. Oct. 22, 1766.
2605. MARY, b. Dec. 11, 1768.
2606. CHARLOTTE, b. Apr. 22, 1771.
2607. JOSEPH, b. July 14, 1773.

ABIGAIL WOOD.

ABIGAIL WOOD (2601), b. Mar. 25, 1750; m. Dec., 1773, Zechariah Whitman. He was the son of Zechariah, son of John, son of Rev. Zechariah, of Hull, who was the youngest son of John Whitman, who came to this country before 1638, and settled in Weymouth, Mass.

Prior to 1780 (the exact date is not recorded), Zechariah and Abigail (Wood) Whitman removed to Westminster, Mass., a newly settled town lying at the foot of

Mt. Wachusett. Here they purchased a section of land, erected buildings, and in 1798 we find in the valuation of homesteads by the government, that of Zechariah Whitman stood second of the one hundred and twenty-five estates.

Of the fourteen children of Zechariah and Abigail (Wood) Whitman, we give a brief record, as follows:

2608. SARAH W., b. June 5, 1775; m. Jos. Spaulding; had 11 children.
2609. ABIGAIL W., b. Aug. 3, 1776; m. Jonas Marshall; had 2 children.
2610. JONATHAN, b. Sept. 6, 1778; m. Anna Jackson and Sally Flint; had 3 children.
2611. ELIZABETH, b. Mar. 7, 1781; m. Caleb Williams; had a large family.
2612. ZECHARIAH, b. May 5, 1782; m. Rebecca Dods; had 3 children.
2613. CATHERINE, b. July 11, 1783; d. unmarried, aged 23 years.
2614. MARY, b. June 13, 1785; m. —— Goss; d. young; no children.
2615. CHARLOTTE, b. Dec. 3, 1786; m. Wm. Rice; had 12 children.
2616. DORCAS, b. Mar. 29, 1788; m. Manasseh Forbush; had 6 children.
2617. JOSEPH, b. Jan. 5, 1790; m. Dolly Mayo; had 9 children.
2618. DOLLY, b. Feb. 20, 1792; m. David Forbush; had 2 children.
2619. SUSANNAH, b. Aug. 6, 1793; d. unmarried, aged 16 years.

Two died in infancy, and names are not recorded.

The father, Zechariah Whitman, d. Aug. 15, 1806, aged 59 years.

The mother, Abigail (Wood) Whitman, d. Feb. 25, 1816, aged 66 years.

The sons: Zechariah Whitman, d. July 21, 1825, aged 43 years.

Jonathan Whitman, d. July 11, 1829, aged 60 years.

Joseph Whitman; d. Oct. 4, 1860, aged 70 years.

The daughters, most of whom lived to an advanced age, were without an exception exemplary wives and mothers, exerting a marked influence on their several families. Our limits will not allow of an extended record of their descendants, who are numerous and widely scattered. Many of them have been noted for moral worth, as well as mental ability and culture, and have held positions of trust and honor.

The two eldest sons died comparatively young, but had held responsible offices, and were regarded as men of integrity and force of character. With their father's aid they built several large substantial houses, one of which was known (and kept for many years) as the "Whitman Tavern." They also built a mill (propelled by water power), where they run a "Grist-Mill" and "Saw-Mill," leasing a part for the manufacture of chairs, which has since become the principal manufacturing interest in the town.

Joseph, the youngest son, engaged early in mercantile pursuits, which, in connection with manufacturing business, and the co-partnership of his two eldest sons, he followed to the close of a long life. He held various town offices of trust and responsibility. He represented the town in the State Legislature, was for many years Justice of the Peace, and Postmaster for twenty-five years prior to his decease. He had eight children, viz:

2620. Maria A., b. June 21, 1820; d. Dec. 12, 1853; unmarried.

2621. Joseph M., b. June 10, 1822; res. Chicago, Ill.; he has 2 sons, Fred. S., and George R.

2622. Jerome, b. Oct. 31, 1824; residence, Westminster, Mass.

2623. ALONZO, b. Feb. 14, 1827; res. Leominster, Mass.; has one son, Frank.

2624. MARCUS, b. July 13, 1829; P. O. address, Westminster, Mass.

The three youngest, Benjamin, Abigail W., and George died of scarlet fever, two the 9th and the other the 11th of March, 1836.

SARAH WOOD (2602), b. in Stow, Apr. 15, 1752; m. ——— Blood. She was not living in 1792, when some property was divided among the heirs of her mother, Abigail (Daby) Wood.

The share of Sarah was ordered paid to her children:

2625. HENRY GARDNER BLOOD.

2626. SARAH BLOOD.

2627. ABIGAIL BLOOD; Oliver Blood, Guardian.

Am informed that Mrs. Soper was a sister of Gardner Blood, and her descendants are Sally, Mary, Jacob, Abigail and Emily, — that the son Jacob only, left descendants; that he married Eliza Tower, of Stow, and left a son and daughter, both living somewhere in the west.

DR. JONATHAN WOOD.

JONATHAN WOOD, JR., M. D. (2603), b. 1761; m. Sarah Leathe, of Watertown, Mass., Sept. 5, 1782. He d. Aug. 29, 1822. They had several children, viz:

2628. JONATHAN WOOD, b. May 8, 1783; m. Jane Proudfit, of Norfolk, Va.; d. March 13, 1847, aged 63 yrs. 10 mos. 5 days.
2629. JOHN WOOD, b. Oct. 15, 1784; d. unmarried.
2630. MARY WOOD, b. June 5, 1786; m. Robert Barber, of Boston, Mass.; d. Jan 7, 1879; had Amelia; d. unmarried.
2631. JEDEDIAH LEATHE WOOD, b. Apr. 4, 1788; d. Oct. 18, 1794.
2632. ABIGAIL DABY WOOD, b. Jan. 16, 1790; m. Timothy Prescott, of Littleton, Mass., Apr. 24, 1814; d. Mar. 22, 1823.
2633. FRANCIS WOOD, b. Oct. 19, 1791; m. Maria Ames, of Va.; d.
2634. SARAH WOOD, b. Feb. 13, 1794; m. Henry Brooks, of Stow, Mass., Mar. 12, 1815; d. May 6, 1859.
2635. HANNAH BLANCHARD WOOD, b. Feb. 24, 1797; m. Charles Jansen, of England, Sept. 23, 1845; d. Mar. 2, 1871.

Dr. Jonathan Wood studied his profession with the famous Dr. Spring of Watertown, Mass.; found his wife there. He practiced largely in Stow until her death, which occurred Jan. 20, 1819. He died soon after, Aug. 29, 1822.

His oldest son, Jonathan, removed to Virginia, afterwards to North Carolina, and thence to Brownsville, Tennessee, where he was a merchant and had a large family.—See records farther on.

John Wood, the next oldest son, went to Norfolk, Va., when a mere lad, and at the early age of 18 was sent to England by his employers to buy goods.

He was quite successful for some years in trade at Richmond, Va., and was there at the burning of the theatre in which so many lives were lost.

He had the youngest brother, Francis, with him in business, and he educated his youngest sister, Hannah, in the best school in Philadelphia, giving her every advantage and accomplishment of the time. He was afterwards in business in Boston, and considered rich, and aided in fitting up the old Wood Mansion in Stow, then owned and occupied by his sister Sally and her husband. He was a man of mark and note at that time, but later was unsuccessful and lost all his property.

His youngest sister, thrown on her own resources, turned her educational accomplishments to advantage by opening a boarding school for young ladies in the old mansion at Stow. This soon became widely known, and was resorted to from the country by the daughters of the best families for finishing their studies. It was sustained by Miss Wood in good repute for fourteen years, until she had earned a competence, and retired from her work. The oldest daughter, Mary, after the death of her husband, in Boston, returned to Stow to live with her sisters, and in 1850, when Mr. and Mrs. Brooks went to Michigan, where their son, John W., was at the head of the Michigan Central Railroad, and the Wood Mansion was sold to strangers, Mary and Hannah removed to Concord, Mass., where they lived beloved and respected to a good old age. Hannah died, aged 75, in 1871, and Mary in 1879, at the great age of 92.

JONATHAN (2628) AND JANE (PROUDFIT) WOOD

AND

THEIR DESCENDANTS.

JONATHAN WOOD, son of Dr. Jonathan and Sarah (Leathe) Wood, was born in Stow, Mass, about 20 miles from Boston, May 8, 1783. He early in life moved to the South, settling at Norfolk, Va., where he engaged in the wholesale mercantile business. For some time he and General Winfield Scott, who was his intimate friend, together kept "bachelors' hall" in Norfolk. In 1811, June 1st, he married Jane Proudfit, dau. of John Proudfit (the large merchant and ship owner of Norfolk, who lost several ships by "French spoliations" in 1800), and of Judith Roane Proudfit, and niece of the distinguished Judge Roane, of the Supreme Court of Virginia.

The wife of Jonathan Wood was a lady of superior qualities of heart and mind—accomplished,—having had the best advantages of education which Philadelphia of that day could afford. Possessed of superior musical culture, and above all endowed with that best jewel of true womanhood—the christian grace which made her so faithful a wife and mother.

Jonathan Wood afterwards moved to North Carolina, living first in Halifax, then in Nash, then in Franklin counties, where he lived many years and reared a large family of children. At that time there was a great impulse of emigration, from both North Carolina and Virginia, to "The West." Accordingly in 1840 we find him leaving two married daughters in the "Old North State," removing with the rest of his family to Tennessee, which was then called "going out west." Indeed, one may now cross the continent in much less time and with far less trouble than was then required to travel from North Carolina to West Tennessee. The "Western District" of

Tennessee was then new and sparsely settled territory; Memphis being but a small village.

In Brownsville, Jonathan Wood again became a merchant, associating with himself in business, his sons, James and Spencer; but his death occurred a few years after his settling in Tennessee. He died March 13, 1847.

His young sons, James and Spencer, continued the business, and through their energy and popularity, soon became successful merchants. Mrs. Jonathan Wood lived to see all of her children married and settled in comfort and prosperity, all being near her excepting Mrs Blount and Mrs. Thorpe in North Carolina. She died in 1856, loved and respected by the entire community.

Jonathan and Jane (Proudfit) Wood had eleven children, — four died in infancy, the remaining seven as follows:

2636. SARAH ANN.
2637. VIRGINIA.
2638. JAMES PROUDFIT.
2639. WILLIAM.
2640. SPENCER ROANE.
2641. JANE.
2642. GEORGIANA.

I.

Sarah Ann Wood (2636), dau. of Jonathan and Jane (Proudfit) Wood, b. July 18, 1815, in Massachusetts; m. Dec. 23, 1834, Benjamin H. Blount. She died Apr. 29, 1883. Had:

2643. GEORGE WASHINGTON BLOUNT, b. Oct. 7, 1836; graduated at University of North Carolina. Is a prominent attorney at law at Wilson, N. C.; Grand Master of Masons in N. C., 1875 and 1876. Now Grand High Priest, G. R. A. Chapter of N. C. A very eminent, cultivated gentleman. He m. Sallie E. Egerton, Nov. 28, 1860; has five children, viz: May Clark, Pauline I., Charles Egerton, Sallie Gertrude, Sue Eloise.

2644. Benjamin James Blount, b. Feb. 4, 1838; d. Dec. 20, 1863; unmarried.

2645. Angelina Blount, b. Aug. 12, 1841; d. Sept. 20, 1841.

2646. Wm. Henry Blount, b. Aug. 4, 1843; editor of *Wilson Mirror*, N. C.; m. Delia Harris, Oct. 17, 1877; no children.

2647. Mary Jane Blount, b. May 25, 1845; m. T. Haywood Best, of Green Co., N. C., Jan. 20, 1876; have Lida Leigh Best and Henry Best.

2648. Thomas Spencer Blount, b. Nov. 25, 1847; d. Aug. 29, 1848.

2649. John Wood Blount, b. Nov. 6, 1849; planter, and attorney at law, at Snow Hill, Green Co., N. C.; m. Bettie Edmundson, Sept. 27, 1877; have two children, Sadie and John.

2650. Sarah Caroline Blount, b. Oct. 16, 1851; m. William T. Barnes, of Wilson, N. C., Nov. 28, 1871; have C. Barnes and Edwina.

2651. Virginia Blount, b. Sept. 22, 1853; m. John T. Weaver, of Wilson, N. C., May 29, 1871; have Kenneth Alva, and Daisy.

2652. Joseph Roane Blount, b. May 25, 1855; d. July 24, 1855.

II.

Virginia Wood (2637), b. in 1817; m. John Thorpe in Nash Co., North Carolina. Had:

2653. Henry Roane Thorpe; he attained distinction as a physician, at Rocky Mount, N. C.; m. Lucie S. Bunn; he died in 1878, aged 42 years; left two children, William Bennett and Lucie Carrie.

2654. John Houston Thorpe, planter and attorney at law, Rocky Mount, N. C.; m. Sallie Eliza Bunn. Has one child, Henry Roane Thorpe, now (1885) in Raleigh, N. C.

2655. William Lewis Thorpe, planter, attorney at law, and merchant, Hilliardston, N. C.; m. Mary E. Armington; has Archibald A. and Virginia.

2656. FRANKLIN JESSE THORPE, physician, at Rocky Mount, N. C.; m. Bettie Battle; has Kate and James.

2657. DANIEL WOOD THORPE, planter at Rocky Mount; age 30 years; m. Mary Blount Tredwell; has one child, John.

2658. ANNIE VIRGINIA THORPE; m. recently, Fletcher Y. Ramsey.

2659. ALEXANDER PROUDFIT THORPE, druggist at Rocky Mount, N. C.

III.

JAMES PROUDFIT WOOD (2638) was born near Louisburg, N. C., Dec. 31, 1819; moved to Brownsville, Tennessee, in 1840; married, Jan. 3, 1848, Anne G. Perkins, dau. of a wealthy planter, of Haywood Co., Tenn.

James P. Wood was distinguished by great energy and activity in business affairs, but not less by those fine social traits, genial disposition and kindliness of heart which endeared him to all.

At fourteen he prevailed upon his parents to allow him to leave school and go into business, and at that early age began his career.

At the contemplation of the building of the first railroad through his section of country he was appointed by the company as general collecting agent, Secretary and Treasurer, and became successively Vice-President and President of the same road (Memphis and Ohio), which latter position he held until the operations of the road were suspended by the great civil war.

After the war he again engaged in mercantile business, and although in infirm health for several years before his death, was engaged in business to the last.

He was a Knight Templar of the order of Free masons and in the communion of the Episcopal Church. His death occurred March, 1879.

His widow is still living, married in 1883, Judge T. M. Jones, of Pulaski, a distinguished Tennesseean, having been several times a member of the State Legislature, a member of the Constitutional Convention of 1870, a Judge of the Supreme Court of Tennessee, &c.

James P. Wood and his wife, Anne G., had only one child, Mary. She has done much to secure the records of her branch.

2660. Mary Wood, dau. of James P. and Anne G. Wood, was born Feb. 3, 1852; she married Dec. 8, 1874, J. W. E. Moore, a leading and distinguished lawyer of the Brownsville bar. Have three children:

2661. Annebel, b. Sept. 21, 1876.

2662. Mary, b. 1879.

2663. Wood, b. April 24, 1881.

IV.

William P. Wood (2639), b. Feb. 14, 1823; married, Nov. 13, 1844, Ariadne Leonard. He was a young lawyer of talent and promise; a graduate of William and Mary College, Va.; a sincere christian, a refined and cultured gentleman, but died at the beginning of his career. He died April, 1850, just one month after the death of his wife. They left three children:

2664. William L., died in infancy.

2665. John Proudfit; m. Fannie Nelson, of Helena, Ark. They have one child, a daughter.

2666. Julia A.; m. R. F. Collins, a wealthy planter below Memphis, Tenn. They have two children, viz: Robert and Sadie.

V.

Spencer Roane Wood (2640), b. in North Carolina, Aug. 2, 1825; married Mary Jane Howell, dau. of Dr.

Wm. Howell, of Brownsville, Tenn., Nov. 17, 1846. Spencer Wood was a popular merchant in Brownsville for some years; was also connected for some time with the Memphis and Ohio Railroad.

In 186–, he moved to Memphis, where he was a partner in a large dry goods house. In May, 1873, he lost his wife and one child from cholera.

In 1876 he returned to Brownsville and married Mrs. M. E. Cole. He died from yellow fever, Oct. 13, 1878. The terrible epidemic of that year also carried off several of his children.

His widow, Mrs. M. E. C. Wood, is still living; residence, Brownsville, Tenn.

CHILDREN OF SPENCER R. (2640) AND MARY JANE (HOWELL) WOOD.

2667. Sarah J., b. Sept. 3, 1847; m. May 18, 1870, L. J. Pettus, of an old Virginia family.

They both died in 1878, of yellow fever, leaving two children, viz: Spencer Wood, and Leroy J. Pettus; both children living (1885) with their paternal grandparents in Virginia.

2668. Margaret Georgiana; died in infancy.
2669. Jonathan, b. Oct. 22, 1852; died of yellow fever, at Memphis, Tenn., Sept. 26, 1878; unmarried.
2670. Junius H., d. in infancy.
2671. William H., d. in infancy.
2672. Virginia Thorpe, b. Sept., 1859; now (1885) living in Brownsville, Tenn.; unmarried.
2673. Henry Taylor, b. Oct. 31, 1861; m. Ida M. Hayes, Sept. 3, 1883; living at Dyersburg, Tenn.; druggist.
2674. Nellie and Emma; both died in infancy.

VI.

Jane Wood (2641), b. March 14, 1828; m. Wm. R. Leigh, Nov., 1845. Had:

2675. Lida; unmarried.
2676. William R. In 186–, was a student at Michigan University; afterwards studied law at Cumberland University, Lebanon, Tenn.; lawyer; resides at Brownsville, Tenn.; unmarried.

Jane, after the death of her first husband, Wm. R. Leigh, married in 1852, W. P. Bond, once member of Legislature of Tenn.; afterwards Judge of Circuit Court, and before the war a wealthy planter.

By second husband had:

2677. Thomas Wood; studied medicine at Louisville College of Medicine. When there was an appeal to the physicians for aid, during the Yellow Fever epidemic at Memphis, in 1878, Dr. T. W. Bond, who was living in Brownsville at the time, promptly responded, and in the cause of suffering humanity nobly fell a victim to the terrible disease, Sept. 16, 1878.
2678. Katherine Pugh; m. C. W. Jacobs, Jan. 1, 1878; has two children, Thomas Bond and William Bond.
2679. Mary; d. in infancy.
2680. James Wood; d. Oct. 6, 1879.
2681. Georgia; was married in 1882 to H. A. Ingram, of Mo.; has one child, James.
2682. Spencer Wood; unmarried.
2683. Edward Hale; unmarried.

VII.

Georgiana Wood (2642), b. July 6, 1835; married, Nov. 4, 1851, to Henry L. Taylor, from the old Virginia family of that name. He was, before the war, a wealthy planter near Brownsville, Tenn.

Georgiana and Henry L. Taylor have four children, viz:

2684. EDMUND H.; educated at Emory and Henry College, Va., and in law at Cumberland University, Tenn. Now (1885) editor *States and Bee*, Brownsville, Tenn.; m. Neppie Harbert; they have four children, Henry, Harbert, Georgiana, and Mary.

2685. WILLIAM WOOD; educated at Emory and Henry College, Va.; studied medicine at Belle Vüe College, N. Y.; now a prominent physician of Memphis, Tenn.

2686. JENNIE; m. Jno. R. Bond, now a prominent lawyer of Brownsville, Tenn.; formerly a member of the Legislature of Tenn. They have six children, Clara, Bate, Mary, Jennie, John, and William.

2687. MARY PETTUS; married R. L. Cochran, a large lumber dealer of Memphis, Tenn. They have two children, William and Marcus.

DESCENDANTS OF ABIGAIL DABY (WOOD) (2632) AND TIMOTHY PRESCOTT.

2788. MARTHA L. PRESCOTT, daughter, b. Apr. 4, 1818; m. John S. Keyes, of Concord, Mass., Sept. 19, 1844. They had:

2789. JOHN KEYES, b. Oct. 13, 1845; d. July 31, 1846.

2790. ANNE S. KEYES, b. May 4, 1847; m. Dr. Edward Waldo Emerson, of Concord, Mass., Sept. 19, 1874.

2791. FLORENCE KEYES, b. Jan. 26, 1850; m. Charles H. Walcott, of Concord, Mass., Sept. 22, 1875; d. Dec., 1877.

2792. MARY E. KEYES, b. July 8, 1853; d. Aug. 9, 1854.

2793. ALICE M. KEYES, b. June 13, 1855.

2794. PRESCOTT KEYES, b. March 26, 1858; m. Alice Reynolds, of Concord, July 6, 1881.

CHILDREN OF DR. EDWARD WALDO

AND

ANNE S. (KEYES) (2790) EMERSON,

CONCORD, MASS.

2795. Ellen T. Emerson.
2796. Florence Emerson.
2797. William F. Emerson.

CHILD OF CHARLES H.

AND

FLORENCE (KEYES) (2791) WALCOTT.

2798. Philip K. Walcott, b. Dec., 1877.

DESCENDANTS OF FRANCIS (2633)

AND

MARIA (AMES) WOOD.

CHILDREN.

2801. Ann Maria, b. Mar. 9, 1816; m. —— LaForest.
2802. Julia A., b. Aug. 27, 1817; d. Aug. 13, 1831; unmarried.
2803. Henry, b. 1820; d. unmarried.
2804. Charles, b. 1823; m. Ann Blaisdell, of Portland, Me.; residence, Aurora, Ill. They had:
2805. Julia, b. 1853; m.; husband dead; no children.
2806. Susan; m. and d.; no children.
2807. Charles; died at 17 years of age.

DESCENDANTS OF SARAH (WOOD) (2634)

AND

HENRY BROOKS.

CHILDREN.

2808. Hannah B. W., b. Apr. 14, 1817; m. June 23, 1840, Wm. Wiley; she d. 1850.

2809. JOHN WOOD BROOKS, b. Aug. 19, 1819; m. Charlotte Louisa Dean, Apr. 21, 1842. He died at Heidelberg, in the Grand Duchy of Baden, Germany, Sept. 16, 1881.

CHILDREN OF HANNAH B. W. (BROOKS) (2808) AND WILLIAM WILEY.

2810. SARAH B. W. WILEY, b. Apr. 12, 1841; m. Lynd Lewis.

2811. WM. WILEY, b. July 15, 1842; killed in the war.

2812. JOHN WILEY; married; one child.

Other children died young.

CHILDREN OF JOHN WOOD (2809) AND CHARLOTTE LOUISA (DEAN) BROOKS.

2813. WALTER DENISON, b. at Rochester, N. Y., Aug. 26, 1845; m. Florence Eveline Williams, dau. of Benj. Webb Williams, of Boston. Walter died in Boston, Apr. 5, 1877.

2814. JOHN HENRY, b. June 20, 1848, at Detroit, Mich.; m. Lucretia Gilbert, dau. of Samuel Gilbert, of Boston, Mass.

2815. ELLA CORA, b. Dec. 21, 1855, at Detroit, Mich.; m. Babson S. Ladd, of Cambridge, Mass.

CHILDREN OF WALTER DENISON (2813) AND FLORENCE E. (WILLIAMS) BROOKS.

2816. JOHN ARTHUR, b. in Milton, Mass., Mar. 27, 1873.

2817. WALTER DENISON, b. in Milton, Mass., Nov. 4, 1877.

CHILDREN OF JOHN HENRY (2814)

AND

LUCRETIA (GILBERT) BROOKS.

2818. John Edward, b. Sept. 14, 1877, in Milton, Mass.
2819. Lawrence, b. Apr. 4, 1880, in Milton, Mass.
2820. Charlotte Louisa, b. May 2, 1883, in Milton, Mass.

CHILD OF ELLA CORA (BROOKS) (2815)

AND

BABSON S. LADD.

2821. Paul Dean Ladd, b. in Boston, Mass., Feb. 16, 1880.

KATHERINE WOOD.

KATHERINE WOOD (2604), dau. of Jonathan and Katherine (Gardner) Wood, b. Oct. 22, 1766; m. Capt. Abram Whitney, Nov. 13, 1796; d. Apr. 7, 1802. They had:

2822. JONATHAN WOOD WHITNEY, b. in Stow, Mass., Sept. 10, 1797.

No information of him excepting that he went west when a young man.

MARY WOOD.

MARY WOOD (2605), dau. of Jonathan and Katherine (Gardner) Wood, b. Dec. 11, 1768; m. Amos Brooks, May 2, 1797. Had:

2823. MARY, b. March, 1800; m. Nathan Brooks, of Bolton, Mass., about 1860; d. in Stow, Mass., June, 1879.

2824. CATHERINE, b. Feb., 1801; d. in Stow, 1878.

2825. CALEB; went to Norfolk, Va., when a young man; married and died there a few years later, leaving a widow and two young children; the eldest daughter:

2826. MARY, d. in her girlhood.

2827. LUCRETIA; m. ——— Johnson, of Norfolk, Va., where she still resides (1885).

CHARLOTTE WOOD.

CHARLOTTE WOOD (2606), dau. of Jonathan and Katherine Gardner, b. Apr. 22, 1771; m. Dr. Charles Whitman, of Stow, Mass., 1798. Had:

2901. CHARLES, b. Aug. 7, 1800; d. Apr. 10, 1812.
2902. ELIZABETH, b. Apr. 17, 1802; m. Edmund Blood, of Bolton Mass., 1824. She d. Feb. 9, 1881.
2903. CHRISTOPHER, b. 1804; m. Nancy Nichols, of Barre, Vt.; res. Lowell, Mass.
2904. CHARLOTTE, b. Feb. 29, 1808; d. Apr. 17, 1880; unmarried.
2905. EMMA, b. Mar. 27, 1812; m. Benj. F. Hartwell, of Groton, Mass. She d. Apr. 22, 1880.

CHILDREN OF EDMUND AND ELIZABETH (WHITMAN) (2902) BLOOD.

2906. ELIZABETH; unmarried.
2907. SUSAN; m. W. C. Allen, of N. Y. She d. 1848.
2908. CHARLOTTE; m. W. C. Allen, in 1851.
2909. ELLEN M.; m. Frank H. Whittemore, of Arlington, Mass., 1867, and had:
2910. LOUIS DOWNING WHITTEMORE, b. 1872.

CHILDREN OF CHRISTOPHER (2903) AND NANCY (NICHOLS) WHITMAN.

2911. CHARLES; unmarried.
2912. NICHOLS; m. and has four daughters, viz:
2913. LIZZIE.
2914. HATTIE.
2915. AMELIA.
2916. EMMA.

CHILDREN OF BENJ. F.
AND
EMMA (WHITMAN) (2905) HARTWELL.

2917. Emma C. (Hartwell) Kennedy, of Zanesville, O., b. May 8, 1843.

2918. Benjamin Hall Hartwell, M. D., of Ayer, Mass., b. Feb. 28, 1845.

2919. Harris C. Hartwell, of Fitchburg, Mass. A prominent lawyer; b. Dec. 28, 1847. He has one son:

2920. Norcross N., b. Dec. 15, 1880.

2921. Lottie E. (Hartwell) Lathrop, of Hartford, Conn., b. Aug. 8, 1851.

CHILDREN OF W. C.
AND
CHARLOTTE (BLOOD) (2908) ALLEN.

2922. Louis Edmund Allen; graduate of Williams College, 1874; studied medicine in Brooklyn and Boston, and received his diploma from Harvard Medical School; located in Boston, Mass.

2923. Frederick F. Allen; d. 1878.

2924. Charlotte H. Allen.

2925. Minnie Allen.

2926. Effie Allen; d. 1881.

2927. Arthur Allen.

First four children b. in New York City, last two in Pittsfield, Mass.

JOSEPH WOOD.

JOSEPH WOOD (2607), son of Jonathan and Katherine, b. July 14, 1773; m. 1798, Betsy Williams, of Stow, who was a dau. of Robert Williams and Lois Wiley.

Lois Wiley's mother was, before her marriage, Miss Phebe Bancroft, and was a descendant of the Richard Bancroft who was made Archbishop of Canterbury by King James I.

Joseph Wood had a portion of the real estate of his father, Jonathan Wood, Esq., but in 1808 removed with his family to Maine. He was Captain, Sheriff, &c.

A man of intelligence and influence. He died at Mobile, Ala., at the age of 47.

CHILDREN OF JOSEPH AND BETSY (WILLIAMS) WOOD.

2928. KATHERINE LOUISA WOOD, b. Aug. 30, 1799.
2929. ELIJAH DOUBLEDAY WOOD, b. Jan. 2, 1802; d. May 13, 1802.
2930. ROBERT WILLIAMS WOOD, b. Apr. 22, 1803.
2931. JOSEPH BARBER WOOD, b. Jan. 4, 1805; d. Jan. 2, 1807.
2932. CHARLOTTE AUGUSTA WOOD, b. Oct. 3, 1807.

Of the above named children of Joseph, Katherine Louisa (2928) m. Jotham Babcock, in Augusta, Me., Apr. 12, 1827. He was b. Apr. 27, 1795, in Augusta, Me., and died there Nov., 1857; his wife d. Sept., 1866.

ROBERT WILLIAMS WOOD.

Robert Williams Wood (2930); graduated at Waterville College, Me., 1829 (now Colby University), and from the Medical school of Bowdoin College, 1832; sailed from Boston for the Hawaiian Islands, Oct., 1838; arrived April, 1839, and by appointments of the American Consul was ten years physician of the Hospital for American Seamen, at Honolulu, 1839 to 1849. For twenty years subsequently was engaged in the growing and manufacture of sugar, a pioneer, and the first financially successful one, in the introduction of this industry into the Hawaiian Islands. He retired from the Islands in 1866, and withdrew his business therefrom, and from all business in 1879. Residence, Jamaica Plain, Boston, Mass. He married June 4, 1833, Delia Morse, dau. of Samuel A. Morse, for many years Collector of U. S. Customs at Machias, and subsequently at Eastport, Maine. Second, married Oct. 31, 1864, Lucy Jane Davis, dau. of the late Charles W. Davis, of Concord, Mass. Her mother was a Hunt; sister of the late Mrs. Dr. Edward Jarvis, of Dorchester, Mass. Davis family of New Ipswich. Remote ancestor, Dolor Davis, of Cambridge, 1634.

Charlotte Augusta Wood (2932); m. 1834, Capt. Wm. Coffin Little, for many years a merchant Captain in the trade between the Hawaiian Islands and the South American coast and China. Wrecked and lost at Mazatlan, Mexico, Nov., 1838. 2d, m. William Hooper, Aug. 17, 1839.

William Hooper was of the well known family of Hoopers of Salem and Marblehead, Mass. He was the third of the name in direct descent and his mother was Miss Sallie Northey, of Salem. He died in 1871.

R. T. Trall

CHILDREN OF JOTHAM
AND
KATHERINE LOUISA (WOOD) (2928) BABCOCK.

ALL BORN IN AUGUSTA, ME.

2933. Anna Elizabeth, b. Mar. 10, 1828; m. George Starrett, Apr. 19, 1849; b. at Weld, Me., June 18, 1824.

2934. Delia Augusta, b. Oct. 12, 1832.

2935. George Augustus, b. June 9, 1834; d. in N. Y., June, 1877.

2936. Charles William, b. June 1, 1839.

2937. Charlotte Louisa, b. Dec. 23, 1840.

CHILD OF DR. ROBERT W. (2930)
AND
LUCY J. (DAVIS) WOOD.

2938. Robert Williams Wood, Jr., b. May 2, 1868.

CHILDREN OF CHARLOTTE A. (WOOD) (2932)

BY FIRST HUSBAND,

WILLIAM C. LITTLE.

2939. William Coffin Little, b. Jan. 15, 1836; m. Sarah Watkins; residence in California.

BY SECOND HUSBAND,

WILLIAM HOOPER.

2940. Edward N. Hooper, b. Mar. 10, 1842; d. Dec. 31, 1878.

2941. Augusta Wood Hooper, b. May 10, 1844; m. Pelham W. Ames.

Mr. Ames is a son of Judge Seth Ames, a grandson of Hon. Fisher Ames, one of our country's early orators and statesmen, and a great-grandson of Dr. Nathaniel Ames, the author of Ames' Almanacs, which were issued from

1726 to 1775, and were the forerunners of Thomas' and the Farmers' Almanacs.

The family residence was Dedham, Mass.

His mother was Miss Margaret Bradford, a direct descendant from William Bradford, the first Governor of Plymouth Colony, and also on a female side, of John Alden and Priscilla Mullen, who are made famous by Longfellow's "Courtship of Miles Standish."

CHILDREN OF GEORGE AND ANNA ELIZABETH (BABCOCK) (2933) STARRETT.

2942. Frederick Wood, b. in Augusta, Me., Jan. 20, 1851.
2943. Mary Katherine, b. in Augusta, Me., Jan. 9, 1853.
2944. Anna Frances, b. in Richmond, Va., Feb. 4, 1855.
2945. George Babcock, b. in Richmond, Va., June 10, 1857.

CHILDREN OF WILLIAM COFFIN (2939) AND SARAH (WATKINS) LITTLE.

2946. Helen Watkins, b. June 8, 1866.
2947. William Hooper, b. Apr. 29, 1868.
2948. Joseph Moss, b. July 21, 1871.
2949. Caroline Halsted, b. June 9, 1873.
2950. Weare Coffin, b. Nov. 25, 1878.

CHILDREN OF PELHAM W. AND AUGUSTA WOOD (HOOPER) (2941) AMES.

2951. Abbie B., b. Apr. 13, 1867; d. Aug. 24, 1868.
2952. Gertrude H., b. June 29, 1868.
2953. Worthington, b. Mar. 16, 1871.
2954. Alice B., b. Sept. 18, 1873.
2955. Elizabeth G., b. June 13, 1877.
2956. Pelham B., b. July 10, 1879.

ELIPHALET WOOD.

ELIPHALET WOOD (12) AND DESCENDANTS.

Eliphalet Wood, the tenth and youngest child of Jeremiah and Dorathy Wood, was born in Littleton, July 19, 1729.

His father, Jeremiah, died July 15, 1730, and his mother became his guardian, she living until Eliphalet was in his twenty-third year. He settled in Harvard, Mass., upon the estate afterwards occupied by his son, Jabez Wood, and still later by Emory Wood, son of Jabez. I notice in the records other lands in Boxboro, deeded by Eliphalet to Jabez, a son by his first wife, Abigail (Child) Wood. Eliphalet Wood of Littleton, m. Abigail Child; marriage recorded in Grafton, Mass.

Upon his gravestone in Harvard Cemetery, we find:

"Eliphalet Wood.

Erected in memory of
Mr. Eliphalet Wood
who died Apr. 16, 1817.
Aet. 87 years, 8 months & 17 days.

Death is a debt to nature due
Which I have paid and so must you"

By his side are the graves of his wife Abigail, who died Jan. 23, 1780, in the 48th year of her age, and second wife Mary, who d. Jan 15, 1829, aged 86 years.

Also upon a gravestone there:

"In memory of
Miss Lucy Wood
daughter of
Mr. Eliphalet and Mrs. Abigail Wood,
who died Nov. 5, 1800,
aged 32 years 4 m. & 11 ds."

Eliphalet's dau. Molly was born June 19, 1763.

I have heard there was a son Jesse, but have no record of him.

Jabez was baptized June 4, 1775, in Harvard, Mass., and a daughter was baptized Apr. 20, 1788. Jabez Wood died March 16, 1850, in his 75th year. Nabby, his wife, died June 8, 1865, at the age of 86 years, 5 months.

They had ten children; none living but Asa, in 1885.

CHILDREN OF JABEZ (2959) AND NABBY WOOD.

2961. BENJAMIN, b. Aug. 22, 1799.
2962. MARY, b. June 10, 1801.
2963. EMORY, b. June 28, 1803.
2964. LUCY, b. July 27, 1805.
2965. FLAVEL, b. Dec. 28, 1807.
2966. ABIGAIL, b. Aug. 23, 1810.
2967. LYDIA, b. Nov. 12, 1812.
2968. JONATHAN, b. Oct. 2, 1815.
2969. JABEZ, b. June 10, 1818.
2970. ASA, b. ——.

Of the above named children, BENJAMIN WOOD (2961), b. Aug. 22, 1799, m. and had:

2971. LEWIS; m. —— Nutting of Groton. No children.
2972. ABBY; d. unmarried.

MARY WOOD (2962), b. June 10, 1801; m. Wm. Taylor of Harvard, Mass. Had children b. in Harvard, Mass:

2973. SAMUEL; m. Emeline ——; 2nd Emily ——; 3rd ——. Had by 1st wife, Jane, Lizzie and Henry.
2974. MARY ANN, b. in Harvard July 9, 1824; m. Barney Phelps of Lancaster, Mass.; he was b. in Milton, Mass., Mar. 28, 1819; and d. Nov. 4, 1880.
2975. JANE; d. young; unmarried.

2976. JOHN ANDREW; m. Sarah Whitcomb, of Littleton; had Edward, b. about 1855, and Warren, b. about 1857; res. Hudson, Mass.

CHILDREN OF MARY ANN (TAYLOR) (2974) AND BARNEY PHELPS.

BIRTHS ALL IN LANCASTER.

2977. CHARLES HERBERT, b. Jan. 26, 1852.

2978. M. ETTA, b. June 19, 1853; m. B. Marshall Pitts; res. Fitchburg, Mass.; proprietor of Fitchburg Cotton Mill. Have two sons: Hiram W. Pitts, b. in Leominster, Mass., June 19, 1878. Earl P. Pitts, b. in Leominster, Oct. 11, 1879.

2979. FLORA ANN, b. Mar. 19, 1866.

EMORY WOOD (2963), b. June 28, 1803; m. Maranda Raymond, of Littleton. She d. Feb. 5, 1838, aged 29 years. Emory m. 2nd, Mrs. Mary Rand, of Harvard, Mass.; he died Nov. 11, 1868; his wife, Mary, d. Mar. 17, 1880.

CHILDREN OF EMORY (2963) AND MARANDA (RAYMOND) WOOD.

2980. ARVILLA A., b. in Harvard, Sept. 15, 1831; m. James Harrington, of Fitchburg, Mass.

2981. RHODA R., b. in Harvard, Mass., May 28, 1834; m. Benjamin L. Heywood.

CHILDREN OF ARVILLA A. (WOOD) (2980) AND JAMES HARRINGTON.

2982. JAMES E., b. Sept. 11, 1850, in Leominster; m. Emma M. Whitney, of Templeton, b. Feb. 11, 1855.

2983. Abbie Arvilla, b. Oct. 7, 1851; m. E. Tyler Greenwood, of Marlboro, N. H. He was in the 14th regiment N. H. Infantry in the late war; d. Nov. 11, 1876.

2984. Clara A., b. Feb. 9, 1853, in Leominster; m. Wm. P. Gay, of Gardiner, Me.

2984*a*. Helen F., b. Aug. 29, 1855, in Fitchburg; d.

2985. Emma Frances, b. in Fitchburg, Nov. 15, 1856; m. Frederick G. Rich, b. in Phillipston, April 11, 1854.

2986. Henry L., b. Mar. 25, 1861, in Fitchburg, Mass.

2987. George H., b. Mar. 7, 1863, in Fitchburg.

2988. Bertha G., b. Mar. 4, 1865, in Fitchburg.

2989. Mary M., b. June 2, 1869, in Fitchburg.

CHILDREN OF RHODA R. (WOOD) (2981) AND BENJAMIN L. HEYWOOD.

2990. Hattie A., b. in Sudbury, Aug. 16, 1857; m. Lawrin H. Pratt, b. in Fitchburg, Mass., Oct. 28, 1846. In jewelry business. Have:

Susie L., b. in Fitchburg, Mass., Sept. 4, 1876.

Alice F., b. in Fitchburg, Mass., Nov. 19, 1882.

Sidney A., b. Oct. 15, 1859, in Winchendon; d. Aug. 8, 1861.

Susie E., b. in Fitchburg, Dec. 20, 1863; d. Sept. 16, 1876.

Sidney L., b. in Sterling, June 5, 1865; d. Apr., 1874.

CHILDREN OF JAMES E. (2982) AND EMMA M. (WHITNEY) HARRINGTON.

2991. Eddie Emory, b. in Fitchburg, June 29, 1872.

2992. Benjamin, b. Apr. 28, 1876, in Akron, O.

CHILDREN OF ABBIE A. (HARRINGTON) (2983) AND E. TYLER GREENWOOD.

2993. Grace, b. in Akron, O., July 20, 1870.
2994. Gertrude Louisa, b. in Akron, O., Feb. 11, 1873.

CHILDREN OF CLARA A. (HARRINGTON) (2984) AND WILLIAM P. GAY.

2994*a*. William P., b. in Fitchburg, Apr. 2, 1874; d. Nov. 20, 1877.
2995. Helen Frances, b. in Fitchburg, Nov., 1878.
2996. Martha Perkins, b. in Boston, 1879.
2997. Richard, b. in Boston, Dec., 1880.
2998. Elenor P., b. in Boston, July, 1882.
2999. Rosco, b. in Boston, June 9, 1884.

CHILD OF EMMA F. (HARRINGTON) (2985) AND FREDERICK G. RICH.

3000. Hattie A. F., b. in Fitchburg, Oct. 26, 1875.

Lucy Wood (2964), b. July 27, 1805; m. and had three children, Abigail Tuttle, Lucy A., and Gloria Ann.

Flavel Wood (2965), b. Dec. 28, 1807.

Abigail Wood (2966), b. Aug. 23, 1810; m. Sylvester Pierce, of Leominster, Mass.; both dead. Had four children, viz: Albert Pierce, m. ——— Wilder, d., of Leominster; Geo. S., m. dau. of Frank Balch; Martha, m. Adin Rice, one son living; Mary Jane, d., m. Charles D. Wilder, of Leominster.

Lydia Wood (2967), b. Nov. 12, 1812; m. Arunia Hall; both d.; had Adeline F. Hall, who was twice m. and had children.

Jonathan Wood (2968), b. Oct. 2, 1815; m. Caroline Worcester; had five children: Albert Wood; Maria, d.; Fanny, d. Jan. 7, 1860, aged 1 yr., 24 da.; and two other children.

Jabez Wood (2969), b. June 10, 1818; m. Mrs. W. Hayden. No children.

Asa Wood, of Troy, N. H. (2970); m. Louise Stone, of Harvard, Mass.; had Ellen Wood and John Wood.

Late in 1849, Jabez Wood, Senior, had twenty-three grandchildren, thirteen great-grandchildren, and thirteen great-great-grandchildren.

The above ends the records of the Jeremiah branch so far as collected. The sons of Jeremiah that had families, named in the order of their birth, were Joseph, Bennet, John, Jonathan and Eliphalet.

The eldest son, Joseph, was traced to descendants now living before the second son Bennet was introduced, and so on until the descendants of Eliphalet, the youngest, closes the Jeremiah branch of "The Wood Brothers Genealogy."

PART SECOND.

CAPT. JOHN WOOD.

John Wood, brother of Jeremiah Wood, married the eldest daughter of Col. Joseph Buckminster of Framingham, Massachusetts.

The following is from the Town Records of Framingham:

"Married, March 3, 1704–5, JOHN WOOD and ELIZABETH BUCKMINSTER, both of this town."

The great-grandfather of Elizabeth (Buckminster) Wood, Thomas Buckmaster, or Buckminster, came to Boston in 1640, from England, and is named in the colonial records of that year. He was made freeman, May 6, 1646. He was the owner of lands at Muddy River, now Brookline, Mass., where he lived. He died there Sept. 20 (Boston records say 28), 1656. He left nine children. In his will he refers to Joseph as one of his youngest sons.

His widow, Johanna, married Sept. 1, 1661, Edward Garfield, of Watertown; died in 1676.

The grandfather of Elizabeth (Buckminster) Wood was Joseph Buckminster, and was the first of that Christian name in this country.

He seems to have succeeded his father and lived on the farm at Brookline.

He married Elizabeth, dau. of Hugh and Elizabeth Clark, of Watertown, in 1665. She was born Jan. 31, 1648. They had two children; Joseph, born July 31,

1666; Elizabeth, baptized Nov. 10, 1668. The father died in 1668.

His widow died in Roxbury; her remains were carried by her son to Framingham, and deposited in the family tomb there, in Church Hill cemetery, where interments of some of the family are still continued.

Joseph Buckminster, second of the name, married May 12, 1686, Martha Sharpe, of Muddy River, now Brookline, Mass.

They were the parents of Elizabeth (Buckminster) Wood, wife of John Wood.

Her father, Joseph Buckminster, was a proprietor of land, and a pioneer in settling Framingham, where his name is first mentioned in 1693.

He took an important part in the establishment and administration of affairs in the place. He was admitted to the Roxbury Church, 1684. In deeds dated 1702, he conveys as of Muddy River (Brookline). He transferred by letter his relations to the church at Framingham, Jan. 5, 1718. His oldest child, Elizabeth, married John Wood in Framingham, March 3, 1705.

The precise date of his removal to Framingham is unknown. The deed, conveying almost the entire estate of Gov. Thomas Danforth to Joseph Buckminster, bears date of March 25, 1699, is on record among the Middlesex deeds. He settled and improved "the famous Brinley Farm," sold to Francis Brinley, Esq., of Roxbury, Feb. 1, 1792, for the sum of £8600 in bills of public credit; hence the name. His estate in the town was large, his title to which involved him in protracted lawsuits, which continued after his death.

He married (2nd), Feb. 7, 1716, Martha Dall, of Boston, who died Feb., 1725.

He was seventeen years Selectman, twelve years Representative to the General Court, and many years Justice of the Peace.

He held several military commissions; commanded a company of Grenadiers in Sir Charles Holley's regiment in the expedition to Port Royal, Sept., 1710; subsequently had the command of a colonial regiment of militia.

Tradition describes him as being tall and athletic, of great physical power, and of a resolute will.

By his first wife, Martha Sharpe, he had eight children. (None by his second wife.) Had:

1. ELIZABETH, b. 1687; married March 3, 1705, to John Wood, of Framingham, as per town records; afterwards settled at what is now Woodville, in the town of Hopkinton, Mass., where descendants now reside. He died in Aug., 1725. His widow married May 6, 1728, Josiah Rice, of Framingham; he died in 1745, and Elizabeth died several years later.

2. JOHANNA BUCKMINSTER, second child of Joseph and Martha (Sharpe), b. 1690; m. June 23, 1712, John Eames, son of John and Elizabeth (Eames) Eames; had ten children. 2d, she m. Mar. 19, 1740, John Butler of Framingham.

3. MARTHA, b. 1693; m. Ebenezer Winchester, of Framingham, Feb. 13, 1718; had seven children. Ebenezer graduated at Harvard College, 1744; was a physician. The father died 1744. His widow m. Nov. 1, 1749, Rev. James Bridgham, of Brimfield.

4. JOSEPH, third of the name, b. 1697, brother of Elizabeth (Buckminster) Wood; m. Sarah Lawson, June 18, 1718; she d. Sept. 11, 1747.

He m. (2d), widow Hannah Kigell; she d. Oct. 25, 1776. He owned a large estate in Framingham; held several commissions; was Colonel about 1738; was twenty-eight years a Selectman; more than thirty years Town Clerk; more than twenty years a Representative at the General Court. He died at the age of 83 years, after a long life of public service and personal worth. He had Joseph, b. March 1, 1720; he was the 4th Joseph Buckminster, in direct succession, and the first to enter the ministry; graduated at Harvard College, 1739, and was pastor at Rutland more than fifty years. Rev. Joseph's son Joseph was b. Oct. 3, 1751; graduated at Yale College, 1770; settled at Portsmouth, N. H.; was a Doctor of Divinity. Dr. Joseph's son, Joseph Stevens Buckminster, b. May 26, 1784; grad. 1800; was ordained over the Brattle Street Church in Boston, Jan. 30, 1805, not 21 years old. His father, Dr. Buckminster, preached the sermon. He died their pastor, June 9, 1812.

James Freeman Clarke, D. D., of Boston, is also a descendant of Col. Joseph Buckminster, Jr.; his father, Dr. Samuel Clarke, was the son of Martha (Curtis) Clarke, who was the dau. of Martha (Buckminster) Curtis, who was the dau. of Col. Joseph Buckminster, Jr. James Freeman Clarke grad. at Harvard College in 1829. His grandmother Clarke, after the death of her husband, Samuel Clarke, married James Freeman, for whom James Freeman Clarke was named; grad. at Harvard College in 1777, D. D., 1811; ordained over King's Chapel, Boston, 1785; was minister there nearly fifty years. Col. Joseph, Jr.'s granddaughter and dau. of Martha (Buckminster) Curtis, Anna Curtis, b. Sept. 18, 1753, m. May 14, 1782, Rev. Jonathan Homer, b. in Boston, 1759; grad. at Harvard College, 1777, D. D.; pastor of 1st Newton Church, sixty years.

Anne Buckminster, b. Dec. 3, 1728, dau. of Col. Joseph, Jr.; m. Sept. 11, 1751, Rev. Abraham Williams, of Sandwich. He was son of Abraham Williams, of Marlboro', who m. a dau. of Rev. Robert Breck, of M.; was b. March 2, 1727; grad. Harvard College, 1744; ordained at Sandwich, June 14, 1749. He died Aug. 12, 1784, aged 58. His widow died Aug. 22, 1810; she was a remarkable woman, of great originality and strength of mind. They had ten children; the eldest, Sarah, b. Sept. 5, 1752; m. Oct. 31, 1771, Rev. Timothy Fuller, of Princeton. Their eldest son was Hon. Timothy Fuller, father of Sarah Margaret Fuller, late Countess Ossili, and Rev. Arthur Buckminster Fuller, Harvard College, 1843, who was a Chaplain in the late Rebellion and killed at Fredericksburg.

William Buckminster, b. Dec. 15, 1736, was son of Col. Joseph, Jr.; he m. Martha Barnes, dau. of Edward and Grace (Newton) Barnes, of Marlboro'. Their children were: William, John, Martha, and Barnes. He settled in Barre. He commanded the minute-men raised in Barre, and immediately marched his company to Cambridge, after the first blood was shed at Lexington. Was on the field the whole day at the battle of Bunker Hill, and was wounded in the right shoulder as they were retreating; although thus dangerously wounded, he continued in the army until the close of the war. He suffered from that wound all his life; he was a man of inflexible integrity and spotless character. He died in Barre, June 23, 1786.

FRANCES, b. Nov. 23, 1738; m. Col. Jonathan Brewer, of Framingham, b. Feb. 23, 1726. He was in the battle of Bunker Hill; was wounded in the arm; died in 1784.

Lawson Buckminster, b. Apr. 19, 1742; m. May 4, 1769, Mary Jones, b. June 19, 1750; dau. of Col. John and Mary (Mellen) Jones, of Hopkinton. Maj. Buckminster served in the war of the Revolution, and was Lieut. under Capt. Winch, at White Plains. He was Town Clerk twenty-five years; Treasurer several years. He inherited three hundred acres of land from his father's estate, where he built a house before his marriage; died there at the age of 89 years, 10 months, Feb. 26, 1832. His wife d. Sept 17, 1842, aged 92 years and 3 months. Had thirteen children, viz: Sally, Betsey, John, Ruth, Lawson, Nancy, William, Jones, Maria, Caroline, Fanny, Harriot, Elizabeth.

Mrs. Ann Maria Buckminster Stevens, dau. of Lawson, of the children just named, resides in Philadelphia. Her husband is Professor of Chemistry and Philosophy in Girard College.

Mrs. Lydia H. Buckminster, second wife of William Buckminster, of the above children, resides in West Roxbury, Mass., and has contributed much to the Buckminster portion of this record. She was born Nov. 26, 1818. Her maiden name was Lydia Nelson Hastings, dau. of Jonathan and Nancy (Adams) Hastings, of Brighton (now a part of Boston, Mass.) Her husband, William Buckminster, entered Harvard College in the class of 1809, but did not graduate, as "the great rebellion" occurred in 1807, and he took part, as he thought, with the oppressed and left college, studied law and was admitted in 1811 to the Middlesex bar, and continued in the practice until 1839; he then became one of the proprietors and sole editor of the *Boston Cultivator*. In 1841 he established an agricultural paper in Boston, the *Massachusetts Ploughman;* was the only editor about four years, when his eldest son, Wm. J. Buckminster, of Harvard College, 1835, was associated with him; (the son died March 2, 1878). He continued this connection until 1862, when he retired to his father's homestead, a portion of the one thousand acres originally owned by his ancestor, Col. Joseph Buckminster, as early as 1693. He gave some attention to inventing, he taking patents for a horse rake, a corn planter, a mill gate, &c.

He died June 9, 1865, and is buried near the Buckminster tomb in Framingham.

His daughter, Mrs. Ellen Buckminster Stone, by first wife, Sally Larrabee, of Malden, resides in Framingham.

Thomas Buckminster, b. Aug. 8, 1751; m. Hannah Rice, of Framingham, dau. of David and Hannah Winch Rice. She d. July 1, 1793, aged 42, and he married (2d), Feb. 4, 1794, Kezia (Perry) Bacon, widow of Wm. Bacon, and dau. of Abel and Kezia (Morse) Perry. He died in Framingham, July 7, 1826. She died Feb., 1833; had thirteen children.

5. Thomas Buckminster, son of Col. Joseph, and brother of Elizabeth (Buckminster) Wood, b. 1699; m. March 1, 1722, Sarah Baxter, of Medfield; had ten children; removed to Brookfield, Mass.

Her sister, Mary Baxter, m. Rev. John Gardner, whose daughter, Katherine Gardner, m. Jonathan Wood, of Stow, son of Jeremiah, thus connecting the Buckminster and Baxter families with both the Jeremiah and John branches of the Wood family.

6. Sarah, dau. of Col. Joseph Buckminster, b. 1702; m. June 23, 1720, Dr. Bezaleel Rice, of Framingham, son of David and Hannah (Walker) Rice; had six children. (Dr. Rice may have been a brother of Josiah Rice, second husband of Elizabeth (Buckminster) Wood).

7. Sybilla, b. 1705; m. Jan. 24, 1728, John White, of Framingham. Had five children.

8. Zerviah, b. July 26, 1710; m. Dec. 19, 1729, William Brintnal, of Framingham, son of Thomas and Hannah (Willard) Brintnal; Yale College, 1721. Was a teacher in Sudbury

and Rutland several years. He also was a minister; died in 1745; interred in the Buckminster lot, Framingham. Had five children.

The family have been honored in its descendants in every generation. The names Thomas, Joseph, Lawson, William, have been conspicuous in different generations. The family—both men and women—have been leaders in public affairs in their own sphere.

Within the cemetery at Framingham, Mass., is a very large and beautiful family yard; an iron fence surrounds it all. In different parts are representatives of the later generations.

Also the following:

"Anno Domini, 1771.
Under this monument lies
JOSEPH BUCKMINSTER, ESQ.,
aged 81 years.
One worthy in his day."

His mother, two wives and many of his descendants are buried there.

DESCENDANTS

OF

CAPT. JOHN WOOD,

AND

ELIZABETH (BUCKMINSTER),

HIS WIFE.

"THE WOOD BROTHERS."

JEREMIAH, born 1678; married 1709; died 1730.
JOHN; married 1705; died 1725.

Joseph Wood

National Biographical Publishing Co.

CAPT. JOHN WOOD.

John Wood, brother of Jeremiah Wood, has been traced from the date of his marriage with the oldest daughter of Col. Joseph Buckminster, of Framingham, Mass.

The following is from the Town Records of Framingham:

CHILDREN OF JOHN (3001)
AND
ELIZABETH (3002) (BUCKMINSTER) WOOD.

3003. John Wood, b. July 24, 1707.
3004. Mary Wood, b. Aug. 4, 1709.
3005. Elizabeth Wood, b. March 3, 1712; d. Apr. 13, 1714.
3006. Benjamin Wood, b. Apr. 15, 1714.
3007. Elizabeth Wood, b. Aug. 4, 1716.
3008. Thomas Wood, b. Sept. 9, 1719.
3009. Joseph Wood, b. Aug. 3, 1722.
3010. Samuel Wood, birth not recorded in Framingham.

Samuel's birth was probably recorded in Hopkinton, as the town completed its organization March 25, 1724, less than a year and eight months after the birth of Joseph, and the father, John Wood, was elected one of the Selectmen. Four sons and one daughter were married in Hopkinton. In the Church Records, May 21, 1723—

"*Voted:* That Mr. John Wood and John How take care that we are constantly provided with a minister to preach with us on Sabbath days."

John Wood was also one of the fifteen original members of the church there, which was organized Sept. 2, 1724, and on the same day the Rev. Samuel Barrett was ordained pastor.

The original members were:

SAMUEL BARRETT,
WILLIAM MONTGOMERY,
*ROBERT HAMILTON,
*SAMUEL WARK,
*BENJAMIN BURNAP,
ROBERT COOK,
*ELNATHAN ALLEN—(See Ward's History of Shrewsbury concerning Allen),
JOHN WOOD,
JOSEPH HAVEN,
ROBERT HUSTON,
*WILLIAM DUNAGHOI,
*PATRICK HAMILTON,
*OBADIAH ALLEN,
JACOB GIBBS.

Those marked with a star (*) were originally from the north part of Ireland.

This indicates that the brothers, John and Jeremiah Wood, were not from Ireland. The tradition is that they were of English origin.

There is a deed in the possession of Col. Albert Wood, of Woodville, Mass., and on record at Cambridge, given Nov. 1, 1714, by "Joseph Buckminster, of Framingham, to *Elnathan Allen*, of Sudbury, in the aforesaid County of Middlesex, yeoman, and *John Wood*, of Framingham aforesaid, yeoman, by each of them one hundred and fifty pounds thereof, &c., containing three hundred acres, situate, lying between townships of Marlboro and Sherborn, in the County aforesaid, which said Cedar Swamp is called, or known by the name of White Hall, and was, together with the uplands thereunto belonging, granted and confirmed unto me, the said Joseph Buckminster, by the Honorable General Court or Assembly of the above province of the Massachusetts Bay, at their session begun and held in Boston in the month of May, in the present year of our Lord, one thousand seven hundred and fourteen (as by Records of said Court may more fully and at large appear)," &c.

Elnathan Allen and John Wood also purchased of the Daniels's two hundred acres, Sept. 12, 1715, and also of and in a saw mill standing on a part of the farm by them purchased of Joseph Buckminster, Esq., called White Hall, all of which premises are situate in Hopkinton. There was an Indenture of Partition of their estate between Allen and Wood, and between Wood and Allen, dated Nov. 25, 1720. John Wood died in Aug., 1725. Elnathan Allen removed to Shrewsbury, Mass.

"An inventory of all goods and chattels of John Wood, Gentleman, deceased," was prized at Hopkinton, on the 14th day of October, 1725, by Henry Walker, Joseph Haven, and Benjamin Burnap, which amounted to 863 pounds, 6 shillings.

The settlement of the estate was long delayed. It was ordered Registered Jan. 27, 1734. Entered Lib. 20, pp. 201, 2, 3, 4.

The following will explain the manner of distribution:

"CAMBRIDGE, Oct. 18, 1731.

This day, upon my citation appeared John Wood, eldest son of the deceased within named, and Daniel Stone, husband of Mary, one of the deceased's daughters, as also Josiah Rice, who married sd. deceased's Widow, together with said Widow, and the returns of the Commissioners within named being read, it appeared that the greatest part of the deceased's Land after the widow's Thirds were set off, were set to said John, and he having refused to accept thereof, and the same being offered to said Stone, he also refused, and whereas the rest of the children are all under age, I direct said Commissioners to distribute the remaining two-thirds of said deceased's estate among sd. deceased's children Viz: Two shares thereof to the eldest son, and to all the rest one Single Share.

JON[N] REMINGTON,
Judge Probate."

Benj. Burnap, Henry Walker, Ebenezer Lock, of Hopkinton, and John Gleazen of Framingham were the Commissioners.

The names of the heirs were Elizabeth Wood alias Rice, Widow's thirds; John, eldest son; Daniel Stone, husband of deceased's child Mary; Benjamin, Elizabeth, Thomas, Joseph and Samuel.

The administration account was dated July 29, 1726, and had this heading:

"The account of Elizabeth Wood, Relict, Widow and administratrix of the estate of Mr. John Wood, late of Hopkinton, in the County of Middlesex, deceased Intestate."

At Cambridge, Oct. 4, 1728, Josiah Rice and Elizabeth Wood alias Rice, made oath to it, and to the heading was added: "now the wife of Josiah Rice, of Framingham in said County, Husbandman." Rev. Mr. Swift reported the marriage, but it is recorded "May 6, 1728. Josiah Rice and Elizabeth Hood, both of Framingham, were married." In the Report of the apprizers of the estate of John Wood, it is written "Capt. John Whood," but in no place so written by members of the family. In Rev. Mr. Parkman's diary, who was about to settle at Westboro, from Watertown, he says: "Returning after I had secured my call, I stopped at Hopkinton at 'Mr. Whood's,' where I fared sumptuously on roast goose, roast pea-hen, baked stuffed venison, beef, pork, &c."

After dinner, he adds: "we smoked a pipe, and read Gov. Shute's 'Memorial to the King.'" This was in 1723. He probably stopped at the house of John Wood, whom he heard called Mr. Whood. His marriage, in Framingham in 1705, is recorded unmistakably John Wood. The Church records of Framingham were lost during Mr. Swift's ministry. A little private journal in the form of a Sabbath diary, kept by Mr. Swift, and extending from Dec. 30, 1716, to July 14, 1728, which the writer has seen, is credited with the following: "John Hood, Fence viewer, 1712, dismissed to found a Church in Hopkinton, Aug. 30, 1724," and was probably the Capt. Hood buried in Hopkinton, Aug. 22, 1725. There was no John Hood among the original members of the Church in Hopkinton, but there was a John Wood.

The mistake of Mr. Swift was very likely caused by the improper pronunciation, but it could be caused by mistaking a W for an H, in some cases, in his diary. His error has been copied by some Genealogists. There are more than one hundred conveyances of land in the index of Hopkinton and Upton lands from 1743 to 1833, by the name of Wood, *but not one by the name of Hood.*

The will of Josiah Rice was made March 2, 1745; was proved Aug. 26, 1745.

EXTRACTS FROM WILL.

"I give my son-in-law, Samuel Wood, one piece of land, containing about twelve acres, be more or less, lying near the Mansion House of Capt. John Wood, late of Hopkinton, deceased, bounded" &c.

"I give and bequeath unto my well beloved wife, Elizabeth, all the remainder of my estate, Real and Personal, wherever it may be found, to be held and enjoyed by her and her heirs forever."

ITEM. I appoint my well beloved wife, Elizabeth, and my son-in-law, Joseph Wood, my Executors.

JOSIAH RICE.

Witnessed by

SAMUEL BARRETT (REV.),
ANN BARRETT."

The same year he gave one-third part of his Grist-Mill to Joseph Wood for five shillings. Other gifts may have been made. Joseph and Samuel were the youngest and were little children when Josiah Rice became their step-father.

JOHN WOOD (3003), the oldest son; m. in Hopkinton, Mary How, in 1727.

MARY WOOD (3004); m. Daniel Stone.

ELIZABETH (3005); b. Mar. 3, 1711–12; d. Apr. 13, 1714.

BENJAMIN WOOD (3006), b. Apr. 15, 1714; m. at Hopkinton, Martha Chamberlain, 1737; had John, b. Apr. 22, 1739.

ELIZABETH WOOD (3007), b. Aug. 4, 1716; m. Thomas Mellen; d. Feb. 25, 1775, aged 58. She left numerous descendants.

THOMAS WOOD (3008), b. Sept. 9, 1719; m. at Hopkinton, Mary Taylor, in 1740; had Thomas; Samuel, b. Dec. 21, 1746; Elizabeth, b. Dec. 11, 1748; John and Benjamin, b. Apr. 30, 1751.

JOSEPH WOOD (3009), b. Aug. 3, 1722; m. Martha Gibson, 1742; had JOSEPH, b. Apr. 18, 1748; HANNAH, b. July 29, 1750; William, second William and Samuel, by wife Martha. She died, aged 33, in 1754; by second wife, Mary Goodwin, Joseph Wood had Polly; WILLIAM, b. in Hopkinton, Oct. 23, 1760; SAMUEL, b. 1761; NATHANIEL GOODWIN, b. in Hopkinton, Aug. 4, 1764; John, Sally, Elizabeth and Martha.

SAMUEL WOOD (3010). He was the youngest son of John and Elizabeth (Buckminster) Wood, and the one to whom was willed some real estate, Mar. 2, 1745, by his step-father, Josiah Rice.

CAPT. JOSEPH WOOD.

Col. Albert Wood, of Woodville, Mass., in a brief sketch of his ancestors, says of his grandfather, "Capt. Joseph Wood (3009), a man of good character, and held important offices in Hopkinton, one of which was a commission as Captain under the King of England." He died at his home in Hopkinton. His gravestone now stands in the old burying-ground, Hopkinton Centre. The following may now be found upon his gravestone:

"Capt. Joseph Wood
Died Sept. 1785, in his 64th year."

On his right lies Martha, his first wife, who died 1754, aged 33, and three sons; William, aged 16 mo.; and William the second, aged 12 years; Samuel, aged 8 years.

On the left lies Polly, the daughter by his second wife, died Apr., 1776, in her 8th year. An inscription on a small stone at the foot reads as follows: "Capt. Joseph Wood and five of his children."

The widow of Capt. Joseph remained a widow for some time; married John Chamberlain, of Hopkinton. John Chamberlain died. The widow remained at Hopkinton Centre for some time, then removed to her son's, William Wood, where she lived a part of the time, and a part with her daughter. She died at her son William's, Feb. 5, 1820, and was buried at Hopkinton, aged 85 years.

The request for administration of Capt. Joseph's estate, was made Oct. 7, 1785. Joseph Wood, of Grafton, Physician, was made administrator. Joseph, the eldest son, asked for but a single share. William was to have the children's share of the estate and pay to his brothers and sisters, viz: Joseph, Samuel, Nathaniel Goodwin,

Hannah, Martha, Sally, Elizabeth and John, their respective shares.

At the close of the settlement and distribution account of said estate, by the Committee appointed, the following certificate and signatures are found in the Probate Records:

"This may certify to the Honorable Judge of Probate, that the subscribers are fully satisfied and contented with the preceding.

Mary Chamberlain,	Samuel Haven,
Joseph Wood,	Isaac Haven,
William Wood,	Sally Wood,
Samuel Wood,	John Newton,
Nathaniel G. Wood,	Joseph Wood, Guardian for John Wood."

DR. JOSEPH WOOD.

I quote from History of Grafton, Mass.

3011. Dr. Joseph Wood, son of Capt. Joseph, b. in Hopkinton, April 18, 1748; m. Miriam Collester.

"Dr. Wood was born in that part of Hopkinton now known by the name of Woodville.

He probably removed to Grafton soon after marriage. He was the physician of the town, and practiced much in the adjoining towns and villages.

Besides being Doctor, he carried on an extensive farm and store in which he sold West India goods. He became quite wealthy and was much respected. His residence was situated on the west side of the common. Was several years Justice of the Peace. A man of decided character, strong convictions of what he thought was right, and liberal in his religious and political views. He held important town offices and was often Representative to the Legislature. He died Oct. 13, 1820.

CHILDREN.

MIRIAM, b. Nov. 28, 1774; d. June 3, 1776.
MIRIAM, b. Nov. 4, 1779; m. Reuben Jenks and —— Holt. Removed to Royalston.
JOSEPH, b. May 20, 1783; m. Phebe Wood.
COLLESTER, b. May 30, 1786; m. Sarah Bowen; 2nd, Eliza Wood.
HARRY, b. Mar. 4, 1791; m. Sarah Brown; d. childless, Aug. 4, 1838.

JOSEPH WOOD, son of Dr. Joseph, b. May 20, 1783; m. Phebe Wood, b. May 19, 1785.

CHILDREN OF JOSEPH AND PHEBE.

PHEBEAN, b. May 3, 1804; m. —— Haskell.
ADELIA, b. Nov. 4, 1805; d. May 19, 1813.
JOSEPH S., b. June 10, 1807; went west.
CLARISSA E., b. Nov. 19, 1809; m. George Bailey; residence Worcester.
WILLIAM F., b. Sept. 27, 1811; m. Emily Curtis.
LEANDER S., b. June 5, 1814; d. Sept. 3, 1839.
AUGUSTUS H., b. July 13, 1816; m. and went west.
LUTHER W., b. Aug. 23, 1818; m. Eunice Gould.

COLLESTER WOOD, son of Dr. Joseph, b. May 30, 1786; m. Sarah Bowen; 2nd, Eliza Wood. He removed to New Boston, Conn., and died there Oct. 2, 1850.

CHILDREN.

1. CHARLES C., b. Jan. 4, 1810; m. Sarah ——, and Harriet Barnes; removed to Dudley.

2. Edwin H., b. Dec. 6, 1811; m. Caroline Chase.

3. Albion B., b. Nov. 4, 1813; m. and removed to Madison, Indiana.

4. Gilbert H., b. Oct. 3, 1816; m. Elizabeth ——, and removed to Iowa. Twins; Sarah C. and Susan A., b. Mar. 2, 1819; both died young."

HANNAH WOOD.

3012. Hannah Wood, dau. of Capt. Joseph, was born July 29, 1750, in Hopkinton, Mass.; m. Samuel Haven, of Hopkinton, Oct. 11, 1770; they afterwards removed to Shrewsbury, Mass., where she died in 1807. The children were all born in Hopkinton:

Samuel, b. May 20, 1773.
Lawson, b. May 14, 1775; d. in Shrewsbury; unmarried.
Joseph, b. Dec. 27, 1776.
Mary, b. Sept. 19, 1778; m. Harvey Nolen, of Boston, Feb. 12, 1804.
Fanny, b. Sept., 1780; m. Col. Joseph Valentine, of Hopkinton, in 1799, and died in 1841. Col. Valentine was a prominent citizen of Hopkinton.
Moses, b. July 7, 1782.
Nancy, bap. May 2, 1786; m. Caleb Leland, Nov. 9, 1805; she died 1810, leaving no issue.
Hannah; bap. Jan. 18, 1789; m. James Hamilton, of Brookfield, Oct. 27, 1805.
Gilbert Wood Haven; bap, Nov. 29, 1795.
Thomas Bucklin; bap. in Shrewsbury, Mass., 1803.

Samuel Haven, the father of the above, was born Dec. 9, 1751; he was son of Dea. Moses Haven, of Hopkinton, b. 1732, who was son of Joseph, b. 1689, and was ruling elder in Hopkinton, 1731 and afterwards, whose father, Moses, was a deacon in Hopkinton, b. in Lynn. 1667., whose father, Richard, came from England, 1645.

3013. SAMUEL WOOD, son of Capt. Joseph, located in Grafton, Mass. (Records further on).

3014. MARTHA, dau. of Capt. Joseph Wood; m. Isaac Haven.

3015. SALLY, dau. of Capt. Joseph; m. ——— Larned (probably Aaron). He built the first hotel at Nahant; afterwards removed to Lansingburg, N. Y., and died there.

3016. ELIZABETH, another dau. of Capt. Joseph Wood; m. John Newton.

3017. JOHN WOOD, son of Joseph, was married and had two children,—a son and a daughter; he died about 1809 or 10.

3018. NATHANIEL GOODWIN WOOD. (Records near the close of the book).

MAJ. WILLIAM WOOD.

3019. MAJ. WILLIAM WOOD, of Woodville, Mass., was born in Hopkinton, Oct. 23, 1760; was in the War of the Revolution, afterwards married Phebe Goulding, of Grafton, Mass., Oct. 10, 1786. They had thirteen children. Maj. William had the homestead of his father, Joseph Wood, which was a portion of the estate of his grandfather, Capt. John Wood, who purchased of his father-in-law, Col. Joseph Buckminster, of Framingham, Mass., in 1714. A Grist-mill was upon this farm. Maj. William Wood built a carding machine, and in 1810 sold his water power and some other lands to the Hopkinton Manufacturing Company, for the purpose of building a Cotton Mill, which was completed in 1811; he having an interest in it.

William Wood was an honest man, and filled important offices in the town of Hopkinton. Was elected Captain of the West company in Hopkinton, and was afterwards elected Major, which positions he filled with honor to himself.

He taught his children to "be up and doing while the day lasts," and impressed upon them the importance of regarding their word in all cases.

He died in Woodville, May 6, 1832, and was there entombed, where a fine granite monument is erected to the memory of his family and his descendants.

3020. PHEBE (GOULDING) WOOD, wife of Maj. William Wood, was born in Grafton, Mass., May 22, 1767. She was truly a helpmeet to her husband, a good manager in his household affairs. She made all persons comfortable who called at her house, and was beloved by all her children and others. She died April 22, 1851, and was nearly 84 years of age. She maintained her faculties up to her last sickness. Her portrait is from an old oil painting.

Phebe Wood

The Fall before her death she called a meeting of her children, an account of which was published in the newspapers of the day, which I will here record:

"A Family Meeting of the Widow and Children of the late William Wood was held in the old Homestead in Woodville, Mass., Oct. 16, 1850.

"Maj. William Wood, the husband of the aged widow, was a soldier in the Army of the Revolution. He was at Saratoga, New York, and at Rhode Island, engaged in active service, and also witnessed the scenes of Bunker Hill.

"After the war was over, he married and became the father of a large family of children. After his decease, his widow received a pension from his country for service rendered in the time of his country's need and peril.

"She was then over 83 years of age, and the remembrance of her husband, vivid and tender, and at the same time her love for her children quick and strong; wishing to give expression to her love of the deceased husband and the surviving children, before she should go hence to be no more, she summoned sons and daughters to meet at her house. They were obedient children and came.

"The eldest a woman of 63 years, the youngest a man of 37 years, and were present in all, five brothers and five sisters, and the widow of a deceased brother,—eleven; these, with their husbands, wives, children, and grandchildren.

"The greetings were glad and hearty as they came and took the aged mother by the hand and spoke of the Heavenly Father's dealings with them. The hours were very short. The family dinner was soon spread and partaken of with the interchange of sweet and tender remembrances of the past, in which the name of the patriot sire was often pronounced.

"As the day drew toward a close, the aged Mother conducted her eleven children into her parlor chamber.

"In the centre of the room stood a table bearing a new silver cup, surrounded by a circle of eleven silver cups of like fashion.

"The centre cup bore the name of the mother and deceased father.

"The old lady then stepped forward and took one from the eleven and presented it to her eldest daughter, a woman of 63 years. It bore the following inscription:

"'Given to ——— — ———, by Phebe Wood, as a part of pension received for services rendered in the U. S. Army by her father, William Wood, in 1776.'

"She received the cup with a mother's blessing and retired to her place.

"Then the next born came forward and received his cup and blessing, and so all in the order of their age until the youngest was blessed and held in his hand the cup bearing his own name and that of his father and mother surmounting the eagle of his country.

"As well as their hearts would allow they sang the beautiful hymn 'Blest be the tie that binds.'

"All hearts in that family circle melted and all eyes overflowed in deep and hallowed affection.

"The Word of God was then read and after mutual exhortation and encouragement, they all bowed together in prayer and thanksgiving to the God of their mercies, their fathers' God, the God of the widow and the fatherless. It was a sweet and heavenly scene.

"After singing the Christian Doxology, and giving the parting hand to the beloved mother and to each other, they separated to meet, probably, no more on earth. And in the homes of the sons and daughters may now be seen the cup on which conjugal and maternal love and patriotism have engraven their joint memorial.

"May the peace of God rest on that aged widow, and on her children and children's children to the latest generation."

The meeting was held Oct. 16, 1850. An anniversary meeting was held the next year, but the aged mother had passed to her final rest. Her youngest son, Samuel, moved "That we hold a Family Meeting of the children of William and Phebe Wood, on or about the 16th of October of each year, and sustain said meetings as long as two of the brothers or sisters are permitted to live." Which was carried.

Samuel was killed the following Spring by being caught in the machinery of his factory, but the meetings have been maintained, — thirty-three meetings up to the present time.

At the twenty-fourth meeting, seventy-four descendants being present, a resolution was adopted by the grand-children to sustain these meetings after the parents had passed away.

I copy from the Secretary's report of the thirty-third meeting:

"WOODVILLE, MASS., Oct. 16, 1884.

"The Thirty-third Reunion of the Descendants of Maj. William and Phebe Wood was held at Reservoir House, Thursday, Oct. 16, 1884.

"Children present as heads of families:

Mrs. Albert Wood.
Mr. and Mrs. Charles Seaver.
Mr. Edward J. Coolidge.

Grandchildren present, twenty-four.
Great-grandchildren, nineteen.
Great-great-grandchildren, two.

"Dinner was served at one o'clock.

"The meeting was called to order at 3 o'clock by the President, S. Eugene Wood.

"The report of the last meeting was read by the Secretary, Leroy E. Coolidge, and was adopted.

"L. E. Coolidge was chosen Secretary for the ensuing year.

"'*Voted:* S. Eugene Wood, Frank Wood and L. E. Coolidge be a Committee to attend to having the Portrait of Phebe Wood, wife of William Wood, bound in the Genealogy of the Wood Family.'

"Remarks were made by many present. Many feeling tributes were spoken in memory of Mrs. Miranda Corbett, who has met with us for the last time here, having departed this life Oct. 24, 1883.

"'*Voted:* to meet again one year from date at the same place.' The meeting closed with singing.

"Supper was served at six o'clock. A social time followed, after which the company disbanded, hoping to meet again the following year."

A statement is drawn from the records of the thirty-three meetings of the above family, giving the number present so far as recorded.

Years.	No. of children by birth or marriage present.	No. Grandchildren present.	No. Great grandchildren present.	No. Great-great-grandchildren present.
1850.	11			
1851.	20	20		
1852.	17	16		
1853.	18	16		
1854.	19	14		
1855.	17	many.		
1856.	15	11		
1857.	16	12		
1858.	15	14		
1859.	17	18		
1860.	15	16		
1861.	17	20		
1862.	13	10		

YEARS.	No. of children by birth or marriage present.	No. Grandchildren present.	No. Great-grandchildren present.	No. Great-great-grandchildren present.
1863.	17	Not recorded.		
1864.	13	"		
1865.	15	"		
1866.	15	19		
1867.	15	Not recorded.		
1868.	12	"		
1869.	11	"		
1870.	12	"		
1871.	12	"		
1873.	8	"		
1875.	9	(64 with Great-grandchildren),		1
1876.	9	34	20	0
1877.	8	31	19	0
1878.	10	33	18	0
1879.	7	27	18	0
1880.	9	16	18	1
1881.	7	33	26	0
1882.	6	24	15	1
1883.	5	29	19	2
1884.	4	24	19	2

FOURTH GENERATION.

CHILDREN OF WILLIAM (3019) AND PHEBE GOULDING (3020) WOOD.

ALL BORN IN HOPKINTON, MASS.

3021. POLLY WOOD, b. June 8, 1787; m. Oct. 13, 1805, Henry Morse (3022); d. Mar. 21 or 23, 1858.

3022. HENRY MORSE, b. in Westboro, Mass.; d. Apr. 8, 1828.

3023. NANCY WOOD, b. Dec. 31, 1788; m. James H. Lewis (3024); d. Aug. 27, 1819.

3024. James H. Lewis, of Marshfield, Mass.; d. Dec. 7, 1813.

3025. Hannah Wood, b. May 22, 1791; m. Eleazer Whitaker (3026); d. Dec. 22, 1871.

3026. Eleazer Whitaker, b. in Seekonk, Mass., Oct. 19, 1789; d. Oct. 4, 1864, aged 75 years.

3027. John G. Wood, b. Mar. 7, 1793; m. Elizabeth C. Read (3028); Rachel Ann Faxon (3029); d. Aug. 4, 1881, in his 89th year.

3028. Elizabeth C. Read, b. in Seekonk, Mass.; m. Nov. 16, 1815; d. Mar. 28, 1832.

3029. Rachel Ann Faxon, of Braintree, Mass.; m. Oct. 9, 1833; d. Sept. 22, 1872.

3030. Miranda Wood, b. Dec. 6, 1794; m. Carleton Corbett (3031); d. Oct. 24, 1883.

3031. Carleton Corbett, b. in Hopkinton; m. May 1, 1839; d. Feb. 29, 1868, aged 86 years.

3032. Russell Wood, b. Dec. 25, 1796; m. Sally Henshaw (3033); d. Sept. 18, 1845.

3033. Sally Henshaw, b. in Brookfield, Mass., Apr. 3, 1793; d. Aug. 14, 1857.

3034. Wm. Bonaparte Wood, b. Apr. 12, 1799; m. Sarah B. Underwood (3035); d. Jan. 14, 1880.

3035. Sarah B. Underwood, of Hopkinton; m. June 16, 1822; d. Feb. 14, 1868.

3036. Albert Wood, b. Aug. 18, 1801; m. Sophia J. Corbett (3037).

3037. Sophia J. Corbett, b. in Hopkinton, Mass.; m. May 25, 1829.

3038. Joseph Wood, b. Oct. 18, 1803; m. Phila T. Freeman (3039); d. Feb. 11, 1873.

3039. Phila T. Freeman, b. in Mendon, Mass., Feb. 12, 1809; m. Aug. 9, 1830; d. Jan. 23, 1882.

3040. Gilman Wood, b. Jan. 1, 1806; d. Jan. 1, 1811.

3041. Phebe Ann Wood, b. Feb. 4, 1808; m. Edward J. Coolidge (3042).

3042. Edward J. Coolidge, b. in Livermore, Me., Oct. 8, 1820.

3043. Martha Haven Wood, b. July 28, 1810; m. Charles Seaver (3044).

3044. CHARLES SEAVER, b. in Mansfield, Mass., Sept. 17, 1808; m. June 20, 1832.

3045. SAMUEL WOOD, b. Aug. 27, 1813; m. Sarah A. Arnold (3046); d. Apr. 21, 1853.

3046. SARAH AMANDA ARNOLD, b. at Coventry, R. I., July 27, 1818; m. Jan. 11, 1843.

COL. ALBERT WOOD, son of Maj. Wm. Wood, was born in Hopkinton, Aug. 18, 1801. He remained with his father until May 1, 1823, when he entered into partnership with his brother, Wm. B. Wood. They continued in the cotton business for nearly twenty years.

They built one stone mill and sixteen dwelling-houses. In November, 1846, the company sold the whole of the property to the City of Boston, in connection with the Water Works, for twenty-five thousand dollars. The Water Power was bought back by Col. Albert Wood and others in 1859. Col. Albert built several dams, and alone, or with another, built more than eighty houses. Was an active business man for many years. Was Colonel of the Fourth Regiment of Massachusetts Militia; held prominent town offices for several years; was twice elected Representative to the General Court.

He has contributed largely to everything that would help to build up the village of Woodville, his home, which was also the home of his father, his grandfather, and his great-grandfather Wood.

Col. Albert Wood's brothers, John G. Wood and Col. Russell Wood, were well known and successful Hotel keepers for many years.

HON. JOSEPH WOOD, son of Major William and Phebe (Goulding) Wood, was born in Hopkinton, Mass., Oct. 18, 1803. His portrait is found at the beginning of Part II. "He entered a cotton factory and had charge of one of the rooms before he was of age; afterwards formed a partnership with Stephen Benedict, and commenced business at Central Falls, Rhode Island, in 1831. This establishment was long known as the 'Benedict and Wood Mill.' In 1847 Mr. Wood also formed a partnership with Mr. John A. Adams and his own brother, Samuel Wood, known as Wood, Adams & Co.; engaged in manufacturing cotton thread. The company was known finally as the Central Falls Thread Co. In 1851, with his brother Samuel, he purchased the Richards Mill, and under the firm name of J. & S. Wood, engaged in manufacturing cotton cloth. This firm was dissolved by the death of Samuel, in 1853, who was killed by being caught in the machinery in the mill.

Samuel's interest being sold to Mr. John A. Adams, the mill was run by Wood and Adams until 1863, when it was sold to the Pawtucket Haircloth Company, and Wood & Adams became connected with the Stafford Manufacturing Company, Mr. Wood as Treasurer. In this position he remained till his death.

A man of great integrity, conscientiousness, industry and perseverance; he acquired a large estate and an enviable reputation. For more than twenty-five years he was superintendent of the Sabbath school of his church. Indeed, no good cause was neglected by him, and his name was a synonym for honor in all business circles. During the Rebellion he lent his voice, strength, and purse to the nation.

After long refusing official honors, he finally consented, in 1872, to accept the nomination of Senator from Lincoln, R. I., and was *unanimously* elected by both parties. He adorned the State Senate, as he had adorned every other circle of life. Mr. Wood died at his residence in Central Falls, Feb. 10, 1873."—[Extracts from biographical sketch of Joseph Wood, in History of Rhode Island.]

FIFTH GENERATION.

CHILDREN OF HENRY (3022) AND POLLY WOOD (3021) MORSE.

3047. William Henry, b. in Westboro, Apr. 13, 1806; m. Hannah Phipps Gamage (3048).

3048. Hannah Phipps Gamage, of Hopkinton, b. July 24, 1810; m. Apr. 9, 1829.

3049. Lovett, b. in Westboro, Apr. 3, 1808; m. Sally Atherton (3050); and Widow Elizabeth Wilbar Hatch (3051); d. May 4, 1880.

3050. Sally Atherton, b. in Dedham, Mass., Dec. 13, 1800; m. Sept. 25, 1828; d. Aug. 7, 1875.

3051. Widow Elizabeth Wilbar Hatch, b. in Taunton, Mass., Nov. 21, 1825; m. Apr. 12, 1876.

3052. Gilman W., b. in Grafton, Mass., Sept. 30, 1810; m. Fanny Atherton (3053); and Amoretta I. Olcott (3054).

3053. Fanny Atherton, b. in Mansfield, 1816; m. Sept. 4, 1834; d. July 19, 1864.

3054. Amoretta I. Olcott, b. in Sterling, 1833; m. June 5, 1866; d. June 8, 1876.

3055. Mary W., b. in Westboro, Feb. 26, 1813; m. Col. Orestes Forbush (3056); Benjamin F. Forbush (3057).

3056. Col. Orestes Forbush, b. in Westboro, July 18, 1797; m. Aug. 11, 1834; d. June 21, 1846.

3057. Benjamin F. Forbush, of Westboro, b. 1802; d. July 9, 1876.

3058. Solomon F., b. in Westboro, Mass., Feb. 7, 1815; m. Caroline Hathaway (3059); d. July 9, 1867.

3059. Caroline Hathaway.

3060. Benjamin F. Morse, b. in Hopkinton, Mass., March 25, 1819; m.

3061. Katie ——; d. 1863. Had four children.

CHILD OF JAMES H. (3024) AND NANCY WOOD (3023) LEWIS.

3062. James H. Lewis, Jr., b. in Marshfield, Mass.; d. (very young) Nov. 23, 1813.

CHILDREN OF ELEAZER (3026) AND HANNAH WOOD (3025) WHITAKER.

3063. Nancy L., b. in Hopkinton, Mass., Feb. 7, 1815; m. Caleb Jacobs (3064).

3064. Caleb Jacobs, b. in Northbridge, Mass.

3065. Mary C., b. in Hopkinton, June 4, 1817; m. Willard Broad (3066) Nov., 1841.

3066. Willard Broad, of Natick, Mass., b. Mar. 25, 1814.

3067. Martha Wood, b. Aug. 17, 1819, in Hopkinton.

3068. Sarah C., b. in Hopkinton, Jan. 21, 1822; m. William Hayward (3069), May 30, 1849.

3069. William Hayward, of North Reading, b. Feb. 20, 1816.

3070. William Wood, b. in Hopkinton, Feb. 27, 1824; m. Charlotte Parker; he was killed on a railroad, Jan. 12, 1882.

3071. Charlotte Parkér.

3072. James L., b. in Hopkinton, Jan. 25, 1826; m. Martha Rockwood (3073), Sept. 11, 1849.

3073. Martha Rockwood, b. in New York.

3074. Joseph Wood, b. in Hopkinton, Sept. 5, 1829; m. Mary E. Winslow (3075), of Lowell, Mass., Oct. 25, 1855. He is paymaster, Boston & Lowell R. R.

3075. Mary E. Winslow, dau. of Louis R. Winslow, Master Mechanic of Boston & Lowell R. R., b. in Lowell, Mar. 31, 1833.

3076. Henry, b. in Ashland, Mass., Nov. 12, 1832; d. Jan. 21, 1837.

CHILDREN OF JOHN G. (3027)

AND

ELIZABETH C. READ (3028) WOOD.

3077. Eliza Ann, b. 1816; d. July 2, 1842.
3078. Charles Austin; m. Caroline E. Wilson; res. Boston, Mass.
3079. Caroline E. Wilson.
3080. Mary M., b. 1819; d. Feb. 12, 1827.
3081. Samuel G.; m. Mary A. Piere; res. Boston, Mass.
3082. Mary A. Piere.
3083. Phebe G., b. Aug., 1826; d. July 29, 1827.

CHILD OF CARLETON (3031)

AND

MIRANDA WOOD (3030) CORBETT.

3084. Mary Miranda, b. in Woodville, Mass., Nov. 1, 1840; m. Sereno B. Johnson (3085).
3085. Sereno B. Johnson, b. in Southboro, Dec. 6, 1842.

CHILDREN OF RUSSELL (3032)

AND

SALLY HENSHAW (3033) WOOD.

3086. Russell Pembroke, b. in Freetown, Mass., Mar. 28, 1824; m. Mary Elizabeth Bigelow Wade (3087).
3087. Mary E. B. Wade, b. in Boston, Mass., Nov. 25, 1823; m. July 7, 1848.
3088. Bowers, b. in Taunton, Mass., July 25, 1826.
3089. Ann Frances, b. in Taunton, Mass., Nov. 28, 1828; m. Robert Henry Peckham (3090).
3090. Robert Henry Peckham, b. in Stonington, Conn., Feb. 26, 1822.
3091. Baylies, b. in Weston, Mass., Apr. 18, 1831; m. Malinda Hutchinson (3092), Apr. 16, 1857.
3092. Malinda Hutchinson, b. in Taunton, Mass., Nov. 16, 1836; d. March 17, 1875.

DESCENDANTS OF WILLIAM B. (3034)

AND

SARAH B. UNDERWOOD (3035) WOOD.

THEY HAD:

3093. Charles Parkman.
3094. Brick Parkman.
3095. Daniel Underwood.
3096. Charles Parkman.
3097. Martha Ann.
} died young.

3098. William Lewis Wood, b. Oct. 19, 1824, in Woodville, Mass.; m. Sula A. Carter (3099).

3099. Sula A. Carter, b. in Templeton, Mass., Mar. 28, 1831.

3100. John Goulding Wood, b. in Woodville, Mass., Mar. 28, 1834; m. Janette Wood (3101); d. Dec., 1879.

3101. Janette Wood, dau. of Robert Wood, of Hopkinton.

3102. Sarah Ann Wood, b. in Woodville, Mass., May 16, 1843; m. Leander A. Collins (3103); she d. June 14, 1885.

3103. Leander A. Collins.

3104. Susan B. Wood; d. aged 23 years.

3105. Emma, dau. of Wm. Lewis Wood, b. Dec. 17, 1853; d. Apr. 8, 1859.

3106. Cora, dau. of L. A. Collins, b. June, 1873.

3107. Viola R. A., dau. of John G. Wood, b. Mar. 26, 1861; m. Wendell E. Belknap (3108); have dau. Ella, b. 1883.

3108. Wendell E. Belknap, b. in Hopkinton, Mass.

CHILDREN OF ALBERT (3036)

AND

SOPHIA J. CORBETT (3037) WOOD.

ALL BORN IN WOODVILLE, MASS.

3109. Augusta, b. Feb. 22, 1830; m. Henry N. Comey (3110).

3110. Henry N. Comey, b. in Hopkinton, Mass.; m. Oct. 16, 1866.

3111. Granby Wood, b. May 26, 1831; boot manufacturer, Woodville, Mass.; m. Ellen Adams (3112); Mary E. Sanger (3113).

3112. Ellen Adams, of Woodville, b. Oct., 1835; d. May 24, 1859.

3113. Mary E. Sanger, of Framingham, Mass., b. Nov. 6, 1842.

3114. Sarah, b. Sept. 13, 1833; d. Nov. 14, 1833.

3115. Francis W. Wood, b. Aug. 12, 1835; boot manufacturer, Woodville, Mass.; m. Sarah Adams (3116).

3116. Sarah Adams, b. in Hopkinton, Mass., Nov. 7, 1843; m. Nov. 10, 1859.

3117. Mary Anna, b. Nov. 2, 1843; m. Joseph A. Gregory (3118).

3118. Joseph A. Gregory, b. in Grafton, Mass., Aug. 11, 1852; m. July 2, 1884.

3119. Helen Phebe, b. Feb. 27, 1852; m. George Kossuth Marshall (3120).

3120. George Kossuth Marshall, b. in Milford, Mass., Apr. 15, 1851; m. Nov. 12, 1873.

CHILDREN OF JOSEPH (3038) AND PHILA T. FREEMAN (3039) WOOD.

3121. Joseph Edward, b. in Central Falls, R. I., June 22, 1839; d. Feb. 19, 1841.

3122. Sarah Frances, b. in Central Falls, R. I., June 25, 1841; m. Rev. Joseph Ward (3123).

3123. Joseph Ward, of Perry Centre, N. Y.

3124. Emma Tiffany, b. in Central Falls, R. I., July 6, 1843; m. Rev. DeWitt Scovill Clarke (3125).

3125. DeWitt Scovill Clarke, b. in Chicopee, Mass., Sept. 11, 1841.

3126. Charles Denny, b. in Central Falls, R. I., Nov. 23, 1844; "Union Metallic Fastening Co.," Boston, Mass.; m. Amanda Eldora Walden (3127). Residence, Lincoln, R. I.

3127. Amanda Eldora Walden, b. in Millville, Mass., Dec. 10, 1848.

3128. Herbert Russell, b. in Central Falls, R. I., July 8, 1846; m. Jane Eliza Mathewson (3129).

3129. Jane Eliza Mathewson, b. in Providence, R. I., Apr. 15, 1849; d. Mar. 22, 1878.

3130. Albert Freeman, b. in Central Falls, R. I., Mar. 28, 1848; m. Martha Peterson (3131).

3131. Martha Peterson, b. in Lardels, Norway, July 2, 1849.

CHILDREN OF EDWARD J. (3042) AND PHEBE ANN WOOD (3041) COOLIDGE.

3132. Angenette Russell, b. in Woodville, Mass., Oct. 25, 1845; m. Marcus M. Woods (3133).

3133. Marcus M. Woods, b. in Woodville, Mass., Oct. 8, 1842.

3134. Leroy Emerson, b. June 12, 1847, in Woodville, Mass.; m. Josie M. Gamage (3135).

3135. Josie M. Gamage, b. in Woodville, Mass., June 13, 1849.

CHILDREN OF CHARLES (3044) AND MARTHA H. WOOD (3043) SEAVER,

WOODVILLE, MASS.

3136. Samuel, b. Feb. 7, 1833; m. Mary E. Adams (3137). He d. Aug. 9, 1876.

3137. Mary E. Adams, b. in Hopkinton.

3138. Benjamin F., b. Sept. 5, 1835; d. May 2, 1836.

3139. Edward B., b. July 13, 1836; d. July 9, 1840.

3140. Charles H., b. Sept. 1, 1838; m. Alice Honey (3141).

3141. ALICE HONEY, of Springfield, California.

3142. EDWARD B. SEAVER, b. Jan. 5, 1841; m. FRANCES BROOKS (3143).

3143. FRANCES BROOKS, b. in New York.

3144. AUGUSTUS, b. Nov. 10, 1842 (Wood & Seaver), "Union Metallic Fastening Co.," Boston, Mass.; m. Marian Thayer (3145).

3145. MARIAN THAYER, b. in Milford, Mass.

3146. AUGUSTA, b. Nov. 10, 1842; d. Aug, 25, 1845.

3147. ELLEN M., b. Mar. 15, 1845; m. W. S. Southworth (3148).

3148. WINFIELD SCOTT SOUTHWORTH, b. in Easton, Mass., res. Brockton, Mass.

3149. ANNETTE, b. Mar. 8, 1847; d. Apr. 12, 1849.

3150. RUSSELL W., b. Aug. 8, 1849; d. May 20, 1851.

3151. JOSEPH W., b. Feb. 23, 1854; d. Feb. 3, 1855.

CHILDREN OF SAMUEL (3045)

AND

SARAH AMANDA ARNOLD (3046) WOOD.

3152. SAMUEL EUGENE, b. in Central Falls, R. I., Nov. 22, 1843; m. Kate Bassett Pond (3153).

3153. KATE BASSETT POND, b. in Bridgeport, Conn., Aug. 2, 1850.

3154. FRANK ARNOLD, b. in Central Falls, Mar. 12, 1846; d.

3155. RUTH ISABEL, b. in Central Falls, Mar. 7, 1847; m. Frank A. Church (3156).

3156. FRANK A. CHURCH, b. in Providence, R. I., Apr. 20, 1844.

3157. ELLA GOULDING, b. in Central Falls, Aug. 11, 1849; m. Joseph A. Dodge (3158).

3158. JOSEPH A. DODGE, b. in Grafton, Mass., Apr. 21, 1846.

3159. ALICE AMELIA, b. in Central Falls, Dec. 4, 1851; the mother, Sarah A. (Arnold) Wood, d. 1885.

SIXTH GENERATION.

CHILDREN OF WM. HENRY (3047) AND HANNAH PHIPPS GAMAGE (3048) MORSE.

3160. CHARLES HENRY, b. in Hopkinton, Mass., May 25, 1830; d. Aug. 7, 1831.

3161. CHARLES HENRY, b. in Hopkinton, Aug. 10, 1832; m. Priscilla A. Stearns (3162), Dec. 11, 1867.

3162. PRISCILLA ALMENA STEARNS, b. in Upton, Mass., June 4, 1839.

3163. BETSEY GAMAGE, b. in Hopkinton, Mar. 16, 1836; m. Abner Holbrook Adams (3164), Nov. 25, 1869.

3164. ABNER HOLBROOK ADAMS, b. in Northboro, Mass., Dec. 8, 1834.

3165. FRANK WM., b. in Westboro, Mass., Apr. 8, 1852; m. Emily Dutton (3166); Abbie Maria Farrington (3167).

3166. EMILY DUTTON, b. in Boston, Mass., 1849; m. June 22, 1874; d. Apr. 27, 1879.

3167. ABBIE MARIA FARRINGTON, b. in Bellingham, Mass., Dec. 28, 1856; m. June 15, 1880.

LOVETT MORSE.

"MR. MORSE was a native of Westboro, Mass., and moved to Taunton, in 1827 or 1828, and was for several years engaged in the hotel business, from which he retired in 1840, turning his attention to financial matters. He was appointed one of the assignees of Crocker and Richmond in 1842, and assisted in settling their large estate. He was also associated with R. S. Dean, as the successors of the above firm in the manufacture of machinery, for some years. He became a director in the Taunton Bank, and was its president for nearly twenty years, retiring in 1869. As a financier he was very successful, accumulating a handsome property. In 1850 he was associated with his sons in the manufacture of nails and tacks, occupying the brick establishment now owned by the Copper Works; but relinquished the business, disposing of it to the above company amid the fluctuations of the war, in 1864. Since that time Mr. Morse has devoted his attention to his private financial affairs and his family, as a gentleman of leisure. He was formerly connected with St. Thomas parish, but subsequently joined the Broadway Congregational Church, which has been the frequent recipient of his liberal contributions, his counsel and co-operation as a member, for more than twenty years. Mr. Morse has been twice married; first with Miss Sally Atherton, by whom he leaves three sons; she died about five years since. His second wife, Mrs. Elizabeth (Wilbar) Hatch, survives him."—[Extract from Obituary notice.]

CHILDREN OF LOVETT (3049)

AND

SALLY ATHERTON (3050) MORSE.

3168. Ellen Maria, b. in Assonet, Aug. 8, 1829; d. Mar. 16, 1832.

3169. Henry Whitfield, b. in Taunton, Mass., June 25, 1831; m. Mary Elizabeth Shepard (3170), Oct. 28, 1857.

3170. Mary Elizabeth Shepard, b. in Wrentham, Mass., May 17, 1834.

3171. Hiram Augustus, b. Sept. 8, 1833; d. Aug. 26, 1834.

3172. Erastus, b. in Taunton, Sept. 5, 1836; m. Sarah Seabury Bassett (3173), Nov. 21, 1860.

3173. Sarah Seabury Bassett, b. in Taunton, Mass., Oct. 26, 1840; d. March 1, 1883.

3174. Francis Leroy, b. in Taunton, Feb. 9, 1844; m. Emma Louise Tisdale (3175), May 21, 1872.

3175. Emma Louise Tisdale, b. in Taunton, May 24. 1846.

CHILDREN OF GILMAN W. MORSE (3052)

BY FIRST WIFE,

FANNY ATHERTON (3053) MORSE.

3176. Alton J., b. in Westboro, Apr. 15, 1851; d. July 2, 1877.

BY SECOND WIFE,

AMORETTA I. OLCOTT (3054) MORSE.

3177. Grace E., b. in Westboro, Apr. 30, 1870.

CHILDREN OF COL. ORESTES (3056) AND MARY WOOD MORSE (3055) FORBUSH.

3178. Mary S., b. in Westboro, Dec. 13, 1835; m. Charles H. Williams (3179), Dec. 31, 1851; d. Oct. 5, 1878.

3179. Charles H. Williams, b. in New York City, Apr. 5, 1829.

3180. Henry W., b. in Westboro, Apr. 23, 1838; d. Jan. 29, 1840.

3181. Martha A., b. in Westboro, Dec. 12, 1840; d. June 5, 1844.

3182. William H., b. in Westboro, June 16, 1843; m. Alice J. Fisher (3183), May 20, 1869; d. Jan. 18, 1881.

3183. Alice J. Fisher, b. in Princeton, Mass., Oct. 27, 1846.

CHILDREN OF CALEB (3064)
AND
NANCY L. WHITAKER (3063) JACOBS.

3184. Henry Jacobs.
3185. Lucy Ann Jacobs.
3186. Martha Jane Jacobs.
3187. Charles Jacobs.

CHILDREN OF JAMES L. (3072)
AND
MARTHA ROCKWOOD (3073) WHITAKER.

3188. James E., b. in Ashland, Mass., Jan. 10, 1851; m. Adeline Louise (3189), dau. of Noah Harding, Oct. 22, 1873.
3189. Adeline Louise Harding, b. in Charlestown, Mass., June 28, 1850.
3190. Mabel, and Irvin; died in infancy.
3191. Milo R., b. in Ashland, Mass., July, 1856; m. Carrie E. (3192), dau. of N. C. Preble, Nov. 29, 1883.
3192. Carrie E. Preble, b. in Boston, Aug. 9, 1859.
3193. Joseph Wood, b. in Medford, Feb. 10, 1862.

CHILDREN OF JOSEPH WOOD (3074)
AND
MARY E. WINSLOW (3075) WHITAKER.

ALL BORN IN CAMBRIDGE, MASS.

3194. Louis Winslow, b. Aug. 15, 1856; d. Sept. 13, 1856.
3195. Mary L. Winslow, b. Nov. 3, 1859; d. Jan. 2, 1872.
3196. Josephine Wood, b. Dec. 18, 1866.

CHILDREN OF CHARLES A. (3078) AND CAROLINE E. WILSON (3079) WOOD.

3197. Mary M. Wood.
3198. Charles Wood, deceased.
3199. Louise Wood, deceased.

CHILDREN OF SAMUEL G. (3081) AND MARY A. P. (3082) WOOD.

3200. William, b. in Dorchester, Mass., Dec. 1, 1850; m. Harriet E. Pierce (3201).
3201. Harriet E. Pierce, b. in Milton, Mass.; m. June 3, 1880.
3202. John G.; d. June 4, 1858.
3203. Samuel G. Wood, Jr., b. in Dorchester, Mass., Nov. 5, 1854; m. Jennie F. Shiverick (3204).
3204. Jennie F. Shiverick, b. in Falmouth, Mass., Mar. 2, 1857; m. Aug. 3, 1875.

CHILD OF SERENO BURGESS (3085) AND MARY MIRANDA CORBETT (3084) JOHNSON.

3205. Mabel Corbett, b. in Woodville, Mass., Aug. 23, 1872.

CHILDREN OF ROBERT HENRY (3090) AND ANN FRANCES WOOD (3089) PECKHAM.

3206. Henry Russell, b. in Taunton, Mass., Oct. 21, 1849; d. Jan. 30, 1856.
3207. Emma Frances, b. in Stonington, Conn., Sept. 17, 1852; m. Benjamin W. Latham (3208).

3208. Benjamin W. Latham, b. in Noank, town of Groton, Conn., Nov. 20, 1849; m. June 16, 1873.
3209. Mary Malinda, b. in Groton, July 16, 1865.

CHILDREN OF HENRY N. (3110) AND AUGUSTA WOOD (3109) COMEY.

3210. Agnes A., b. in Woburn, Mass., Sept. 19, 1869.
3211. Mary A., b. in Woburn, Mass., Dec. 27, 1870.

CHILDREN OF GRANBY (3111) AND MARY E. SANGER (3113) WOOD.

ALL BORN IN WOODVILLE, MASS.

3212. Clarence Corbett, b. Aug. 10, 1865.
3213. Florence Augusta, b. Feb. 8, 1869.
3214. Edith Sanger, b. Aug. 27, 1874.

CHILDREN OF FRANCIS W. (3115) AND SARAH ADAMS (3116) WOOD.

3215. Fred. Albert, b. in Woodville, Mass., Sept. 4, 1862.
3216. Wilber A., b. in Woodville, Mass., Feb. 4, 1865.

CHILDREN OF GEORGE KOSSUTH (3120) AND HELEN PHEBE WOOD (3119) MARSHALL.

ALL BORN IN MILLVILLE.

3217. Jessie Corbett, b. July 14, 1874.
3218. Anna Wood, b. Nov. 5, 1877.
3219. Hilton Albert, b. Nov. 19, 1879.

CHILDREN OF JOSEPH (3123)
AND
SARAH FRANCES WOOD (3122) WARD.

ALL BORN AT YANKTON, DAKOTA TERRITORY.

3220. Joseph Wood, b. Nov. 12, 1871; d. Oct. 1, 1873.
3221. Ethel Tufts, b. July 15, 1873.
3222. Donald Butler, b. Oct. 1, 1876.
3223. Freeman, b. Aug. 9, 1879.
3224. Sheldon, b. Mar. 27, 1882.

CHILDREN OF DeWITT SCOVILL (3125)
AND
EMMA TIFFANY WOOD (3124) CLARKE.

3225. Garit DeWitt, b. in Clinton, Mass., Aug. 7, 1873.
3226. Leigh Freeman, b. in Clinton, Mass., Feb. 9, 1878.
3227. Hilda Goulding, b. in Salem, Mass., Sept. 25, 1883.

CHILD OF CHARLES DENNY (3126)
AND
AMANDA ELDORA WALDEN (3127) WOOD.

3228. Carrie Walden, b. in Brooklyn, N. Y., May 7, 1871.

CHILDREN OF HERBERT RUSSELL (3128)
AND
JANE ELIZA MATHEWSON (3129) WOOD.

3229. Ida Mathewson, b. in Pawtucket, R. I., Apr. 30, 1873.
3230. Joseph, b. in Pawtucket, R. I., Sept. 7, 1875.

CHILDREN OF ALBERT FREEMAN (3130) AND MARTHA PETERSON (3131) WOOD.

ALL BORN IN DAKOTA TERRITORY.

3231. Mabel, b. May 5, 1876.
3232. Emma Tiffany, b. Aug. 4, 1879.
3233. Charles Goulding, b. Nov. 22, 1880.
3234. Bertha Capron, b. June 11, 1883.

CHILDREN OF MARCUS M. (3133) AND ANGENETTE R. (3132) WOODS.

ALL BORN IN HOPKINTON, MASS.

3235. Bertha C., b. June 6, 1875.
3236. Effie L., b. Sept. 17, 1876.
3237. Clara L., b. June 23, 1881.

CHILD OF SAMUEL (3136) AND MARY E. ADAMS (3137) SEAVER.

3238. Charles W., b. in Ashland, Mass.

CHILDREN OF CHARLES H. (3140) AND ALICE HONEY (3141) SEAVER.

3239. Laura, b. in Springfield, Cal., Aug. 31, 1864.
3240. Franklin Chester, b. in Springfield, Cal., Dec. 17, 1867.
3241. Minnie, b. in California, Aug. 11, 1873.
3242. Charles, b. in Springfield, Cal., Apr. 5, 1875.

CHILD OF AUGUSTUS (3144) AND MARIAN THAYER (3145) SEAVER.

3243. Augustus Seaver, b. in Milford, Mass., Apr. 5, 1875.

CHILDREN OF SAMUEL EUGENE (3152) AND KATE BASSETT POND (3153) WOOD.

3244. Kenneth Foster, b. in Central Falls, R. I., May 24, 1873.

3245. Ruth Goulding, b. in Central Falls, Jan 29, 1875.

CHILDREN OF FRANK A. (3156) AND RUTH ISABEL WOOD (3155) CHURCH.

3246. Butler Lane, b. in Central Falls, May 6, 1873.

3247. Ernest Clinton, b. in Central Falls, Aug. 12, 1876.

CHILDREN OF JOSEPH A. (3158) AND ELLA GOULDING WOOD (3157) DODGE.

ALL BORN IN GRAFTON, MASS.

3248. Irving Bigelow, b. Jan. 5, 1876.

3249. Kathrina Arnold, b. Feb. 22, 1879.

3250. Louise Whitney, b. Mar. 5, 1881.

SEVENTH GENERATION.

CHILDREN OF CHARLES HENRY (3161)

AND

PRISCILLA A. STEARNS (3162) MORSE.

3251. EMMA, b. in Hopkinton, Feb. 12, 1869.
3252. WILLIAM STEARNS, b. in Hopkinton, Feb. 24, 1871.
3253. AGNES MARIA, b. in Hopkinton, Oct. 7, 1874.

CHILD OF HENRY WHITFIELD (3169)

AND

MARY ELIZABETH SHEPARD (3170) MORSE.

3254. FANNY, b. in Taunton, Mass., Aug. 24, 1858.

CHILDREN OF ERASTUS (3172)

AND

SARAH SEABURY BASSETT (3173) MORSE.

3255. JOHN LOVETT, b. in Taunton, Apr. 21, 1865.
3256. ELIZABETH BASSETT, b. in Taunton, Apr. 31, 1874; d. June 15, 1875.
3257. SALLY HOLMES, b. in Taunton, May 6, 1879.

CHILD OF FRANCIS LEROY (3174)

AND

EMMA LOUISE TISDALE (3175) MORSE.

3258. ELIZABETH TISDALE, b. in Taunton, Mass., May 15, 1881.

CHILDREN OF MARY S. FORBUSH (3178) AND CHARLES H. WILLIAMS (3179).

3259. CHARLES H. WILLIAMS, JR., b. in Westboro, Sept. 12, 1853.
3260. JENNIE S., b. in Westboro, Aug. 29, 1856; m. Mahlon L. Barber (3261).
3261. MAHLON L. BARBER; m. March, 1876.
3262. NELLIE G., b. in Westboro, Apr. 3, 1871; d. Apr. 12, 1875.
3263. MARY F., b. in Westboro, Oct. 8, 1873; d. Apr. 23, 1875.
3264. EVA I., b. in Westboro, June 20, 1876.

CHILD OF JAMES E. (3188) AND ADELINE LOUISE HARDING (3189) WHITAKER.

3265. CHESTER LELAND, b. in Somerville, Mass., Oct. 15, 1882.

CHILD OF MILO R. (3191) AND CARRIE E. PREBLE (3192) WHITAKER.

3266. SARAH B., b. in Somerville, Mass., Sept. 6, 1884.

CHILDREN OF SAMUEL G. (3203) AND JENNIE F. SHIVERICK (3204) WOOD, (JR.).

3267. FLORENCE MARY, b. in Neponset, Mass., Jan. 25, 1876.
3268. CARRIE S., b. in Neponset, Mass., Feb. 20, 1882.

CHILD OF BENJAMIN W. (3208)

AND

EMMA FRANCES PECKHAM (3207) LATHAM.

3269. Ethel Wood, b. in Noank, Conn., Dec. 30, 1883.

EIGHTH GENERATION.

CHILDREN OF JENNIE S. WILLIAMS (3260)

AND

MAHLON L. BARBER (3261).

3270. Leonard O. Barber, b. in Westboro, Mass., Dec. 17, 1876.

3271. Ernest L. Barber, b. in Westboro, Sept. 28, 1879.

SAMUEL WOOD.

"Samuel Wood, brother of Maj. William and Nathaniel, and half brother of Dr. Joseph, b. in Hopkinton, 1761; m. Sept. 28, 1788, Elizabeth Kimball, b. 1770; d. Sept. 15, 1824.

"He removed to this town from Woodville, Hopkinton, when quite a young man, and was employed by his brother, Dr. Joseph Wood, on his farm and in his store. He was noted for his activity. He was for a number of years the principal inn-keeper in the town. He erected the Grafton Hotel, and kept it until his death, Sept. 30, 1813.

CHILDREN.

1. Betsey, b. May 10, 1789; d. Sept. 12, 1792.
2. Samuel, b. Sept. 5, 1792; d. Sept. 13, 1792.
3. Samuel, b. Dec. 16, 1793; m. Sarah Bruce and Hannah P. Adams.
4. Betsey, b. Nov. 1, 1801; d. May 16, 1816.

"HON. SAMUEL WOOD, son of Samuel, b. Dec. 16, 1793; m. Sarah Bruce, d. June 1817; m. Hannah P. Adams. He was born in Grafton, and always resided here, with but the exception of one or two years of temporary absence.

"After the death of his father he became proprietor of the Hassanamisco House, which he conducted with success, and sold to Lovell Baker, Senior, when he purchased of Dr. Lamb and built him a fine residence.

"He was for a number of years a very large shoe manufacturer, in company with Noah Kimball; Wood, Kimball & Co. He held all the town offices,—town clerk, assessor, selectman, and representative for a number of years. He was also a member of the Senate of the Massachusetts legislature from the Worcester District, and a member of the council of Gov. George N. Briggs.

"During this time he was the most influential man in this section, especially in his town.

CHILDREN.

1. SARAH E., b. May 17, 1817; m. Nicholas H. Brigham; res. in New York city.
2. HANNAH M., b. Aug. 2, 1820; m. Rufus E. Warren.
3. AMELIA W., b. Dec. 23, 1823; d. unmarried.
4. JANE A., b. Dec. 2, 1827; d. Sept., 1875; unmarried."

—[History of Grafton, Mass.]

NATHANIEL GOODWIN WOOD.

NATHANIEL GOODWIN WOOD (3018), was born in Hopkinton, Mass., Aug. 4, 1764; m. Levina Hayden; Patty Green; Prudence Spooner.

Levina Hayden was born in Bridgewater, Mass., Apr. 1, 1773; died Feb. 14, 1819, at West Boylston, Mass.

Patty Green, b. in Northboro, Mass., Nov., 1772; d. Dec., 1829, at Hopkinton.

Prudence Spooner died in Westboro.

FOURTH GENERATION.

DESCENDANTS OF NATHANIEL GOODWIN (3018) AND LEVINA (HAYDEN) WOOD.

CHILDREN.

4272. MERRITT WOOD, b. in Grafton, Mass., Jan. 21, 1794; m. 1st, Belinda Holt (4273); 2d, Mary E. Fairbank (4274); d. Nov. 3, 1873, in Leominster.

4273. BELINDA HOLT, b. in West Boylston, Mass., Oct. 4, 1798; d. Dec. 17, 1845, in Leominster.

4274. MARY E. FAIRBANK, b. in West Boylston, Jan. 24, 1806; d. June, 1879, in Leominster.

4275. PATTY WOOD, b. in Grafton, Mass., Nov. 5, 1795; d. Oct. 30, 1796, in Grafton, Mass.

4276. NATHANIEL WOOD, b. in Holden, Aug. 29, 1797: m. Louise Holman (4277); d. Aug. 2, 1876, in Fitchburg, Mass.

4277. LOUISE HOLMAN, b. in Bolton, Nov. 30, 1803; residence, Fitchburg.

NATHANIEL WOOD graduated from Harvard University in the class of 1821,—was tutor of Mathematics there two years,—practised law in Fitchburg, Mass., till two years before his death. Often represented the town in the Massachusetts General Court,—was one of the influential citizens. Burns's epitaph would apply to him:—

"An honest man here lies at rest,
As e'er God with his image blest;
The friend of man, the friend of truth;
The friend of age, the guide of youth;
Few hearts, like his, with virtue warm'd,
Few heads, with knowledge so inform'd."

4278. JONATHAN WOOD, b. in Holden, Dec. 14, 1799; d. Nov. 16, 1819, in West Boylston.

4279. SABRINA WOOD, b. in Holden, Dec. 6, 1803; m. John O. Benthall (4280); d. March 26, 1883, in Leominster.

4280. JOHN O. BENTHALL, b. in East Greenwich, R. I.; d. Nov. 27, 1854, in Dubuque, Iowa.

4281. GOODWIN WOOD, b. in Westminster, Mass., Oct. 6, 1803; m. Sally Bascom (4282); Mrs. Mary L. Hale (4283); d. June, 1862, in Princeton.

4282. SALLY BASCOM.

4283. MARY L. HALE, b. in Newburyport; died there; no children.

4284. A DAUGHTER, b. in Westminster, Aug. 10, 1805; lived only a few days.

4285. MARY WOOD, b. in Westminster, Mar. 6, 1808; m. George Leonard (4286); d. in Ripon, Wis., Aug. 10, 1876.

4286. GEORGE LEONARD, b. in Westminster, Nov. 29, 1800; d. in Lowell, Mass., July 17, 1870.

4287. MOSES WOOD, b. in Westminster, Oct. 10, 1811; m. Mary Ann Bridges (4288); Julia Ann Howe (4289); Mrs. Addie M. Blake (4290).

4288. MARY ANN BRIDGES, b. in Holliston, Mass., June 12, 1811; d. in Westboro, May 29, 1845.

4289. JULIA ANN HOWE, b. in Worcester, Mass., Oct. 6, 1825; d. in Westboro, Aug. 17, 1856.

4290. ADDIE M. BLAKE, b. in Walpole, Mass., Aug. 31, 1830.

Moses Wood is a jeweller in Westboro, Mass., and has been in the same business there for forty-eight years.

4291. Otis Wood, b. in West Boylston, Sept. 1, 1813; m. Josephine Lucena Keach (4292); d. in Princeton, Mass., Aug. 14, 1878.

4292. Josephine L. Keach, b. in St. Johnsbury, Vt., Dec. 13, 1823; residence, Princeton; no children.

FIFTH GENERATION.

CHILDREN OF MERRITT (4272) AND BELINDA HOLT (4273) WOOD.

4293. Alonzo Hayden, b. in West Boylston, Oct. 12, 1818; m. Emily Jane Gerden (4294); Phebe H. Stratton (4295); d. in Worcester, Dec. 24, 1870.

4294. Emily Jane Gerden, b. in Hancock, Me.; d. in Lowell, May, 1845.

4295. Phebe H. Stratton, b. in Hancock, Me.; residence, Boston, Mass.

4296. Martha Levina, b. in West Boylston, Apr. 13, 1820; m. Henry Fairbank Holt (4297); res. Leominster.

4297. Henry F. Holt, b. in South Berwick, Me., Nov. 25, 1816; d. Dec. 23, 1882, in Leominster. Mrs. Holt has done much to secure the records of her branch.

4298. Merritt Milton, b. Sept. 9, 1823; d. Mar. 4, 1824, in Leominster.

4299. Nathaniel Goodwin, b. in Leominster, Dec. 5, 1824; m. Maria Sizer Johnson (4300); residence, Boston, Mass.

4300. Maria S. Johnson, b. in Leominster, Mar. 22, 1826.

NATHANIEL GOODWIN WOOD.

Nathaniel Goodwin Wood (4299), son of Merritt, and grandson of Nathaniel Goodwin Wood, went early into the jewelry business. He was with Moses Wood for a time, then engaged with Wm. P. McKay & Co., of Boston, to finish his trade and learn the general business; he remained with them about three years, after which he went to Saco, Maine,—established a jewelry store on Factory Island, so called;—after about eighteen months he established another store in Biddeford, Me., and continued the two for about eighteen months.

He moved to Boston in 1848, and has been eminently successful there, and is a man of wealth and influence.

He does not forget the home of his father, and is a large real estate owner there, as I learn from the tax list of Leominster, Mass. He has been ably assisted by his sons in his business.

His portrait is presented upon the opposite page.

CHILDREN OF NATHANIEL (4276)

AND

LOUISE HOLMAN (4277) WOOD.

4301. Frederick Nathaniel, b. in Fitchburg, Mass., May 2, 1829; d. Dec. 6, 1837.

4302. Louise, b. in Fitchburg, July 6, 1832; d. June, 1833.

4303. Louise Holman, b. in Fitchburg, July 14, 1834; m. James Ripley Wellman (4304); residence, Fitchburg, Mass.

4304. James Ripley Wellman, b. in Cornish, N. H., July 27, 1829; d. in Cornish, N. H.

Dr. Wellman studied medicine at Dartmouth College, N. H.; also in Europe, and practised his profession in Fitchburg, Mass.

N. G. Wood

CHILDREN OF JOHN O. (4280)

AND

SABRINA WOOD (4279) BENTHALL.

4305. JOHN MILTON, b. in Princeton, Mass., Sept. 12, 1832; m. Mary Elizabeth Stratton (4306); Elizabeth D. Wilson (4307); res. Quasqueton, Iowa.

4306. MARY E. STRATTON, b. in Hancock, Me., Mar. 20, 1837; d. in Quasqueton, Iowa, Mar. 20, 1858.

4307. ELIZABETH D. WILSON, b. in Middlebury, N. Y., Dec. 18, 1839.

J. M. Benthall enlisted in the 10th Minnesota Vol. Infantry, Aug. 26, 1862; was discharged Aug. 26, 1865. 1st year in Minnesota in the Indian War; 2d year, St. Louis, Memphis and Nashville; 3d year, New Orleans, Mobile, and in battles of Tupelo, Nashville, Spanish Fort, taking of Mobile, &c.

4308. MARY LEVINA, b. in Princeton, Oct. 30, 1834; m. Julian Victor Keyes (4309); d. in Lawrence, Sept. 2, 1856.

4309. JULIAN V. KEYES, b. in Westford, Mass.; res. Lowell, Mass.; no children.

CHILD OF GEORGE (4286)

AND

MARY (WOOD) (4285) LEONARD.

4310. GEORGE ENOCH, b. in Princeton, Mass., Oct. 4, 1829; m. Maria E. Walker (4311); res. Lowell, Mass.

4311. MARIA E. WALKER, b. in Shirley, Mass., Jan. 5, 1834.

CHILDREN OF MOSES (4287)

AND

MARY ANN BRIDGES (4288) WOOD.

4312. EMILY L., b. in Hopkinton, Mass.; d. in Westboro, Mass.

4313. MELVILLE, b. in Hopkinton, July 11, 1834; m. Oct. 3, 1855, Catherine A. Forbush (4314).

4314. CATHERINE A. FORBUSH, dau. of Benj. F. and Susan (Warren) Forbush, b. in Westboro, Mar. 30, 1836. Optician and jeweller, Kansas City, Mo.

Melville Wood enlisted, 1861, in Regimental Band, and after one year of service was, by an Act of Congress, discharged; he was in the battles of Roanoke and New Berne.

4315. MARY, b. in Westboro, Jan. 2, 1839; m. William Clemens (4316); res. Northboro, Mass.

4316. WILLIAM CLEMENS, b. in Northboro, 1837.

4317. ELLEN, b. in Westboro; d. in Manchester, N. H., 1842.

4318. ALONZO, b. and d. in Westboro.

4319. JOSEPHINE, b. in Westboro, Jan. 2, 1844; m. Charles Edwin Boyles (4320).

4320. CHARLES E. BOYLES, b. in Princeton, Aug. 27, 1836; res. Sterling, Mass.

C. E. Boyles enlisted in 25th Regimental Band in 1861; in one year was discharged by Act of Congress. Was in the battles of Roanoke and New Berne.

SIXTH GENERATION.

CHILD OF ALONZO H. (4293)

AND

EMILY JANE GERDEN (4294) WOOD.

4321. EMILY JANE, b. in Lowell, Mass., Sept. 17, 1843; m. Frank Albert Tufts (4322); d. in Worcester, May 22, 1869.

4322. FRANK ALBERT TUFTS, b. in Sterling, Mass.; d. in New York, July, 1883.

CHILD OF HENRY F. (4297)

AND

MARTHA L. WOOD (4296) HOLT.

4323. John Milton Benthall Holt, b. in West Boylston, Sept. 22, 1856; d. in West Boylston, Jan. 30, 1859.

CHILDREN OF NATHANIEL G. (4299)

AND

MARIA S. JOHNSON (4300) WOOD.

4324. Albert Nathaniel, b. in Saco, Me., Jan. 30, 1848. A very successful business man. In jewelry business with his father, 444 Washington St., Boston, Mass.; m. Clara Annah Barrett (4325); res. Boston, Mass.

4325. Clara A. Barrett, b. in West Townsend, Mass., Jan. 6, 1849.

4326. A Daughter, b. and d. in Boston, a few weeks old.

4327. George Melville, b. in Boston, Mar., 1855; d. in Leominster, Apr., 1858.

4328. Fred. Marshall, b. in Boston, May 6, 1861; m. Annie Baker Thayer (4329); res. Boston.

4329. Annie B. Thayer, b. in Boston, Oct. 18, 1861.

4330. Arthur Goodwin, b. in Boston, July 10, 1868; residence Boston.

CHILDREN OF JOHN MILTON BENTHALL (4305)

BY FIRST WIFE,

MARY E. STRATTON (4306).

4331. John Frederick, b. in Quasqueton, Iowa, Sept. 10, 1857; m. Jennie Evelyn Barker (4332); res. Waltham.

4332. Jennie E. Barker, b. in Essex, Me., May 12, 1863.

BY SECOND WIFE,

ELIZABETH D. WILSON (4307).

4333. Eugene Delafield, b. in Quasqueton, Iowa, Dec. 7, 1871.

4334. Mary Ejista, b. in Quasqueton, Feb. 3, 1877.

CHILDREN OF MELVILLE (4313) AND CATHERINE A. FORBUSH (4314) WOOD.

RESIDENCE KANSAS CITY, MO.

4335. Florence Nightingale, b. in Leominster, Mass., July 25, 1856; d. in Portsmouth, Va., Oct. 19, 1865.

4336. Virginia Franklin, b. Feb. 27, 1861, in Worcester, Mass.

4337. Rosa Bell (always called Nannie), b. in Worcester, Mass., Feb. 10, 1864.

4338. } Twins. { Herbert Carl Wood, } b. in Norfolk,
4339. } { Harry Earl Wood, } Virginia, Nov. 8, 1870.

CHILDREN OF WILLIAM (4316) AND MARY WOOD (4315) CLEMENS.

4340. Charles, b. in Northboro, Mass., 1866.

4341. Forester, b. in Westboro, June 27, 1868.

CHILDREN OF CHARLES E. (4320) AND JOSEPHINE WOOD (4319) BOYLES.

4342. Mabel Louise, b. in Sterling, Mass., June 10, 1868.

4343. Susie Wood, b. in Sterling, Oct. 27, 1869.

All the descendants of Capt. John Wood have been traced to the second or third generations, as shown upon page 232.

The descendants of Joseph Wood, son of Capt. John, have been traced to the present in the line of his sons who had families, and in the line of his daughters to times within the remembrance of those now living.

All the descendants of Maj. William Wood and Nathaniel Goodwin Wood, are supposed to be here recorded to the year 1885.

INDEX

OF

HEADS OF FAMILIES.

Two references are made here to each Family Record, through :—

1st. The name of the Father.

2nd. The name of the Mother before the marriage.

INDEX A.

HEADS OF FAMILIES BY THE NAME OF WOOD.

[The figures refer to pages.]

T.

V.

W.

INDEX B.

HEADS OF FAMILIES OTHER THAN WOOD.

[The figures refer to pages.]

C.

D.

E.

F.

J.

K.

N.

O.

P.

U.

V.

Y.

www.ingramcontent.com/pod-product-compliance
Lightning Source LLC
Chambersburg PA
CBHW071639270326
41928CB00010B/1987
* 9 7 8 0 7 8 8 4 1 6 4 6 0 *